MARTIN LUTHER'S THEOLOGY
of
BEAUTY

MARTIN LUTHER'S
THEOLOGY
of
BEAUTY

» A REAPPRAISAL «

MARK C. MATTES

B
Baker Academic
a division of Baker Publishing Group
Grand Rapids, Michigan

Published by Baker Academic
a division of Baker Publishing Group
P.O. Box 6287, Grand Rapids, MI 49516-6287
www.bakeracademic.com

Printed in the United States of America

Library of Congress Cataloging-in-Publication Data
Names: Mattes, Mark C., author.
Title: Martin Luther's theology of beauty : a reappraisal / Mark C. Mattes.
Description: Grand Rapids : Baker Academic, 2017. | Includes bibliographical references and index.
Identifiers: LCCN 2017004116 | ISBN 9780801098376 (cloth)
Subjects: LCSH: Luther, Martin, 1483–1546. | Aesthetics—Religious aspects—Christianity. |
    Theology of the cross. | Philosophical theology.
Classification: LCC BR333.3 .M364 2017 | DDC 230.01—dc23
LC record available at https://lccn.loc.gov/2017004116

17 18 19 20 21 22 23   7 6 5 4 3 2 1

Dedicated to the memory of my father,
Donald Athalbert Mattes,
and to the honor of my mother,
Betty Joan Nyquist Mattes,
who both nurtured me in the faith

Contents

Acknowledgments

There are many pleasures that come with writing, but the chief one is the fellowship established in the community of scholars that writing facilitates. Writing is solitary, but it is never isolated. Instead, this book, in spite of whatever flaws that may exist in it, has benefited mightily from extensive comments received from Paul Rorem, Robert Kolb, Oswald Bayer, and Steve Paulson. I am grateful for and indebted to the fellowship that exists in and is garnered by the journal *Lutheran Quarterly*, which the aforementioned friends find as a point of reference for their work in English-speaking circles. I am heartened by and indebted to the many suggestions that these scholars have brought.

This work has benefited as well from a less international but no less important support system: my colleagues and friends at Grand View University, which, professionally speaking, has been my home for over twenty years. Thanks are especially to be given to Ken Sundet Jones, who was often the first to read the pages in this book and who generously and in detail commented on them. Likewise thanks go out to John Lyden and Kathryn Pohlmann Duffy for their critique and support. Sheri Roberts and Cara Stone, Grand View librarians, assisted with providing numerous interlibrary loan resources. Most importantly, I am grateful to the board of trustees of Grand View for granting me a sabbatical in the fall of 2015 for the purpose of finishing this book. In particular, Dean Ross Wastvedt aided in the sabbatical application process. At Princeton Seminary, Mark Dixon was helpful in finding copies of Nicholas of Lyra's biblical commentaries, with which I compared Luther's *Lectures on Genesis*; Miles Hopgood likewise was helpful in retrieving several important bibliographic references for me. Additionally, John Pless, Oliver Olson, Russ

Lackey, Kevin McClain, Roger Burdette, and Mary Jane Haemig provided encouragement and moral support through the writing process. Thanks to my wife, Carol, and children, Joseph, Peter, and Emma, who were patient with me as I carved out time to finish this project. Finally, thanks are due to editors Dave Nelson and Tim West at Baker Academic for shepherding this manuscript through the editorial process and to publication.

A number of these chapters were originally presented orally in various settings, and I wish to acknowledge those institutions that invited me to share this work. Chapter 2 is a revision of "Luther's Use of Philosophy," which originally was given as a plenary address to the Twelfth International Luther Congress in Helsinki in August 2012. The substance of chapter 3, "Luther on Goodness," was presented in October 2014 during "Weekend with the Word," a conference sponsored by the Lutheran Church of the Master, Corona del Mar, California. I am grateful to Pastor Mark Anderson for hosting me at this event. Chapter 4, "The Early Luther on Beauty," was presented in a working group at the North American Luther Research Forum held at Concordia Seminary in St. Louis, Missouri, in April 2014. Chapter 6, "Luther on the Theology and Beauty of Music," was a keynote presentation for the Vi Messerli Lectures at Concordia University in River Forest, Illinois, in October 2015. Finally, a condensed version of chapters 4 and 5, dealing with both the early and the mature Luther on beauty, was presented at the 2016 Symposium on the Confessions, Concordia Theological Seminary, Ft. Wayne, Indiana, and at the North American Luther Forum held at Luther Seminary in April 2016. Thanks are due to David Scaer for his invitation to lecture in Ft. Wayne and to Mary Jane Haemig for the invitation to present in St. Paul.

Chapter 2, "Luther's Use of Philosophy," originally appeared in *Luther-jahrbuch* 80 (2013): 110–41, and is used here with permission. Fortress Press and Concordia Publishing House have kindly granted permission to cite at length from *Luther's Works*, 55 volumes (Philadelphia: Fortress; St. Louis: Concordia, 1955–86).

Abbreviations

ACW	Ancient Christian Writers
ANF	*The Ante-Nicene Fathers*. Edited by Alexander Roberts and James Donaldson. 1885–87. 10 vols. Reprint, Peabody, MA: Hendrickson, 1994.
AUSS	*Andrews University Seminary Studies*
BC	*The Book of Concord*. Edited by Robert Kolb and Timothy J. Wengert. Minneapolis: Fortress, 2000. Passages are cited by page and margin number.
BSELK	*Die Bekenntnisschriften der Evangelisch-Lutherischen Kirche*. Edited by Irene Dingel et al. Göttingen: Vandenhoeck & Ruprecht, 2014. Passages are cited by page and margin number.
CH	*Church History*
Colloq	*Colloquium*
CTQ	*Concordia Theological Quarterly*
CurTM	*Currents in Theology and Mission*
JMEMS	*Journal of Medieval and Early Modern Studies*
KD	*Kerygma und Dogma*
LBW	*Lutheran Book of Worship*. Minneapolis: Augsburg, 1978.
LCL	Loeb Classical Library
LQ	*Lutheran Quarterly*
LW	*Luther's Works* (American edition). Edited by Jaroslav Pelikan and Helmut T. Lehmann. 55 vols. Philadelphia: Fortress; St. Louis: Concordia, 1955–86. New series, vols. 56–82. St. Louis: Concordia, 2009–.
MQ	*Musical Quarterly*
NPNF[1]	*A Select Library of Nicene and Post-Nicene Fathers of the Christian Church*. 1st series. Edited by Philip Schaff. 14 vols. New York: Christian Literature, 1886–89. Reprint, Peabody, MA: Hendrickson, 1994.
NZSTh	*Neue Zeitschrift für systematische Theologie und Religionsphilosophie*
PL	Patrologia Latina. Edited by Jacques-Paul Migne. 217 vols. Paris, 1844–64.
SRR	*Seminary Ridge Review*
ST	*Studia Theologica*

WA   *D. Martin Luthers Werke: Kritische Gesamtausgabe; Schriften.* 73 vols. Wei-
         mar: H. Böhlau, 1883–2009. Passages are cited according to volume, page,
         and line.
WA BR   *D. Martin Luthers Werke: Kritische Gesamtausgabe; Briefwechsel.* 18 vols.
         Weimar: H. Böhlau, 1930–85.
WA DB   *D. Martin Luthers Werke: Kritische Gesamtausgabe; Bibel.* 12 vols. Weimar:
         H. Böhlau, 1906–61.
WA TR   *D. Martin Luthers Werke: Kritische Gesamtausgabe; Tischreden.* 6 vols. Wei-
         mar: H. Böhlau, 1912–21.

≫ 1 ≪

Introduction

In modern Luther research there has been a steady stream of articles and books devoted to Luther's appreciation for music and his defense of icons and the visual arts in the face of the iconoclastic protests of other Reformers. Likewise, there have been numerous studies devoted to Luther's view of worship and the liturgy. But the topic of beauty in Luther has rarely been examined.[1] This study seeks to cover new ground on a theme that was important for Luther but that we would not anticipate. After all, how can a thinker who struggled so much with God, who distinguished a "hidden" or an "absconded" God from a revealed God, and who differentiated a "theology of the cross" from that of "glory" possibly have anything to contribute to a theology of beauty? Beauty conveys a tranquility that hardly seems to square with the Reformer's spirituality, marked so often by chronic conflict with God, which he actually understood as assault (*tentatio*) from God. Among all the major Reformers, Luther would seem the least likely source for finding anything of significance for beauty. Indeed, prima facie we might think of Luther as the enemy of beauty. After all, the medieval Catholic system was apt to see union with beauty itself in the beatific vision as a reward for cultivating the habits of faith, hope, and love, provided that grace initiated this cultivation. In his quest to challenge and abolish the tradition of interpreting grace through the lens of merit, it would seem that Luther is the great foe of beauty. This study indicates otherwise. In many respects, the gospel as Luther understood

---

1. An important exception is Miikka Anttila, "Die Ästhetik Luthers," *KD* 58 (2012): 244–55.

it opens a horizon that gives sinners access to beauty and a message that is itself so beautiful that desperate, repentant sinners crave it. The God who is like the waiting father in the parable of the prodigal son (Luke 15:11–32) or who stands with Jesus as he defends the woman caught in adultery (John 8:2–11) is exactly the one whom sinners can identify as beauty itself, because nothing is quite as wondrous or joyful as the full and free forgiveness given through Jesus Christ and the new life it imparts. This study aims to present a different image of Luther—one in which the Reformer has not only "existentialist" depth but also cosmic and eschatological breadth.[2]

Insofar as it accomplishes that goal, it is indebted to newer Luther research that refuses to limit the Reformer's insights solely to an "existentialist" interpretation of the doctrine of justification by grace alone through faith alone. I put "existentialist" in quotation marks because it is anachronistic to peg Luther as an existentialist.[3] The intent behind that label is to acknowledge that Luther's theology is highly experiential but without experience serving as a criterion of truth. Justification by grace alone through faith alone, so central for Luther, also bears on how we are to understand creation (since creation exists after all apart from human worthiness or merit), and eschatology, how God is bringing about a new creation. Increasingly, Luther scholars have been dissatisfied with a "thin" description of Luther that reduces the Reformer's teachings to the doctrine of justification interpreted in existentialist terms. Instead, they have brought to the fore a "thick" description[4] that shows how the doctrine articulates a social dimension such as the "three estates" (the church, the household, and the civil government),[5] as well as

2. Clearly this approach is indebted to the work of Oswald Bayer. See Bayer, *Theology the Lutheran Way*, trans. Jeffrey Silcock and Mark Mattes (Grand Rapids: Eerdmans, 2007).

3. Søren Kierkegaard (1813–55) developed existentialism as a response to the totalizing tendencies in G. W. F. Hegel (1770–1831) and other idealists. In all existentialism, it is the individual who wrests a meaning out of life grounded either in a leap of faith in an allegedly irrational paradox, such as the God-man Jesus Christ, as with Kierkegaard, or in the face of irrational meaninglessness, as with atheist existentialists such as Jean-Paul Sartre. But Kierkegaard's view of faith as affirming life in the face of meaninglessness is a different context than Luther's believing in the promise in the face of the accusing law. There is no religion-neutral, secular space for Luther as there is in theory for Kierkegaard. Luther's world is not secular. The public realm's three estates are channels where God works, albeit in a hidden way. Nor is the paradox of God becoming human in Jesus Christ wholly irrational: its inner logic is the development of "for us and for our salvation."

4. Admittedly, I am playing fast and loose with Clifford Geertz's categories of "thick" and "thin" description, since for Geertz thick description acknowledges that all description comes with interpretation; there is no neutral objectivity per se. But the parallel between my use here and Geertz's is that adequate interpretation is not reductionistic. See Geertz, *The Interpretation of Cultures* (New York: Basic Books, 1973), 5–6, 9–10.

5. See Oswald Bayer, *Martin Luther's Theology: A Contemporary Interpretation*, trans. Thomas Trapp (Grand Rapids: Eerdmans, 2008), 120–53.

an acknowledgment of the Word of God as embodied, administered in the sacraments or in preaching. This latter teaching—the embodiment of the Word—is rich in significance for our work since it acknowledges that faith at its core is markedly aesthetic, awakening the senses, opening receptivity, kindling wonder, and evoking gratitude. Such an aesthetic core to the faith is expressed in worship that is sensitive not only to ecstatic joy but also to complaint or accusation against God when life seems terribly unfair, seen for instance in the laments in the Psalter, and even spiritual attack or *Anfechtung* when God appears to be against us. The latter is an inevitable result of Luther's threefold spirituality of prayer, meditation, and attack (*oratio, meditatio, tentatio*).[6] Current Luther research is attuned to the fact that it cannot be reductionistic; it must acknowledge that justification bears on all the articles of faith and, just as importantly, on daily life. It also seeks to situate Luther within his late medieval context.[7] Luther was not primarily the herald of the modern era as much as a medieval thinker seeking truth. His work inexorably changed the future—whether through intended or unintended consequences. But it is deeply embedded within the mystical piety of the monastery, the nominalist approaches to logic he learned at the university, humanism's call to return to primary sources, and his deep engagement with the Scriptures through teaching, prayer, and study.[8] He reworked all these and other matters and made them conform to evangelical faith.

In a word, what we learn from Luther about beauty is that while God's alien work (wrath) is indeed terrifying, not beautiful, God's proper work (mercy) is most beautiful indeed. And that proper work of granting Jesus Christ as gift[9] or sacrament to all who believe regenerates believers such that their senses are renewed and they experience the world more aware of the beauty that God has worked into it. As wasted by sinners, Jesus Christ had "no form nor comeliness" (Isa. 53:2 KJV), but the ugliness that sinners imprint upon him is the basis on which God works to remake such sinners as beautiful in his eyes. God does not find sinners to be attractive. Instead, in the gospel, God makes these sinners to be attractive and beautiful for Jesus's

6. See ibid., 30–36.

7. In this regard I am indebted to Finnish scholar Miikka E. Anttila. See Anttila, *Luther's Theology of Music: Spiritual Beauty and Pleasure* (Berlin: de Gruyter, 2013). Obviously Anttila and I are not on the same page concerning forensic justification, but his work, more than any other, has helped me work through Luther's approach to beauty, and I am grateful for it.

8. See Berndt Hamm, *The Early Luther: Stages in a Reformation Reorientation*, trans. Martin J. Lohrmann (Grand Rapids: Eerdmans, 2014).

9. For an excellent article showing the nonreciprocity of exchange in Luther's notion of gift, see Berndt Hamm, "Martin Luther's Revolutionary Theology of Pure Gift without Reciprocation," *LQ* 29 (2015): 125–61.

sake. As an "innocent delight,"[10] music by nature points to this joy. Icons or visual imagery can be an acceptable aid in worship since the Word of God is itself already embodied. Idolatry in any case is a matter of the heart, not the eye. Hence, for Luther, through the gospel the creation can be a place of innocent delight, things that can be enjoyed. As Oswald Bayer describes one of Luther's sermons:

> The ungrateful nature of the human being is depicted in a multifaceted repetition—drastically, distinctly, concretely: if we had our eyes and ears open, then the flowers would speak to us, as would our possessions and money: "even the grain would talk to us: 'Be joyful in God, eat, drink, use me and serve your neighbor with me.'" But what comes instead of this: ingratitude and covetousness. "Thus we ruin the joy for ourselves with cares and coveting, so that we shame our Lord, God." "Your cares and coveting" do not run their full course because of God's long-suffering nature and patience, because of "his profound goodness," not because of us. "We are not worthy [that even] a bird should sing and that we should hear a sow grunt."[11]

If humans were attuned to God's generosity, they could quite innocently enjoy creation for what it is and from that enjoyment be empowered to serve others in need. While beauty might not be the first of Luther's priorities, it is important, and it provides access to a new perspective on Luther, one that gives cosmic, historical, and social breadth as a counterweight or balance to the "existential" depth that earlier generations of scholars have so ably described. Beauty is one way that those alive in Christ appreciate the world. Believers undergo not only dying with Christ but also rising with Christ (Rom. 6:1–11). Appreciating beauty is one way that sinners have it confirmed for them that God's creation is good, that they can be at home in the world, that the world or life is not only or even primarily task, but also and especially gift. Now it is obviously not the case that only believers appreciate beauty. But it is not clear that, in the long run, nonbelievers' appreciation for beauty leads to their salvation. Rather, just as not honoring God's goodness condemns, so likewise not appreciating beauty.

Luther lived in a time of transition for aesthetic sensibilities, in which Europeans increasingly looked away from the tradition stemming from Augustine (354–430), which tended to intellectualize beauty, seeing it as a way to ascend beyond the senses, and instead looked toward sense experience itself as

---

10. WA 30/2:696.8; translated in Robin Leaver, *Luther's Liturgical Music: Principles and Implications* (Grand Rapids: Eerdmans, 2007), 86.

11. Bayer, *Martin Luther's Theology*, 109–10. For the Luther sermon, see WA 46:494.

pleasing the affects, and the mind as acknowledging such with appreciation. Luther himself contributed to this trend. Likewise, Luther shared important convictions of German humanists that also shaped his aesthetics. Concerned with educating civil servants, early Italian Renaissance humanists perceived the medieval model of learning (the *trivium* and the *quadrivium*) as inadequate to prepare courtiers and diplomats. As an alternative, they focused on the *ars dictaminis* (elegant writing), Latin grammar, and classical Greek to cultivate persuasive leaders.[12] This milieu influenced northern Europe and provided a context for Erasmus to develop his critical edition of the New Testament (1516), a move crucial for Luther's translation of the New Testament (1521).

The early Luther was fond of associating his work with the likes of Lorenzo Valla and Giovanni Pico della Mirandola.[13] Renaissance humanism, emphasizing formal Latin rhetoric and elegance in style by means of mastering linguistic skills and textual criticism, and critiquing Scholastic method, influenced Luther's approach to composing treatises, devotional literature, letters, and his translation of the Bible. Humanists employed erudition and ornament in their writings precisely in order to evoke an affective and ethical response in readers. This was not beauty for its own sake, but instead attractiveness as a means to persuade. It is noteworthy that Renaissance humanists, like their medieval predecessors, did not associate beauty with the arts per se but instead based their views of beauty on ancient or classical models.[14]

But in order to properly situate him, it is valuable to understand the continuities and discontinuities between Luther and the previous medieval tradition on beauty, which, as identified by Thomas Aquinas (1225–74), included proportion, clarity, and integrity as criteria for beauty. As we shall see, Luther's understanding of the gospel significantly altered that tradition. Likewise, in a sense, those three standards fall short of God's creativity, which is much more wondrous and delightful than even these three standards could ever fully assess.

Luther's own great artistic achievement, even more than his beautiful hymns, was his translation of both the Old and New Testaments into German.[15] His translation had a profound and lasting impact on the German language, providing not only a standard language, in contrast to the many dialects, but also turns of phrase without which it would be impossible to imagine German today. Through such verbal artistry, Luther has shaped almost a half millennium of

12. Paul Oskar Kristeller, *Renaissance Thought II: Papers on Humanism and the Arts* (New York: Harper & Row, 1965), 4–5.

13. Erika Rummel, *Biblical Humanism and Scholasticism in the Age of Erasmus* (Leiden: Brill, 2008), 4.

14. Kristeller, *Renaissance Thought II*, 186.

15. See Birgit Stolt, "Luther's Translation of the Bible," *LQ* 27 (2014): 373–400.

German spirituality, not only in Protestant churches but among Roman Catholics as well. This achievement, in turn, has influenced Protestant musicians, artists, poets, and architects not only in Germany but also throughout the world—and again, not only self-identified Lutherans but also Roman Catholics, Reformed, and even fairly secular people. Minimally such a list would include musicians such as Heinrich Schütz (1585–1672), Johann Sebastian Bach (1685–1750), Felix Mendelssohn (1809–47), F. Melius Christianson (1871–1955), Hugo Distler (1908–42), and Heinz Werner Zimmermann (born 1930);[16] painters such as Albrecht Dürer (1471–1528) and his pupil Hans Balding (1484–1545), Lucas Cranach the Elder (1472–1553), and Franz Timmermann (1515–40), but also Reformed painters whose work testifies to and is rooted in Luther's understanding of the gospel and his appreciation of ordinary life, such as Rembrandt van Rijn (1606–69) and Vincent van Gogh (1853–90). Naturally, other artists to include are Caspar David Friedrich (1774–1840), Julius Schnorr von Carolsfeld (1764–1841), and sculptors Bertel Thorvaldsen (1770–1846) and Paul Granlund (1925–2003).[17] Hymn writers influenced by Luther's approach to faith include Paul Gerhardt (1607–76), Thomas Hansen Kingo (1634–1703), and N. F. S. Grundtvig (1783–1872), and writers such as Thomas Mann (1875–1955), Conrad Richter (1890–1968), Ole Edvard Rølvaag (1876–1931), and John Updike (1932–2009). Such lists could be greatly amplified.

Foundation in Scripture

In many ways, Luther's approach to beauty is commentary on Scripture. Isaiah notes, "Your eyes will behold the king in his beauty; / they will see a land that stretches afar" (Isa. 33:17). Believers' faith is evoked by God's beauty:

> One thing have I asked of the LORD,
>   that will I seek after:
> that I may dwell in the house of the LORD
>   all the days of my life,
> to gaze upon the beauty of the LORD,
>   and to inquire in his temple. (Ps. 27:4)

16. For the impact of Luther's valuation of music among Protestants, see J. Andreas Loewe, "Why Do Lutherans Sing? Lutherans, Music, and the Gospel in the First Century of the Reformation," *CH* 82 (2013): 69–89; and Paul Helmer, "The Catholic Luther and Worship Music," in *The Global Luther: A Theologian for Modern Times*, ed. Christine Helmer (Minneapolis: Fortress, 2009), 151–72.

17. For an extensive discussion, see Werner Hofmann, ed., *Luther und die Folgen für die Kunst* (Munich: Prestel, 1983).

The gospel lays out a stance on beauty that transgresses the tendency to encompass beauty within matters such as proportion (so important for Augustine) or light (the basis of beauty for Pseudo-Dionysius [late fifth to early sixth centuries]) or integrity (crucial for Aquinas, who also adopted the views of Augustine and Pseudo-Dionysius). Instead, in the biblical view of atonement, in the servant who has "no form nor comeliness" and the cross that seems the very embodiment of impotence and foolishness, beauty is to be found. This truth is not apparent to fallen human aesthetics but is the beauty-in-giving that is God's ultimate beauty. Likewise, the question of proportion is also a question of order and disorder, and thus genuine ugliness, nothing other than the adversary's disruption of our proper perception of how God orders the world, and so a part of the eschatological battle unavoidable for all people.[18] That "all things work together for good" (Rom. 8:28) is a promise for those now walking by faith and not sight germane to the outcome of such cosmic conflict. Through Christ believers in the face of the adversary's attack claim not only goodness but also beauty: that is not only their birthright but also their inheritance.

The creation as good is beautiful. "Eden" is a garden of "delight." For God's covenant people, the concept of beauty is enfolded into that of abundance or "blessing," the assurance that God will provide sustenance, abundance, and safety for his people. Likewise the new creation (expressed as the new Jerusalem in Rev. 21–22) is beautiful, a place of consolation, harmony, and fulfillment. Indeed, in the Old Testament, beauty is often enclosed within goodness, particularly the goodness of God's abundance. Echoing the theme of a delightful garden of plenty as the dénouement after Judah's trials due to rebellion and idolatry, Jeremiah writes:

> For the LORD has ransomed Jacob
>   and has redeemed him from hands too strong for him.
> They shall come and sing aloud on the height of Zion,
>   and they shall be radiant over the goodness of the LORD,
> over the grain, the wine, and the oil,
>   and over the young of the flock and the herd;
> their life shall be like a watered garden,
>   and they shall languish no more.
> Then shall the young women rejoice in the dance,
>   and the young men and the old shall be merry.
> I will turn their mourning into joy;
>   I will comfort them, and give them gladness for sorrow.
>   (Jer. 31:11–13)

18. For this insight I am indebted to Robert Kolb.

Echoing the prophet's appreciation of abundance or blessing as an eschato-logical promise, other biblical authors are not silent about the wonder and grandeur of creation (Gen. 1–2; Job 38–39; Ps. 8).[19]

Naturally, Israel's cycle of rebellion and punishment depicted throughout Scripture is not beautiful, but the fact that God remains faithful to his people is. This is the truth that situates beauty at the core of the gospel. This truth is typified in the command that Hosea marry a harlot and find beauty in her. Hence, in Scripture, we have a view of beauty that would catch ancient Greeks and Romans totally off guard: beauty is the offshoot of love, and not vice versa. In God's dealings with his covenant people, it is not that like is attracted to like, but that the ugly is covered with the beautiful garment of God's love. In that embrace, those who are ugly, distorted, or sinful are granted new life, a new identity. In such a view, God is committed to be faithful to his people in spite of the ugliness of their idolatry and injustice.[20] We hear its pathos in Hosea 11:8–9, where God announces:

> How can I give you up, O Ephraim?
>   How can I hand you over, O Israel?
> How can I make you like Admah?
>   How can I treat you like Zeboiim?
> My heart recoils within me;
>   my compassion grows warm and tender.
> I will not execute my burning anger;
>   I will not again destroy Ephraim;
> for I am God and not a man,
>   the Holy One in your midst,
>   and I will not come in wrath.

Gospel beauty is found in the fidelity of love, which "bears all things, believes all things, hopes all things, endures all things" (1 Cor. 13:7). This is the basis for the attractiveness of the suffering servant. It is beautiful that he remained faithful to his vocation leading to the salvation of sinners in spite of the fact that he was wasted and made ugly at the very hands of sinners.

God's theophanies, whether to Moses (Exod. 3) or Isaiah (Isa. 6) or Eze-kiel (Ezek. 1), are not beautiful but instead numinously overpowering, as is also the transfiguration (Mark 9:2–13) or John's encounter with the risen

---

19. For Luther's view of creation as a place of wonder and mystery, see Charles Arand, "God's World of Daily Wonders," in *Dona Gratis Donata: Essays in Honor of Norman Nagel on the Occasion of His Ninetieth Birthday*, ed. Jon Vieker, Bart Day, and Albert Collver III (Manchester, MO: The Nagel Festschrift Committee, 2015), 197–215.

20. See Anttila, "Die Ästhetik Luthers," 245.

and glorified Jesus (Rev. 1:9–20). Again, such matters are not "sublime" in any Burkean or Kantian sense because by no means can the beholder withstand God. The beholder remains alive through sheer grace before God, whom no one can see and still live (Exod. 33:20). But the Bible witnesses to beauty—for instance, in the Song of Solomon's love poems and even in the formal structures of the Hebrew language (i.e., the parallelism and chiasms found throughout Scripture). Likewise, the Bible appeals to the importance of fine craftsmanship when it discusses the making of the ark of the covenant (Exod. 25:10–22), the appointments and furnishing for the tabernacle (Exod. 25–27) and the temple (2 Chron. 4), the clothes of the priests (Exod. 28), and the like. Such furnishings reinforce Luther's conviction that God ever and only works through specific and concrete means, offering humans something tangible through which faith can steady itself and apprehend or hold onto Christ.

Overview of the Book

As noted, Luther's views of beauty are deeply indebted to Scripture, especially the Psalter, which he prayed regularly in the friary as a young man and so knew by heart. But the theology of beauty that developed in the Middle Ages was also deeply informed by philosophical views of beauty stemming from the ancient Greeks, especially Plato. The three criteria for beauty defined by Thomas Aquinas—proportion, light or color, and integrity or perfection—find their roots in Plato's thinking. Along with Augustine and Pseudo-Dionysius the Areopagite, Aquinas reworked these themes, and they became a standard part of his theology.

Late medieval nominalists and mystics were not interested in the theme of beauty as such. Obviously these two approaches to faith deeply influenced Luther. His university professors trained him in rigorous methods of nominalist logic, while Luther the friar, in conversation with his mentor Johann von Staupitz (1460–1524), had an appreciation for and thoroughly studied mystics such as Johannes Tauler (ca. 1300–1361) and the anonymous author of the *Theologia Germanica*. Even if beauty was not a central topic of discussion in Luther's milieu, the related topic of desire was never far from medieval theologians, since they believed that God worked through desire to reorder the human heart and focus its interests in the eternal, divine matters to be enjoyed, as opposed to the temporal, earthly matters to be used. Sin effaces this proper ordering and causes people to enjoy the temporal and use the eternal, just the opposite of how they should behave.

Chapter 2, then, examines Luther's use of philosophy. Since the biblical
concepts of beauty employed by medieval thinkers had been shaped by philosophy, it is important to discern how Luther approached philosophy and the
value that he found in it for theology. Luther's approach, we will see, is best
designated as eclectic. That is, his first loyalty was not to a philosophical school,
although he claimed to belong to the Ockhamist or "terminist" school. While
indebted to nominalism in important ways, such as in his use of supposition
theory in logic or his view of the divine will apart from or outside of Christ as
voluntaristic, Luther was no lackey of this school. Instead, after his discovery
that law and gospel are not the same word of God but two different words,
one conveying expectations or demands and the other a promise, the Reformer
evaluated philosophical tools and perspectives in light of the law-and-gospel
distinction. Certainly there is nothing arbitrary about the "proper work" of
God; it exists precisely to create and nurture faith in men and women. While
not a realist, Luther however did affirm a view of participation, believers' dying
and rising daily with Christ, shorn of Platonic assumptions of a hierarchical
ascent into the divine.[21] Thus Luther's theology undermines the "analogy of
being" as the best description of the relation between beings and Being or
between good works and the Good. Plato, who knows only an eternal law but
no eternal gospel, would never comprehend such death to the "old being." But
by the same token the new life in Christ is no merely nominal designation that
Christians as individuals belong to the set of those who have appropriated
Christ. Instead, in a sense, the reality of the new being, the basis for a new
clean heart in the Christian, is Christ himself, the ultimate agent working in
and through Christians, renewing their very being, identity, or "form." While
philosophy does not set the conditions for how theology is to be done, it still
retains its status as a "handmaid," as medieval thinkers put it, a servant of
theology, helping to provide logical consistency and rigor for terms whose
meaning ultimately is situated within the grammar of faith.

Like chapter 2, chapter 3 also prepares the reader for the heart of Luther's
views of beauty by dealing with Luther's views of goodness. Medieval thinkers
of various schools tended to associate beauty with goodness. For some, this
was because both goodness and beauty were "transcendentals" describing the
structure of being as such. The transcendentals included oneness, goodness,
being, and truth. For many medieval thinkers, beauty was added to this list
because even if not a transcendental it was still closely associated with goodness. In general, for medieval thinkers, goodness was descriptive of all realities
participating in God as Goodness itself. However, the gravitational force of

---

21. See "Nominalism and Realism" in chap. 2 (pp. 20–26) for further discussion.

this truth was to be found more at the top of the hierarchy, in being itself as self-sufficient and not transient, the ultimate desire or goal for all *viatores*, pilgrims on their journey to God as their ultimate good.

Luther's approach to goodness departs from this Platonic itinerary and instead resituates goodness as God's favor, granted surprisingly to sinners who neither earn nor deserve it. He exposes the itinerary itself as reinforcing incurvation, since sinners underpin their own attempts to achieve status before God as opposed to simply receiving mercy from God. Hence, Luther identifies an alien work of God, which painfully slays the old Adam or Eve (who think that grace is at most supplementary) so that a new being completely dependent on God's mercy emerges. God's genuine beauty then is to be found in the word as "clothed," granted sacramentally in the embodied word of promise, in baptism, the Lord's Supper, the absolution, and preaching. Beauty is confirmed not through metaphysics but through Jesus Christ, paradoxically seen *sub contrario* (under the sign of the opposite) as the one who had "no form nor comeliness" at least in sinners' eyes but who is the chosen servant of God.

The heart of this book as an essay in historical theology is to be found in chapters 4 and 5, which deal with Luther's specific views of beauty both early and late in his career. There is marked consistency in Luther's views of beauty throughout his life. At one level, human existence before God, including the three criteria articulated by Aquinas, is demolished, and at another level, human existence before the world is maintained. From early in his career and sustaining him throughout, Luther claimed that God creates out of nothing. Even the new creation that God begins within believers through regeneration is dependent on God re-creating a new humanity out of the nothingness of sin and death. Hence, those who refuse to acknowledge their dependence on God at all times and places, who think that they can claim some turf or independence as their own, something that they could offer God in exchange for mercy, will be brought to nothing. They will experience the alien work of God, reducing them to despair of themselves, proving to them that faith alone is the only posture that makes sense when humans deal with God, since on their own they truly have nothing to offer God.

This view will put Luther at odds with the stance known as "pancalism"— meaning that *all things* (pan-) to one degree or another are beautiful (*kalos* in Greek)—maintained by many medieval thinkers. We can find hints of such pancalism in Luther at the earliest stage of his career, but as he matures, this view is increasingly challenged. It aids and abets the notion that humans could have something to offer God, but that is nothing other than an illusion. It feeds a cruelty that hammers at people, crushing them with its demands. But God's hidden or alien work is precisely to challenge that supposition so that sinners might look to God's mercy found in Christ alone and find God's goodness and beauty established in Christ alone as God's favor granted to sinners—an absolving word that effectuates new life through apprehending Christ. So, while pancalism is ruled out as leverage for old beings, a basis from which to justify themselves through works, the new being in Christ enjoys creation as God's gift and appreciates the beauty that is in fact crafted in it throughout. Indeed, Christ himself is beautiful because he assures sinful men and women that for his sake they are embraced by God. Sinners in fact cannot get enough of this beauteous message in worship and so crave gospel proclamation, and not just the expectations of law. Again, beauty is established not on a metaphysical basis, as in the legacy of Plato appropriated in the medieval church, but on the basis of Christ, who right-wises sinners and assures them of God's mercy. This absolving word also regenerates, brings about new beings alongside the old who appreciate the wonder and mystery apparent in all created things. We can distinguish a creation beauty, particularly in seeing how Luther assumes proportion, color or clarity, and integrity or perfection in his portrayal of the creation of Adam, from a gospel beauty in which God's love does not find a beauty to which it is attracted but instead as regenerative love creates a new being as an object of its attraction. Again, this new being can experience the world as an environment of delight or innocent pleasure.

Chapters 6 and 7 show how Luther's view of beauty can be seen in his love of music and his appreciation of visual imaging. Luther belonged to an era that was in the process of appreciating music not because it was a "science" akin to mathematics, as Augustine, and Plato before him, maintained, but because it was an art that alters human moods and affects, builds up community, and expresses delight. In the stance arising from late antiquity, performing music was actually considered a lower appreciation of music than studying the mathematics of its harmonies and rhythms. Luther was not totally opposed to this early musical tradition since he saw value in a cosmic approach to music—that is, that the heavenly spheres themselves produce harmonies as they traverse their circular patterns—but overall with respect to music he did not pit emotion against intellect. Indeed, he felt that not just the words but even the notes conveyed meaning and truth. For Christians, Christ himself is the *cantus firmus* or melody that makes sense of life.

In Luther on visual imaging, we see how the Reformer was aware that icons and visual depictions of the faith were vulnerable to being misused in late medieval piety. Luther's concern was less over the biblical injunction against "graven images" and more about whether such images would become idols within the heart. For Luther, it is not the eyes but the heart where genuine worship or idolatry takes place. Images or pictures can be valuable not only in educating the illiterate and spreading the faith but also—and even more importantly, given that humans are creatures who inescapably image—in providing a tangible, concrete reminder that God grants his mercy in sacramental forms, such as water, bread and wine, and the preached, oral word. Icons certainly do not mediate grace, but they are on a continuum with all reality, which masks God. Only in the promise is God's mercy unmasked, made available for sinners. Luther thus does not support the strict dichotomy between word and image of which Protestants are usually accused. For Luther, there is no God to be had apart from some "covering" or "wrapper," whether that wrapper is God masking himself in created, material realities or giving himself sacramentally in the church.

Finally, in chapters 8 and 9, I seek to move beyond historical theology and draw out the implications of Luther's view of beauty for contemporary theology. The most important ventures into theological aesthetics in the last several decades are the voluminous works of Hans Urs von Balthasar and those of the apologist David Bentley Hart. Both thinkers' works are grounded in the *nouvelle théologie* spearheaded by Henri de Lubac (1896–1991). Both thinkers retrieve the analogy of being in order to help secular humanity reason from beauty evident in the world to Beauty itself as the foundation for beautiful things. The analogy of being honors a "still greater dissimilarity"[22] in the midst of such significant similarity between God and the world. Hence, one can talk of real similarities between God and creatures all the while honoring the apophatic dimension of God. Hart employs the analogy of being to show that the seemingly irreconcilable, violent power struggles identified by postmodern thinkers ultimately find their place or peace in infinity, which is metaphysically construed as beauty itself. Likewise, von Balthasar identifies all creaturely realities as shaped by some form or another that grants them a luminosity that points them beyond themselves to the divine, which accords them their ultimate meaning and significance. Both thinkers, quite rightly, challenge secularism's "disenchantment" of the cosmos.[23] Such disenchantment sees no deeper meaning in material reality other than how humans can exploit it for their own purposes.

Luther's thinking in no way contributes to a disenchanted or secular perspective. True enough, his thinking undermines the realist approach, which layers

---

22. Eberhard Jüngel, *God as the Mystery of the World: On the Foundation of the Theology of the Crucified One in the Dispute between Theism and Atheism*, trans. Darrell L. Guder (Grand Rapids: Eerdmans, 1983), 288.

23. See Max Weber, *Essays in Sociology*, trans. and ed. H. H. Gerth (London: Routledge, 2009), 139.

reality as a series of ascending spiritual spheres that participate more accurately and fully in truth, goodness, and beauty. Instead, for Luther, Jesus Christ is the fulcrum through which life, and most specifically truth, goodness, and beauty, are to be understood. The itinerary established through Christ does not see the creation as the lowest step on a ladder ascending to the eternal. Rather, if the ladder metaphor is at all appropriate, it is a downward staircase. Due to Christ's humility and death, and later resurrection and exaltation (Phil. 2), we have a downward staircase, one that Christ descends to rescue smug, self-satisfied sinners and thereby refocus them in faith to live from love and service, like Christ, in the world. One can have an enchanted world without the Platonic itinerary leading one beyond the senses to the intellect, and from the intellect to the soul, and from the soul to the divine. Luther does not rule out analogy altogether, but analogy is best established ex post facto: through the light of Christ's resurrection such analogies become obvious in nature and human relations. Otherwise one is apt to develop an aesthetics fueling a theology of glory instead of an aesthetics shaped by the theology of the cross. The cross offers a *strange beauty* in that it is defined through Christ as deliverer, one who absorbs our sins bodily on the tree of the cross in opposition to propelling sinners to ascend into heaven through merit. Hence, genuine participation in God is baptismally configured as dying and rising in Christ and not as greater degrees of mimetically embodying beauty or goodness.

Finally, in chapter 9, Luther outlines for us an aesthetics not of perfection but of freedom. It is gospel beauty, in which Christ absorbs the ugliness and impurity of sin and bears it away never to be found, that opens the horizon of appreciating creation beauty and restoring humans to creation as gift, the paradise that God intends this good earth to be. Therefore, in the gospel, God can be acknowledged as beautiful based on the goodness of his gifts of creation and salvation. Secular views of beauty are shown to be inadequate because they fail to account for the wonder and mystery in reality that people actually experience. In contrast to contemporary aesthetics, which have a hard time discerning a wider purpose to life and the world, gospel beauty permits believers to feel at home in the world. This comfort with creation is iterated each time the gospel is preached.

Perhaps the most treasured hymn of American Lutherans of whatever synodical affiliation is "Beautiful Savior." Hopefully, this study will indicate why it is natural that that hymn would be so beloved. To associate beauty with the risen Jesus Christ, the Savior and Lord, is part and parcel of Lutheran identity, encoded within the doctrine of justification by grace alone through faith alone. The following study seeks to draw out the theological and spiritual implications of that truth.

» 2 «

Luther's Use of Philosophy

nyone who assumes that Luther believed that philosophy had no positive contribution to make to theology simply fails to deal with Luther's
corpus. Undoubtedly, Luther puts his finger on an irresolvable tension between
philosophy and theology, especially as the latter is obliged to articulate faith-
fully the gospel as *promissio* (of which philosophy knows nothing). However,
first, there is no question that Luther found philosophy, especially logic, to be
a helpful tool by which to establish doctrinal clarity through the use of syllogisms when properly following the grammar of the "new tongue" (*nova lingua*)
of theology.[1] As such, logic helps ward off heresy and clarifies true doctrine.[2]

1. However, we must keep in mind that
even the study of grammar that Luther praised so highly and gave pride of place to in the
trivium is not something that theology can follow uncritically, for it also reflects certain
biases and the linguistic conventions of the day. The way that key theological terms are
used, such as the words "God" and "human being," "creator" and "creature," proves
disastrous for theology. The world of sin, the old world, also has its own "old language."
. . . In this sense "the Holy Spirit," who makes the old world and its old language new,
"has his own grammar" [WA 39/2:104.24]. Indeed, "grammar operates in all fields, but
when the subject is greater than can be comprehended by the rules of grammar and philosophy, it must be left behind" [WA 39/2:104.24–26]. Grammar confirms and strengthens
the "philosophical argument," that "there is no relation between the creature and the
creator, between the finite and the infinite," between a beginning in time and eternity.
"We, on the other hand, assert not only a relation, but [even] the union of the finite and
the infinite" [WA 39/2:112.15–19]. (Oswald Bayer, *Theology the Lutheran Way*, trans.
Jeff Silcock and Mark Mattes [Grand Rapids: Eerdmans, 2007], 81)
Luther particularly employed syllogistic reasoning in his Christology. See his comments on
Heb. 1 at WA 10/I, 1:151.12–20 (LW 75:260), or on the deity of Christ at WA 28:92.29–36;
37:44.10–14. See also Siegbert Becker, *The Foolishness of God: The Place of Reason in the
Theology of Martin Luther* (Milwaukee: Northwestern, 2009), 82–87.
2. "Reason is used to understand the object of faith in an area formed by the center and
circumscribed by the boundary. When attacks from the boundary threaten to erode the center,

Second, however, very early in his career, Luther could employ not merely the formalism of logic but also the substance of Platonic thinking (in opposition to that of Aristotle) since he saw its apophaticism[3] as better able to honor God's hiddenness and more compatible with a theology of the cross (*theologia crucis*). Extending the "way of negation" (*via negativa*), Luther claimed that the theology of the cross enables us to distinguish appearance and reality with respect to God and our works, since we become aware that, while our works appear meritorious and God's appear evil, in fact just the opposite is the case. As we shall see, particularly in chapter 8, which analyzes the *nouvelle théologie*, the overall trajectory of Luther's theology substantially diverges from Plato's philosophy, especially Plato's positing an ontological hierarchy in which humans have the potential to rise higher and thereby perfect themselves. More generally, for the Reformer, philosophical concepts, including metaphysical ones, must first be "bathed" before they can become useful in theology.[4]

Third, with respect to the divergent schools of nominalism and realism, Luther comes across as somewhat eclectic—borrowing ideas from and rejecting aspects of both—making it challenging to peg him under those categories. The overall shape of relating philosophy and theology in terms of "two spheres"[5]—

---

or when the certainty of the center is shaken, the theological task begins" (Christine Helmer, *The Trinity and Martin Luther: A Study on the Relationship between Genre, Language and the Trinity in Luther's Works [1523–1546]* [Mainz: von Zabern, 1999], 3).

3. Knut Alfsvåg, who places Luther within the wider Platonic-Augustinian-mystical apophatic tradition, defines apophaticism as the path that systematically rejects all necessary predicates of God, and then again rejects the rejections, locating the presence of God in an area beyond all positive conceptualities, including the concepts of being and not-being. See Alfsvåg, *What No Mind Has Conceived: On the Significance of Christological Apophaticism* (Leuven: Peeters, 2010), 1.

4. See Sammeli Juntunen, "Luther and Metaphysics," in *Union with Christ: The New Finnish Interpretation of Luther*, ed. Carl Braaten and Robert Jenson (Grand Rapids: Eerdmans, 1998), 134. "Si tamen vultis uti vocabulis istis, prius quaeso illa bene purgate, füret sie mal zum Bade" (WA 39/1:229.16–19): "If, nevertheless, you wish these terms to be used, I ask first that they be well washed; get thee to a bath!"

5. Usually Luther distinguishes philosophy as dealing with the temporal while theology deals with the eternal (LW 13:199; WA 51:243.10–18), but sometimes he distinguishes them as "present" (philosophy) and "future" (theology) (LW 25:361; WA 56:371.30). Bayer helpfully situates the relation between philosophy and theology as parallel to "humanity in general and Christians in particular."

> Luther's distinction between knowledge and certainty is along the same lines as that between "holy" and "saved" that we find in his *Confession* (1528). This distinction is highly illuminating for his definition of the relationship between philosophy and theology. God orders his creation within three orders. The basic order of all human life is "holy" because it is "grounded in God's word and commandment." "However, none of the orders is a way of salvation. There is only one way beyond all these, the way of faith in Jesus Christ. For to be holy and to be saved are two entirely different things. We are

(1) philosophy, aligned with temporal matters, and (2) theology, aligned with eternal ones—as well as his view of the inscrutability of God's will,[6] seems to be indebted to nominalism. However, in theology, Luther is not averse to using a participatory approach, similar to but clearly not the same as realism, especially when commending the believer's union with Christ. When Luther says that believers are "one loaf" with Christ or "cemented" to Christ, or that they have the "form" of Christ or the "form" of God, giving themselves as a "Christ" to their neighbors,[7] such talk is not merely nominal, as if "Christian" were merely the name given to the set of those aligned with Christ and who behave in Christlike ways. Instead, the new being of the Christian is in fact Christ himself, who allows the believer to participate in him through daily dying and rising, granted through the agencies of baptism and absolution. The absolving word that imputes forgiveness simultaneously effectuates new being. Hence, in no sense does believers' participation in Christ entail their ability to develop their potential toward perfection before God. Instead, it is the securing of the soul as cemented to Christ through the word, which exchanges the soul's liabilities for Christ's righteousness. Progress made in this life ever returns believers to the waters of baptism. Progress in the life to come is solely in God's good hands as he brings believers to their fulfillment.

Luther's training was in nominalist logic, but his spirituality was deeply indebted to mysticism, which, seeing the soul as a bride and Christ as a groom, is apt to honor images of the believer's union with Christ.[8] Luther reworks both traditions in light of the gospel. Because God in his being is not merely or solely equivalent to, coterminous with, or reducible to eternal law, as nominalism taught, Luther discovered that God in his proper work is merciful and loving. Likewise, union with Christ is no reward for piety but

---

saved through Christ alone. But we become holy through this faith as well as through these divine institutions and orders. Even the godless can have much about them that is holy, but they are not for that reason saved inwardly. (*Theology the Lutheran Way*, 75; Bayer refers to LW 37:365 [WA 26:505.16–21])

6. Luther writes against Erasmus,

I say that the righteous God does not deplore the death of His people which He Himself works in them, but He deplores the death which He finds in His people and desires to remove from them. God preached works to the end that sin and death may be taken away, and we may be saved. "He sent His word and healed them" (Ps. 107.20). But God hidden in Majesty neither deplores nor takes away death, but works life, and death, and all in all; nor has He set bounds to Himself by His Word, but has kept Himself free over all things. (*The Bondage of the Will* [1525], trans. J. I. Packer and O. R. Johnston [New York: Revell, 1957], 170 [WA 18:685.18–24])

7. For "cemented" to Christ, see LW 26:168 (WA 40/1:285.24); for "one loaf," see LW 24:226 (WA 45:667.32–668.3); and for "Christ to my neighbor," see LW 31:367 (WA 7:35.35).

8. See Patricia Wilson-Kastner, "On Partaking of the Divine Nature: Luther's Dependence on Augustine," *AUSS* 22 (1984): 123.

a gift received in faith. Luther's eclecticism is not inconsistent, because his standard for evaluating philosophy is primarily the requirement of clarifying and advancing the gospel, which philosophy is called upon to serve. Luther's theological ontology is not one that pits relationality against participation; instead, divine favor (relation) grants a new being (participation).

Fourth, in Luther's view, when philosophy is applied to practical matters in the temporal realm, it can positively contribute to human flourishing. Just as the law is valuable for directing human conduct before the world (*coram mundo*) but has no say as a way for self-justification before God (*coram deo*), so philosophy works in tandem with the law to help people determine more productive ways to support the common good.

Finally, philosophy needs to come with a warning label. It is not neutral turf but can be exploited by the purposes of the old Adam. If philosophy opts to encroach upon theology, Luther sets clear demarcations for it.[9] He will not allow it to be misused to bury the risen Christ, who seeks to raise those dead in sin.[10] Indeed, this risen Christ renders all theoreticians guided by "the innate ambition to be like God" (*ambitio divinitatis*)[11] quite passive *coram deo*. It is Christ as the *novum* (the new) to whom every thought, including philosophical ones, must be taken captive. In so doing, *philosophia* can serve "not as mistress but as maidservant and bondwoman and most beautiful helper" for theology.[12]

The Scope of Philosophy in the Late Medieval University

Philosophia in the late Middle Ages was a demonstrative science based on Aristotle's *Posterior Analytics*, established through analytic deductions and

9. "To be sure, theology encroaches upon the rules of philosophy, but, contrariwise, philosophy itself encroaches more often upon the rules of theology" ("Disputation concerning the Passage: 'The Word Was Made Flesh'" [1539], thesis 15, in LW 38:240 [WA 39/2:4.22–27]).

10. "Disputation concerning the Passage: 'The Word Was Made Flesh,'" in LW 38:248 (WA 39/2:13.15).

11. In his letter to George Spalatin (June 30, 1530), Luther writes, "Be strong in the Lord, and on my behalf continuously admonish Philip [Melanchthon] not to become like God [Gen. 3:5], but to fight that innate ambition to be like God, which was planted in us in paradise by the devil. This [ambition] doesn't do us any good. It drove Adam from paradise, and it alone also drives us away, and drives peace away from us. In summary: we are to be men and not God; it will not be otherwise, or eternal anxiety and affliction will be our reward" (LW 49:337 [WA BR 5:415.41–46]).

12. "Disputation concerning the Passage: 'The Word Was Made Flesh,'" in LW 38:257 (WA 39/2:24.24). In general, Luther represents the view that philosophy is an *ancilla theologiae* or "servant of faith." See WA 39/2:24.20–26 and WA 1:355.1–5. Luther says, "Theology shall be empress. Philosophy and other good arts shall be her servants. They are not to rule or to govern" (WA TR 5:616; trans. Becker, *Foolishness of God*, 85).

syllogisms. It included those subdisciplines present in contemporary philosophy, such as metaphysics and ethics, but was wider than the discipline as presently defined since it included what we would call the natural sciences.[13] The most important subject for the bachelor's degree was logic.[14] The master's degree continued the study of logic, investigating Aristotle's *Topics* and his philosophy of nature.[15] Martin Brecht notes that Luther's Erfurt philosophy teachers, Jodocus Trutvetter and Bartholomäus Arnoldi von Usingen, following the *via moderna*, "did not question the superior authority of revelation and the Bible over against philosophy."[16] Nevertheless, all *moderni* acknowledged that theology was not a science, a theoretical system of truth established via demonstration. Reason could work within theology, but its fundamental axioms were accepted on the basis of authority.[17]

The foundation for all study in medieval universities was the *trivium*, composed of grammar, logic, and rhetoric. For Scholastics, the study of grammar included semantical and logical analysis. Luther was grounded in these disciplines at Erfurt. However, Luther was also influenced by humanism, best understood not as a philosophical system but as a cultural program.[18] Especially in northern Europe, the humanists' call was a return to the sources (*ad fontes*) of classical and biblical texts in their original languages. In contrast to Scholasticism, humanists were primarily lexicographers, recounting matters within a text, and not analysts, who are better served by syllogistic reasoning.

The public exercise of logic in the university for the sake of establishing clarity and truth culminated in academic disputations, a dialectic between two people, a master and a respondent. "Disputations were a regular part of academic life, which occurred publicly at fixed points on the academic

13. Graham White, *Luther as Nominalist: A Study of the Logical Methods Used in Martin Luther's Disputations in the Light of Their Medieval Background* (Helsinki: Luther-Agricola-Society, 1994), 86–88. As White and others note, philosophy in Luther's day was guided by semantic and ontological concerns, not epistemological ones as has been the case since Descartes and Hobbes.

14. The primary textbook on logic was the thirteenth-century compendium of Petrus Hispanus. However, the Neoplatonist Porphyry's commentary on Aristotle (called the "old art" [*ars vetus*]) was also studied, culminating in a reading of Aristotle's *Prior Analytics* and *Posterior Analytics*, and his work dealing with fallacies. See Martin Brecht, *Martin Luther: His Road to Reformation, 1483–1521*, trans. James Schaaf (Minneapolis: Fortress, 1993), 32–38.

15. Aristotle's philosophy of nature included *On the Heavens*, *On Generation and Corruption*, *Meteorology*, *On the Soul*, and *Parva Naturalia*.

16. Brecht, *Martin Luther*, 35.

17. Indeed, Luther regarded Trutvetter as the one "who first taught him that belief is to be accorded only to the biblical books, and all others are to be accepted with critical judgment," a precursory formulation of the "scriptural principle," as Brecht notes, making possible a kind of coexistence of philosophy and theology (ibid.).

18. Alister E. McGrath, *Luther's Theology of the Cross* (Oxford: Blackwell, 1985), 40.

calendar, as part of graduation exercises, and in private between pupils and masters."[19] The goal of such disputations, which all made extensive use of syllogistic reasoning, was to establish theological truth (though not the agenda or grounds for truth) in the face of heresies threatening the catholic faith or to clarify specific loci. Early in the Reformation, between the years 1522 and 1533, there were practically no disputations held at Wittenberg. However, when Luther was dean of the theological faculty, after 1533, the practice was revived. It is likely that Luther, who had a reputation as a skillful interlocutor in disputations, valued them "because it was through them . . . that he made his most important breakthroughs in 1518 (Heidelberg) and 1519 (Leipzig)."[20]

Nominalism and Realism

Insofar as Luther's thinking is beholden (as he claims) to William of Ockham (ca. 1287–1347), Luther too takes a position that rejects not only a radical separation (and complete isolation) of faith from reason but also a synthesis of faith and reason. For Luther, the relation between philosophy and theology is not determined by the relation between nature and grace (as it was for nominalists and realists). Instead, it is guided by the distinction between law and gospel, which construes philosophy as a suitable instrument for service in this world, including theology as an academic endeavor.[21] For Luther, in stark

19. R. Scott Clark, "*Iustitia Imputata Christi*: Alien or Proper to Luther's Doctrine of Justification," *CTQ* 70 (2006): 297. In an academic disputation, theses written by a professor were presented. In the course of the disputation, opponents (*opponentes*) would provide arguments attacking the theses, while it was the responsibility of the respondent (*respondens*), usually a doctoral candidate, to reply to these arguments. The respondent's job was not to argue for the theses but to find fault with the opposing syllogisms of the opponents. Given that the primary vocation of the theological faculty was the training of clergy, it is clear that what in contemporary parlance is called "critical thinking" was deemed requisite for successful pastoral leadership. It staggers the imagination to think of such public disputations being required of today's pastoral and doctoral candidates. Additionally, disputation as a social practice indicates the high value that was placed on rigorous, clear thinking in the attempt to establish theological truth.

20. Ibid.

21. Ingolf Dalferth notes,

The difference may be described as the transition from an additive co-ordination of the two perspectives of Faith and Reason to an internal reconstruction of the perspective of Reason within the perspective of Faith. What used to be an external contrast between Nature and Grace is now re-created as an internal differentiation of the perspective of Faith in terms of Law (*lex*) and Gospel (*evangelium*), viz. the knowledge of God, world and human existence *extra Christum* and *in Christo*. This is a purely theological distinction. But by relating two theological perspectives, not a theological and a non-theological one, the theological perspective is universalized and made independent of the philosophical perspective. Theology is seen strictly in the service of the explication

contrast to Aristotle's valuation of philosophy as contemplative, theology is a practical and not a contemplative discipline. Early in his career he defined it as experiential wisdom (*sapientia experimentalis*), which, as Oswald Bayer notes, means that, as wisdom, it includes science, unites theory and practice, and grounds both in an experiential or receptive life (*vita passiva*). Again, as Bayer indicates, experiential wisdom would be a contradiction in terms for Aristotle. Nothing historical or experiential can serve as a ground for knowledge in Aristotle's perspective.[22]

While the subject matter of philosophy in the medieval German university centered primarily (though not solely) on Aristotle's works, these writings were interpreted through the lens of two opposing perspectives, realism and nominalism. The heart of the philosophical debate between these schools was over the nature of universals. Realists held that universals either had their being apart from their instantiations in particular things (the Platonic view, as seen in William of Champeaux [1070–1121]), or—while not fully accounted for by those instantiations—did not have their being apart from them (the Aristotelian view, as seen in Thomas Aquinas). In contrast, extreme nominalists (like Roscelin [1050–1125]) held that general terms like "whiteness" did not refer to universals, but simply were different names for the particulars of which they were predicated. For nominalists like Ockham, all that exists are particular entities having particular qualities. As noted, Luther was educated in the Ockhamist (nominalist) tradition.[23] However, his teachers were more eclectic in their approach to the status of universals than they supposed. While the approach of Luther's teacher Trutvetter to logic and semantics was shaped by nominalism, in metaphysics Trutvetter assumed a theory of participation of creatures in God, which is closer to a realist position on the status of universals as objective realities.[24]

---

of faith in Christ and its vision of reality. . . . Hence it constitutes the decisive point of reference for interpreting the totality of reality, and requires all theological thinking about God, the world, and human existence to be christologically determined. (*Theology and Philosophy* [Oxford: Blackwell, 1988], 76)

22. Bayer, *Theology the Lutheran Way*, 28–29.

23. See Dennis Bielfeldt, "Clarity with Respect to Realism," *Disputationes* (blog), January 10, 2009, http://disputationes.blogspot.com/2009/01/clarity-with-respect-to-realism.html.

24. Juntunen writes:

Luther's teachers Jodocus Trutvetter and Bartholomaus Usingen, who wanted to renew teaching at the University of Erfurt and bring it into line with orthodox Ockhamist tradition, were actually themselves Ockhamist only in their logic. When they treated themes like creation or the existence of creatures in their natural philosophy, they could imply the concept of *participatio* in a way that was contradictory to Ockham's basic intentions. . . . That his teachers did not pay much attention to contradiction between the use of the *suppositio* theory and the ontological use of the concept of participation leads one to

Luther referred to himself as a "terminist" (a nominalist), and to Ock-ham as his teacher (*magister meus*).[25] It is likely, however, that his approach, similar to that of his teachers, is more fluid than his self-designation would indicate. When he calls himself a *modernus*, he is referring to semantic and logical skills he gained from disputational methodology. However, he is also indebted to the *via moderna* for its greater emphases on disconti-nuity between philosophy and theology than that of the *via antiqua*. In Luther's judgment, philosophy and theology constitute two quite different spheres whose boundaries must be properly honored if both philosophy and theology are to do their respective work.[26] Broadly construed, he rejected Aristotelian essentialism (that our duty in life is to realize our fixed poten-tials in a hierarchical scheme), but he thinks in terms of "natures" as sets of possibilities by which we generalize and classify objects in the world.[27] In theology, however, he could at times think in terms or appropriate language very similar to that of realists. For instance, when he describes Christ as the *forma* of faith,[28] in which believers share the same form as the object

think that Luther might have understood created being as participation in God, though as a good "terminist" he should not have done so. ("Luther and Metaphysics," 150)

25. See WA 38:160.3; see also McGrath, *Luther's Theology of the Cross*, 36.

26. Bruce Marshall helpfully indicates that theology, unlike philosophy, deals with the *whole* of reality:

Theology and philosophy each has its own "sphere"; neither provides the content for the other's discourse, and each has its own rules for forming true sentences. But this distinc-tion turns out to be a way of insisting that theology has to keep its epistemic priorities straight. Theology's "sphere" ends up being the whole; theology puts philosophy in its place by defining philosophy's sphere, that is, by marking out the boundaries within which its rules for forming true sentences may apply (viz., wherever they do not conflict with the truth of Scripture and creed taken in their natural sense). ("Faith and Reason Reconsidered: Aquinas and Luther on Deciding What Is True," *The Thomist* 63 [1999]: 46)

27. For this insight I am indebted to Paul Hinlicky, email correspondence, August 17, 2011.

28. See LW 26:130 (WA 40/1:229.22–32) and Tuomo Mannermaa, *Christ Present in Faith: Luther's View of Justification*, trans. Kirsi Stjerna (Minneapolis: Fortress, 2005), 57–58. With respect to the relation between God's favor and God's gift in justification, which is disputed between advocates of "forensic" justification and the Mannermaa school, Risto Saarinen makes headway: "While it is true that God's benevolence and God's gift appear together, one also needs to say that God's gift needs to be preconditioned by benevolence in order that it can be a gift. . . . In this very specific and limited sense, there is a conceptual priority of favor over the gift." Saarinen goes on to caution that "adherents to forensic justification readily affirm the primacy of merciful favor, but they fail to see the dynamics of one's being both recipient and beneficiary. Adherents of effective justification grasp this dynamic, but they do not see the fine differences between the concepts of favor and gift" ("Finnish Luther Studies," in *Engaging Luther: A (New) Theological Assessment*, ed. Olli-Pekka Vainio [Eugene, OR: Cascade, 2010], 23–24). However, for all Saarinen's protestations, I find his position here to be hardly different from my own ("Christ is so for us that he becomes one with us in this marriage of the con-science to Christ"; see Mark Mattes, "A Future for Lutheran Theology?," *LQ* 19 [2005]: 446), which he describes on pp. 21–22. For a thorough critique of the Finnish school, see William W.

of their knowledge, Christ, then Christ is the reality as such, the universal (if you will), and believers as "Christs" have their reality as participating in Christ, as Christ's instantiations in the world.

The *via antiqua* hearkened back to Thomas Aquinas, who as much as possible sought to harmonize the Christian faith and Aristotelian philosophy. "Observing that in Christ grace and nature are combined, Aquinas argued that a commonality exists between God and the creature whereby grace perfects nature, and nature serves as a vehicle for grace. But this also means for the later Thomists that reason is a necessary starting point for theology, and that philosophy and theology are completely intertwined."[29] In contrast, the *via moderna* left open "the question of the coherence of reality, of the commonality between the Creator and the creature."[30] The *via moderna* held faith to be a separate realm of truth, though not a demonstrative science, and so "not subject to the same methods and standards of proof."[31] For the Ockhamists, theology and philosophy do not dissolve into a unity of truth. When Ockham asserted that there were "many kings" governing a plurality of academic

Schumacher, *Who Do I Say That You Are? Anthropology and the Theology of* Theosis *in the Finnish School of Tuomo Mannermaa* (Eugene, OR: Wipf & Stock, 2010). Commenting on LW 13:71 (WA 31/1:217.4–17) Schumacher writes,

> In this mature, evangelical view, such human existence is properly connected to God— "deified"—precisely to the extent that it is concretely played out in the divinely ordered (divinely "spoken") sphere of very *human* activity: parents, children, master, servants. The "divine" character of such people has nothing to do with overcoming or transcending who they are as human creatures, but depends directly on what God says. God's word blesses, sanctifies—even *deifies*—precisely in the midst of created human life. (113)

Simply said, united with Christ, believers share in both natures of Christ—they are being not only "deified" but also "humanized." Hence, in *Two Kinds of Righteousness* (LW 31:302–3 [WA 2:148.33–149.16]), Luther writes,

> If one has wisdom, righteousness, or power with which one can excel others and boast in the "form of God," so to speak, one should not keep all this to himself, but surrender it to God and become altogether as if he did not possess it [2 Cor. 6:10], as one of those who lack it. Paul's meaning is that when each person has forgotten himself and emptied himself of God's gifts, he should conduct himself as if his neighbor's weakness, sin, and foolishness were his very own. He should not boast or get puffed up. Nor should he despise or triumph over his neighbor as if he were his god or equal to God. Since God's prerogatives ought to be left to God alone, it becomes robbery when a man in haughty foolhardiness ignores this fact. . . . And if we do not free desire to put off that form of God and take on the form of a servant, let us be compelled to do so against our will.

29. Rosalene Bradbury, *Cross Theology: The Classical* Theologia Crucis *and Karl Barth's Modern Theology of the Cross* (Eugene, OR: Pickwick, 2010), 49. For an extensive discussion of the relation between Luther and Aquinas, see Denis Janz, *Luther on Thomas Aquinas: The Angelic Doctor in the Thought of the Reformer* (Stuttgart: Steiner, 1989).

30. Bradbury, *Cross Theology*, 50.

31. Ibid.

disciplines, it would seem that he was opposing Aristotle's dictum that the "rule of many is not good; let one [reason] be the ruler."[32] Hence, Ockham countenances the possibility of conflict between faith and reason that is irresolvable in this life. Such a distinction between (though not a separation of) philosophy and theology influenced Luther's view. Upping the ante, Luther's conviction that the gospel is a *promise*, a word that creates new life from the nothingness of sin and death, and is neither a directive nor a description of a state of affairs, further situates philosophy as belonging to the temporal realm and not the eternal realm.[33]

In general, the realists affirmed a continuum between nature and grace, in which grace is able to perfect nature by healing the wound of sin and elevating finite, created being to the infinite, uncreated Being, God. For realists, it was possible to establish a synthesis of all knowledge achieved through various gradations of reality as instantiating the triune life. By contrast, nominalists felt that the analogical transparency of such gradations violated the very divinity of God, which for them was anchored in God's will and not God's intellect. Nominalists focused on the divine will as inscrutable, while realists focused on God's intellect, which is imprinted in the various gradations of order attested to in the world. Realism affirmed that the analogy of being (*analogia entis*) assumes a still greater difference in the midst of such great similarity between the uncreated God and the created world. By contrast, nominalism focused not on the analogy of being but on "being" as a univocally shared concept between the infinite and the finite in the fact that both realities *are*. As we shall see, Luther's view of beauty is indebted not to the analogy of being but to God's faithfulness to his own, given in the one who himself had

32. Bayer writes that
Luther does not agree with this sole or absolute rule of reason, nor does William of Ockham whose philosophy of science Luther had become acquainted with through his Erfurt teacher and his own study of Biel's *Collectorium*, especially the prologue, which deals with the questions of the philosophy of science. Ockham is skeptical of the Aristotelian idea that science should rule supreme. His remark at the end of book 12 of Aristotle's *Metaphysics*, that there is not just one king but many kings, can no doubt be understood as a counter-metaphor. (*Theology the Lutheran Way*, 28–29)

33. In "A Brief Instruction on What to Look for and Expect in the Gospels" (LW 35:117; WA 10/I, 1:9.11–15), Luther notes,
Gospel is and should be nothing else than a discourse or story about Christ, just as happens among men when one writes a book about a king or a prince, telling what he did, said, and suffered in his day. Such a story can be told in various ways; one spins it out, and the other is brief. Thus the gospel is and should be nothing else than a chronicle, a story, a narrative about Christ, telling who he is, what he did, said, and suffered—a subject which one describes briefly, another more fully, one this way, another that way.
Of course, the gospel as a creative word that creates out of nothing stands in contrast to the philosophical axiom that "out of nothing, nothing comes."

"no form nor comeliness," who was "despised and rejected" by people. Christ alone is the fulcrum for enjoying beauty.

For nominalists, grace elevates nature by requiring humans to honor what God has enjoined them to do via covenant (*pactum*), while for realists, grace perfects humans as they more and more conform to eternal law. For Luther, both views fail to love God for his own sake because we seek our own self-fulfillment as we exercise our potential even in our quest for salvation.[34] Both views could appeal to the Aristotelian dictum "reason pleads for the best."[35] Hence, Luther was adverse to Aristotle's voice in matters pertaining to salvation, although he would find a place for Aristotle in logic and ethics for the good of worldly affairs (including theological inquiry). Likewise, for Luther, there is a sense in which nature as created good needs not perfection as a human endeavor but liberation—from sin, death, and the accusations of the law. So, for Luther, theology does not perfect philosophy (realism) nor is it parallel to philosophy (nominalism); instead, it sets limits to philosophy, which surreptitiously seeks to enter theology's arena (matters of infinitude and/or grace) and also exploits its logical tools for rigorous clarification of doctrine.

For some time there has been a tendency to cast Aquinas as a veritable "rationalist" in order to place his view of faith and reason in opposition to Ockham's alleged "fideism." But as Alfred Freddoso notes, this opposition engenders "exaggerated estimates of the degree of confidence that Aquinas and Scotus repose in natural reason."[36] All medieval theologians believed that "divine revelation is absolutely necessary" for humans to flourish and "that, as far as ultimate metaphysical and moral questions are concerned, we remain in an utterly perilous state of ignorance without it."[37] Even in Thomas Aquinas's

34. See Theodor Dieter, "Why Does Luther's Doctrine of Justification Matter Today?," in *The Global Luther: A Theologian for Modern Times*, ed. Christine Helmer (Minneapolis: Fortress, 2009), 194–96.

35. Luther was fond of criticizing this expropriation of Aristotle's thinking for late medieval Scholastic soteriology. See LW 1:143 (WA 42:107.34–38), where Luther indicates that "when they say: 'Reason pleads for the best,' you should say: 'For the best in a mundane sense that is, in things about which reason can judge.' There it directs and leads to what is honorable and useful in respect to the body or the flesh." Luther makes a sharp distinction between the temporal and the eternal and situates philosophy as appropriate in the former while theology alone is appropriate in the latter.

36. Alfred J. Freddoso, "Ockham on Faith and Reason," in *The Cambridge Companion to Ockham*, ed. Paul Vincent Spade (Cambridge: Cambridge University Press, 1999), 329.

37. Freddoso notes that Aquinas divides "divinely revealed truths into what he elsewhere calls the *mysteries* [or: *articles*] of the faith, which 'altogether exceed the capability of human reason,' and the *preambles* of the faith, which can at least in principle be established by the light of natural reason. Ockham draws a similar distinction between theological truths that we are naturally able to have evident cognition of and theological truths that we can have cognition of only supernaturally" (ibid., 332 [italics original]).

approach to reason and faith, philosophy and theology, "theological inquir-
ers cannot have *scientia* with respect to the conclusions of theology. This is
a point Ockham emphasizes repeatedly in his critique of the claim that 'our
theology' counts as a science."[38] Ockham offers an "irenic separatism" that
rejects "the prototypically Catholic intellectual project of unifying classical
philosophy and the Christian faith in such a way as to exhibit the latter as
the perfection of the former, and yet that stops short of disdaining the light
of natural reason in the manner of radical intellectual separatism." Overall,
such an Ockhamist spirit seems to be operative in Luther's distinction between
philosophy and theology as "two spheres." If anything, Luther—less irenic
than Ockham—accentuates the distinction between philosophy and theology
since he will indulge no *mixing* of philosophy and theology,[39] providing no
philosophical fuel that might aid the free will in its conviction that it can make
progress in righteousness *coram deo* and so marginalize faith.

Luther's Divergences from Nominalism

Nominalism's assumption of a covenant or *pactum* between God and humanity in which God will give his grace to those who do their very best (*facere
quod in se est*), maintained by Gabriel Biel, was Luther's chief target in his
early attempt to understand the true nature of human justification *coram
deo*. In spite of Luther's self-identification as a "terminist," it is hard to
imagine that his rejection of a nominalist view of salvation would have no
impact whatsoever on his reception of philosophy. Bengt Hägglund pointed
out that, unlike nominalist psychology, which assumed reason's capacity to

---

38. Freddoso indicates that "Aquinas cites approvingly Aristotle's dictum that natural reason
is as incapable of comprehending the most intelligible natures as the eye of an owl is of viewing
the sun." Hence, for both Thomas and Ockham, "philosophical inquiry unaided by divine revelation can help foster logical skills and intellectual habits that are required for the articulation
of true wisdom within Christian theology; it can even provide Christian thinkers with new and
useful conceptual resources. But it cannot on its own make any noteworthy progress toward
providing us with the substance of absolute wisdom" (ibid., 335).

39. Luther maintains that the Scholastics' mistaken notion of seeing faith as a habit is due
to the fact that they have obscured faith by mixing Aristotelian philosophy with theology. See
Lectures on Genesis, in LW 8:261 (WA 44:770–71). Hence, he notes,

> philosophy and theology must be carefully distinguished. Philosophy also speaks of a
> good will and of right reason, and the sophists are forced to admit that a work is not
> morally good unless a good will is present first. And yet they are such stupid asses when
> they proceed to theology. They want to prescribe a work before the good will, although
> in philosophy it is necessary for the person to be justified morally before the work. Thus
> the tree is prior to the fruit, both in essence and in nature. (*Lectures on Galatians* [1535],
> in LW 26:261 [WA 40/1:410.14–20])

submit itself to the imperative to conform to the truth that God as the Supreme Being ought to be loved above all things, Luther affirmed instead that we rebel against grace and are unable to control our interior will.[40] Nor for Luther is grace to be understood as an infused new quality in the regenerate but instead is "the divine mercy that brings about the forgiveness of sins. As the Spirit of God gives life, so grace confers that eternal life which is given us in and with the forgiveness of sins."[41] But given that the nominalists held that God of his absolute power (*de potentia absoluta*) could declare humans "righteous only because God accepts" them "as such quite apart from any infusion of grace" (the doctrine of acceptance),[42] Luther was decisively anti-nominalist. For Luther, "imputation is nothing else but the work of grace. And grace, *instead of being the arbitrary will of God*, works the justification of the sinner because of Jesus Christ."[43] Nominalist views of justification as construed either through the lens of *de potentia ordinata* (God's ordained power) or *de potentia absoluta* (God's absolute power) fail to acknowledge that our justification is *propter Christum* (for the sake of Christ).

Jettisoning any saving efficacy for the law, Luther heightens the distinction between faith and works. Works are crucial for the well-being of the neighbor, not for human salvation. Luther construes philosophy as parallel to works or law and theology as parallel to God's favor or grace. With respect to salvation, "Christ alone" (*solus Christus*) means that the law codified as the *pactum* offers nothing *coram deo*. No longer given the aura of a manual to salvation, the law is restored as a way to order life *coram mundo*. It is relegated to temporal matters and loses any potency in eternal matters. But Luther notes that the nominalist perspective also appeals to philosophy as a way to affirm human activity *coram deo*. In so doing, such "sophist" mixing of philosophy with theology marginalizes the efficacious role of an active Christ. Speaking against the faculty of the Sorbonne, Luther in 1539 writes:

> But here we especially oppose the men at the Sorbonne who allow such things as the forgiveness of sins and the mystery of the incarnation and eternal life to be deduced by logic. They have asserted that they are there and can be obtained by living according to the law and through philosophy. This we deny. For they speak thus and allege that whoever has done what he was able to do is justified and merits grace according to his fitness, and afterward even in strict justice. This we deny. What use would there be here for Christ? He would be set aside

40. Bengt Hägglund, "Was Luther a Nominalist?," *Theology* 59 (1956): 227.
41. Ibid., 228.
42. Ibid., 229.
43. Ibid. (italics added).

and buried completely. For when they want to be justified altogether without Christ, what else are they doing than consigning Christ to oblivion so that Christ might be completely useless for us and have died in vain? We admit that philosophy teaches and all men know by nature that theft is unlawful, as are many other things. But we cannot and ought not tolerate the fact that these chief theological articles—for whose sake alone Scripture was given—namely, those concerning justification, the forgiveness of sins, liberation from eternal death, are actually attributed to philosophy and human powers.[44]

In a word, philosophy knows nothing of grace—which is the most important thing to know.[45] Just as an active, unburied Christ relativizes law and gives it its appropriate locus in temporal matters, so philosophy is similarly relativized by the gospel *promissio*, a move that, given their soteriology of human contribution to justification, nominalists could not make. For Luther, philosophy has its full voice in temporal matters, not eternal matters. In the same disputation he notes, "We say that theology does not contradict philosophy because the latter speaks only about matrimony, obedience, chastity, liberality, and other virtues. But it is one thing to believe in the Son of God, to possess and to expect eternal life, and something else again to be chaste, to marry, to live honestly in the world, to be liberal, meek, obedient, kind, and peaceable."[46]

As noted above, for Aristotle, reason had a divine status in the theoretical, contemplative life. In contrast, Luther shifts the focus of the divine dimension of human reason to the "active life" of human beings, where reason is capable of making sound decisions about the economy, politics, and natural sciences. Luther reverses the Augustinian and Scholastic distinction between a superior part (*portio superior*) and an inferior part (*portio inferior*) of reason with respect to faith. In the traditional Augustinian scheme, the superior part of reason

is directed toward the *aeterna*, or eternal things, and the inferior part is directed toward the *temporalia*, the temporal objects. This distinction also reflects two different acts of knowledge: the superior part of reason is intellectual (*intelligere*), knowing something in its simple wholeness, and the inferior part employs discursive thinking (*ratiocinari*). This distinction in other words is

44. "Disputation concerning the Passage: 'The Word Was Made Flesh,'" argument 6, in LW 38:248 (WA 39/2:13.10–14.6).
45. Luther writes that philosophers know nothing of mercy and truth. See *Lectures on Genesis*, in LW 4:148 (WA 43:242.21–22).
46. "Disputation concerning the Passage: 'The Word Was Made Flesh,'" argument 6, in LW 38:248 (WA 39/2:14.8–13).

the distinction between wisdom and science. The Scholastics, like Augustine, distinguished between use (*uti*) and enjoyment (*frui*), which means that all *temporalia* are meant to be used by us, and all *aeterna* are meant to be enjoyed by us—and not to be used.[47]

Luther rejects this classic distinction between the superior and inferior parts of reason and distinguishes instead between reason (*ratio*) and faith (*fides*): "Any relationship between human beings and God (and all eternal things) is not conceived by reason—not even by a superior part of reason. Faith alone is the vehicle and instrument by which the human person is related to the triune God. . . . Reason is, thereby, freed by faith from any illusions of attaining God on its own capacity."[48]

While demarcating philosophy as a demonstrable science in contradistinction to theology as grounded in revelation that is to be accepted on the basis of authority, Hägglund noted that nominalism also affirmed that

> not only are certain theological truths accessible to reason and that those that rest on a supernatural revelation can, after the event, become the object of rational speculation. Theological knowledge is, so to speak, on the same level as rational knowledge. The chief difference between them is that the former presupposes revelation and faith, faith being conceived as the submission of the will to the authority of revealed truth.[49]

For nominalists, humans are capable of producing saving faith on the basis of one's natural powers. "Free will is then capable of adhering to truths of faith which ecclesiastical authority proposes to it."[50] When useful for theology, *recta ratio* (right reason) is defined not from nature but from grace. Such reasoning will follow the narrative of the gospel as outlined and presented in Scripture.

Repeatedly Luther cautions that when there is conflict between philosophy and theology (as invariably there must be since philosophy knows nothing of God's grace, nor can it encompass God's infinity, which transcends all human conceptuality), then "all thought (no doubt this also includes philosophy) is to be taken captive to the obedience of Christ (2 Cor. 10:5),"[51] and following

47. Hans-Peter Grosshans, "Luther on Faith and Reason: The Light of Reason at the Twilight of the World," in Helmer, *Global Luther*, 181.
48. Ibid.
49. Hägglund, "Was Luther a Nominalist?," 231.
50. Ibid.
51. "Disputation concerning the Passage: 'The Word Was Made Flesh,'" thesis 8, in LW 38:239 (WA 39/2:4.6–7).

Ambrose he argues that "the dialecticians have to give way where the apostolic fishermen are to be trusted."[52] Syllogistic reasoning is an excellent approach to academic inquiry, but it is useful only to the extent that it conveys the subject matter. And the subject matter of theology, the sinful human needing justification and the God who justifies in Christ, cannot be encompassed by reason. Rather, it is reason that must be subject to Christ.

The means by which Luther limits the scope of philosophy to temporal matters is nothing other than his distinction between law and gospel. "The meaning of the law is, under various circumstances, known to the philosophers. But the promises of God belong to theology, and the gospel is not known to every creature because it is a mystery hidden from the world."[53] Philosophy is akin to law as theology is akin to gospel. Just as God's promise actually affirms the law by situating it within *temporalia*, where it properly belongs, indicating that antinomianism is inappropriate, so also there is no "antinomianism of philosophy." Even as the law abides for sinners as an instructor and accuser, so philosophy abides as practical thinking about furthering human life, community, and service. It also, as we shall see, can provide theology useful logical tools to establish sound doctrine, once thinking is taken captive to Christ (and not vice versa).

Aristotle's Inadequacies and Adequacies

As is well known, Luther at times disparaged Aristotle (designated by medieval theologians as "the philosopher") for his divergences from Scripture and the misuse of Aristotelian reasoning in nominalist schemes of salvation.[54] Luther repeatedly noted that neither Aristotle's cosmology nor his psychology squares with Scripture. For Aristotle, the world is eternal while the soul is mortal, a reversal of scriptural truth.[55] Even so, Luther appeals to Aristotle's conviction that the goal of life is happiness. Here, Aristotle has an inkling of the truth.[56] The problem is that Aristotle's God, who cares nothing for the

52. "Disputation concerning the Passage: 'The Word Was Made Flesh,'" thesis 9, in LW 38:239 (WA 39/2:4.8–9).
53. "Disputation concerning the Passage: 'The Word Was Made Flesh,'" argument 24, in LW 38:258 (WA 39/2:5.3–4).
54. For the most thorough recent study of Luther on Aristotle, see Theodor Dieter, *Der junge Luther und Aristoteles: Eine historisch-systematische Untersuchung zum Verhältnis von Theologie und Philosophie* (Berlin: de Gruyter, 2001).
55. *Lectures on Genesis*, in LW 1:3–4 (WA 42:3.31–4.1).
56. See *Lectures on Genesis*, in LW 1:131 (WA 42:98.13–26):
    Aristotle says something worthwhile when he declares that the goal of man is happiness, which consists in a virtuous life. But in view of the weakness of our nature who

world but only for himself, can never be the *telos* of human life. Aristotle's God knows nothing of grace. While God exists for Aristotle, his God simply does not communicate with humans, which is vital for Luther's understanding of God. Hence, Luther is quick to respond that this Aristotelian God "means nothing to us."[57] However, Luther's rapport with Aristotle is far broader than this. As can be seen in the "Disputation concerning Man" (1536), Luther does not reject Aristotle's theory of fourfold causality consisting of the efficient (from whence does the matter come?), material (in what does it consist?), formal (as what does it exist?), and final (toward what does it aim?) causes but does indicate its inadequacy for theological anthropology. What is problematic is the limited epistemological access that humans have about themselves with respect to ultimate matters. Here, philosophy offers only "fragmentary, fleeting, and exceedingly material" knowledge.[58] We scarcely perceive humanity's material cause sufficiently, and philosophy does not know the efficient and final causes for certain.[59] Instead, it is through scriptural revelation that we learn that "man is a creature of God consisting of body and a living soul, made in the beginning after the image of God, without sin, so that he should procreate and rule over the created things, and never die."[60] The problem is not with reason as such, which is "most excellent," indeed "a sun and a kind of god appointed to administer these things in this life." (Indeed, after the fall, God did not "take away this majesty of reason, but rather confirmed it.")[61] Rather, the problem is that we finite and sinful creatures are too distanced from these truths. It is through Paul that we properly understand that it is justification by faith alone that briefly sums up the definition of humanity.[62]

---

can reach this goal? Even those who are the most fortunate encounter discomforts of various kinds, which both misfortune and the ill will and meanness of men bring on. For such happiness peace of mind is necessary. But who can always preserve this amid the great changes of fortune? It is vain, therefore, to point out this goal which no one reaches. The main goal, then, to which Scripture points is that man is created according to the likeness of God; in eternity, therefore, he is to live with God, and while he is here on earth, he is to preach God, thank Him, and patiently obey His Word. In this life we lay hold of this goal in ever so weak a manner; but in the future life we shall attain it fully. This the philosophers do not know. Therefore the world with its greatest wisdom is most ignorant when it does not take advantage of Holy Scripture or of theology. Human beings know neither their beginning nor their end when they are without the Word.

57. LW 4:145 (WA 43:240.30), translation altered.
58. "Disputation concerning Man," thesis 19, in LW 34:138 (WA 39/1:175.3–4).
59. "Disputation concerning Man," theses 12–13, in LW 34:138 (WA 39/1:175.26–29).
60. "Disputation concerning Man," thesis 21, in LW 34:138 (WA 39/1:176.7–9).
61. "Disputation concerning Man," thesis 11, in LW 34:137–38 (WA 39/1:175.24–25).
62. "Disputation concerning Man," thesis 32, in LW 34:139 (WA 39/1:176.33–35).

Early Appropriation of Plato

In spite of Luther's rejection of a hierarchy between *portio superior* and *portio inferior*, we can discern an appropriation of aspects of Plato's thinking, especially in his early theology. This appropriation of Plato's thinking over Aristotle's is likely traced to his intense reading of Augustine as well as German mystics such as Johannes Tauler and the anonymous author of *Theologia Germanica*, a book he edited early in his career. In his explanation of thesis 36 of the philosophical theses of the *Heidelberg Disputation* (1518), Luther argued that Aristotle, who "insists on the priority of the sensible," only *seems* to give knowledge of reality.[63] As Knut Alfsvåg notes, for Luther, Aristotle's epistemology is grounded in the senses. So, for Aristotle, if knowledge is to obtain, then (unlike Plato) form and matter cannot be separated. But for Luther, such an approach is tied to the "instability" and uncertainty of the senses and thus fails to convey the eternal. In fact, with Plato, we should affirm the "priority of the infinite and divine. True knowledge is according to Luther dependent on the acceptance of unknowability."[64] There is no *proportio* (proportion) between the Creator and created things, and thus no ladder between what we can perceive and the "invisible things of God" that can be constructed for the *viator* (pilgrim). Hence, the "visible and manifest things of God" are to be seen only "through suffering and the cross."[65] So, in thesis 37, Luther argues that Pythagoras and especially Plato, unlike Aristotle, appropriately integrate the infinite and the finite in the concept of participation.[66] Alfsvåg notes:

> As evidence for the latter, Luther explicitly refers to what he calls the most beautiful discussion of oneness in Parmenides, where the author first deprives oneness of everything until it is reduced to nothing, and then gives everything back until there is nothing left in which oneness is not. There is thus nothing that does not exist through oneness, which in this way at the same time is outside of and in everything.[67]

63. See Alfsvåg, *What No Mind Has Conceived*, 194. For a translation of the *Heidelberg Disputation*'s philosophical theses into German, see Helmar Junghans, "Die Probationes zu den philosophischen Thesen der Heidelberger Disputation Luthers im Jahre 1518," *Lutherjahrbuch* 46 (1979): 10–59. This article contains both Latin and German. Thesis 36 reads: "Aristotle wrongly finds fault with and derides the ideas of Plato, which actually are better than his own" (LW 31:42 [WA 1:355]).

64. Alfsvåg, *What No Mind Has Conceived*, 194.

65. *Heidelberg Disputation* (1518), thesis 19, in LW 31:40 (WA 1:354).

66. Thesis 37 reads: "The mathematical order of material things is ingeniously maintained by Pythagoras, but more ingenious is the interaction of ideas maintained by Plato" (*Heidelberg Disputation*, in LW 31:42 [WA 1:355]).

67. Alfsvåg, *What No Mind Has Conceived*, 195.

Since God is incomprehensible and invisible, we simply cannot move, as Luther notes in the theological theses of the *Heidelberg Disputation*, from knowledge of creatures to their Creator. This truth is decisive for his rejection of a "theology of glory" and his approval of a "theology of the cross." As important as this move is for Luther's theological development in distinguishing law from gospel and associating the gospel with a word of promise, Luther would increasingly challenge the "speculation" inherent in Platonism and Christian Platonists' neglect of the word of God. Or, said differently, a consistent *via negativa* leads not only to negating divine attributes and then negating these negations, but also to the negation or death of theologians themselves since such an apophatic approach gains us only the *deus absconditus* (hidden God) and thus functions as God's *opus alienum* (alien work). Only in the word does God wish to be found.[68] But as we shall see in later chapters, this word comes ever in embodied form—with water, or bread and wine, or some other tangible presence.

Nevertheless, Luther's consistent perspective that God is a given for all people, not especially needing demonstration, seems to be grounded in a Platonic view of anamnesis, as can be seen in Luther's description of the terrified sailors who flee to God in his *Lectures on Jonah* (1526). Luther perceives the general revelation of God less through the lens of inference on the basis of design in nature or the goal of human life and more through an anamnesis in which all people have a memory that there is a God.[69]

For Luther, the existence of God is never in doubt. But God's disposition toward humankind is. "That there is a God, by whom all things were made, that you know from his works . . . but God himself, who he is, what sort of divine Being he is, and how he is disposed toward you—this you can never discover nor experience from the outside."[70] True knowledge of God must acknowledge awareness that God cares for his world. This divine love is foreign to philosophers, even the likes of Plato.

> Philosophers argue and ask speculative questions about God and arrive at some kind of knowledge, just as Plato looks at and acknowledges the government of God. But everything is merely objective; it is not yet that knowledge which Joseph has, that God cares, that He hears the afflicted and helps them. Plato cannot determine this; he remains in his metaphysical thinking, as a cow looks at a new door.[71]

68. See Alfsvåg's discussion in ibid., 197.
69. LW 19:53 (WA 19:205.27–206.7).
70. "Predigt am 6 Sonntag nach Epiphania, January 31, 1546," in WA 51:150.42–151.3 (trans. Becker, *Foolishness of God*, 40).
71. *Lectures on Genesis*, in LW 8:17 (WA 44:591.34–39).

If we are to have true knowledge of God, we cannot escape the forensic, *pro nobis* (for us) dimension if such knowledge is in fact true.

> You have the true knowledge of God when you believe and know that God and Christ are your God and your Christ. This the devil and the false Christians cannot believe. Thus this knowledge is nothing else than the true Christian faith; for when you know God and Christ in this way, you will rely on Him with all your heart and trust in Him in good fortune and misfortune, in life and death.[72]

To call Luther's view of knowledge of God "existentialist" would be anachronistic, but it is true to say that Luther's perspective is highly experiential without permitting experience to be a source or norm for theology. Of course, our experience with God is often quite painful, for "it is by living—no, not living, but by dying and giving ourselves up to hell that we become theologians, not by understanding, reading, and speculating."[73]

The Question of Double Truth

In his 1539 "Disputation concerning the Passage: 'The Word Was Made Flesh,'" Luther maintains that even though "every truth is in agreement with every other truth," still "what is true in one field of learning is not always true in other fields of learning."[74] His chief example is the christological principle that in theology "it is true that the Word was made flesh" but in philosophy the "statement is simply impossible and absurd."[75] Was Luther an advocate of the "double truth" theory, that what is true in philosophy may be false in theology and vice versa?

In this disputation, Luther takes the Scholastic axiom *nulla est proportio finite ad infiniti* ("There is no relationship between the finite and the infinite") as a philosophical given. The infinite cannot be made finite and still remain infinite.[76]

---

72. "Sermons on the Second Epistle of St. Peter," in LW 30:152 (WA 14:16).

73. *Operationes in Psalmos* (1519–21), in WA 5:163.28–29 (trans. Bayer, *Theology the Lutheran Way*, 23).

74. "Disputation concerning the Passage: 'The Word Was Made Flesh,'" thesis 1, in LW 38:239 (WA 39/2:3.1–2).

75. "Disputation concerning the Passage: 'The Word Was Made Flesh,'" thesis 2, in LW 38:239 (WA 39/2:3.3–4).

76. The phrase as such can be traced to Duns Scotus, but it can be found throughout medieval Scholasticism, including Thomas Aquinas and Bonaventure. The phrase was used by these earlier figures as "just one aspect of the *analogia entis*, to be complemented by the notion of a likeness or relation between God and humanity. The nominalists, in opposing Thomistic Christology, emphasize the distinction in a stronger way than their predecessors" (David W. Congdon, "*Nova Lingua Dei*: The Problem of Chalcedonian Metaphysics and the Promise of

But this is exactly what has happened in the incarnation. Luther proceeds by developing a series of syllogisms, which are formally sound philosophically but which result in false conclusions in theology. He also provides examples from the "other arts and sciences that the same thing is not true in all of them," for instance, an incommensurability between the measurements of lines and weights.[77]

Luther rejects the position of the Sorbonne that the same is true in philosophy and theology. His point is that in their attempt to defend univocal truth in both philosophy and theology, they equivocate on the nature of humanity as shared by all people and Christ. The Sorbonne's position represents a reaction against the "double truth" theory of Latin Averroism (radical Aristotelianism), which had been championed by Siger of Brabant (ca. 1235–ca. 1282).[78] Following upon Parisian bishop Stephen Tempier's general condemnation (219 condemnations) of Latin Averroism on March 7, 1277,[79] Robert Kilwardby, archbishop of Canterbury, on March 18, 1277, published thirty prohibited propositions, known as the Oxford Condemnation. The first two condemned theses read:

1. *Quod contraria simul possunt esse vera in aliqua materia* (that contraries can be simultaneously true in a certain subject matter).

2. *Item quod syllogismus pecans in material non est sillogismus* (that the syllogism which is materially erroneous [with respect to a subject matter] is not a syllogism).[80]

---

the *Genus Tapeinoticon* in Luther's Later Theology" [unpublished paper, Princeton Theological Seminary, 2011], 42n126).

77. "Disputation concerning the Passage: 'The Word Was Made Flesh,'" thesis 32, in LW 38:242 (WA 39/2:5.19–20). Theses 16–25 develop syllogisms that are structurally sound philosophically but conclude with false beliefs theologically. Theses 29–37 offer examples of matters true in one discipline but not in another.

78. This position can be traced to the Muslim philosopher Averroës (1126–98), known as the "Commentator" on Aristotle. Since Averroës judged Aristotle to be the pinnacle of human intellect despite his views not always corresponding with the Qur'an, Averroës proposed a double truth. "This does not mean that . . . a proposition can be true in philosophy and false in theology or vice versa: his theory is that one and the same truth is understood clearly in philosophy and expressed allegorically in theology. The scientific formulation of truth is achieved only in philosophy, but the same truth is expressed in theology, only in a different manner" (Congdon, "*Nova Lingua Dei*," 29–30, quoting Frederick Copleston). While privileging philosophy over theology, Averroës still maintained the unity of truth. In contrast, Siger of Brabant allowed philosophy to contradict theology in favor of philosophy.

79. Here Bishop Tempier rejected the perspective that "certain views were true according to philosophy, but not according to Catholic faith, 'as if there were two contrary truths'" (Hans Thijssen, "Condemnation of 1277," *Stanford Encyclopedia of Philosophy*, ed. Edward N. Zalta, https://plato.stanford.edu/entries/condemnation).

80. Heinrich Denifle and Emile Chatelaine, eds., *Chartularium Universitatis Parisiensis* (Paris: Delalain, 1889–97), 1:558, as quoted by Congdon, "*Nova Lingua Dei*," 31 (translation modified).

As David Congdon writes,

> By rejecting the first thesis, Kilwardby seems to affirm that truth is univocal;
> there can only be one kind of attribution of truth. In rejecting the second thesis,
> it is affirmed that as long as a syllogism is formally correct, it remains rational
> regardless of the subject-matter. These theses, along with the others, together
> imply a rejection of any contradiction between philosophy and theology; what
> is rational and true in one subject-matter must be rational and true in the other.[81]

Luther is no advocate of "double truth" theory, but he does maintain that
philosophy and theology constitute two distinct spheres with their own distinct
logics. The univocal approach to truth advocated by the Sorbonne would result
in the "articles of faith" to be "subject to the judgment of human reason."[82]

In their attempt to establish univocal truth in philosophy and theology,
the faculty of the Sorbonne actually equivocate. The word "man" ends up
meaning one thing in reference to humans generally and another in reference
to the Word made flesh. Hence, to expose the inaccurate reasoning of the
Sorbonne, Luther proposes this theologically inaccurate syllogism:

(1) Every man is a creature.

(2) Christ is a man.

(3) Therefore, Christ is a creature.[83]

Luther noted that this is a sound syllogism in philosophy but that in theology
it has an erroneous conclusion. As Reijo Työrinoja claims, "According to the
philosophical argumentation, there is no proportion between the Creator and
a creature, infinite and finite. But in theology, Luther states, there is not only a
proportion, but in Christ the unity of finite and infinite (*unitas finiti et infiniti*).
Therefore the predicates of God and man are the same."[84] The point is that
the above syllogism fails to follow theological grammar. Luther claimed that

81. Congdon, "*Nova Lingua Dei*," 31.

82. "Disputation concerning the Passage: 'The Word Was Made Flesh,'" thesis 6, in LW
38:239 (WA 39/2:4.2–3).

83. "Disputation concerning the Passage: 'The Word Was Made Flesh,'" argument 4, in LW
38:246 (WA 39/2:10 [argumentum 4]), translation altered.

84. Reijo Työrinoja, "*Nova Vocabula et Nova Lingua*: Luther's Conception of Doctrinal
Formulas," in *Thesaurus Lutheri: Auf der Suche nach neuen Paradigmen der Luther-Forschung*,
ed. Tuomo Mannermaa et al. (Helsinki: Luther-Agricola-Society, 1987), 229. As a rule, Luther
does not generalize expressions like "unity of finite and infinite," but limits them very concretely
to the incarnation and the person of Christ. Melanchthon, Chemnitz, and others make it more
explicit perhaps, or emphasize it more, but Luther does not argue for a general unity of the
finite and the infinite, limiting it to the person of Christ.

with respect to such syllogistic reasoning the fault is not due to a "defect of the syllogistic form but because of the lofty character and majesty of the matter which cannot be enclosed in the narrow confines of reason or syllogism. So the matter is not indeed something contrary to, but is outside, within, above, below, before, and beyond all logical truth."[85] While the "syllogism is a most excellent form . . . it is useless with regard to the matter itself. Therefore, in articles of faith one must have recourse to another dialectic and philosophy, which is called the word of God and faith."[86]

Priority of Grammar over Logic

For Luther, philosophy, including logic, is beholden to grammar (semantical analysis). His view came to the fore in his debates with Ulrich Zwingli (1484–1531) and Johannes Oecolampadius (1482–1531) over the nature of the Lord's Supper.[87] Following the Roman rhetorician Quintilian (35–100) on the nature of metaphor or "transfers of words" (new words or tropes) produced according to the rules of comparison, Luther indicated that a word such as "vine" has both an old and a new meaning. In the old sense it means simply the stock in the vineyard. But "according to the new it means Christ, John 15[:5]: 'I am the vine.'"[88] Luther explained how Christ himself is the basis on which the comparison is made. "For Christ is not a likeness of the vine, but on the contrary the vine is a likeness of Christ." Explaining the word "seed" in "the seed is the word of God" (Luke 8:11), Luther says, "Here the word 'seed' does not indicate the grain, which is a simile of the gospel, but as a new word or trope should, signifies the gospel, the true, new seed itself, which is not a likeness. And so forth; all tropes in Scripture signify the true, new object, and not the simile of this new object."[89]

Luther agreed with his opponents that "it is undeniably true that two diverse substances cannot be one substance. For example, an ass cannot be an ox, a man cannot be a stone or a piece of wood."[90] This, of course, follows

85. "Disputation concerning the Passage: 'The Word Was Made Flesh,'" thesis 21, in LW 38:241 (WA 39/2:4.34–35).

86. "Disputation concerning the Passage: 'The Word Was Made Flesh,'" thesis 27, in LW 38:241 (WA 39/2:5.9–10).

87. See "The Law of Identical Predication" in *Confession concerning Christ's Supper* (1528), in LW 37:294–303 (WA 26:437–45). For a sound commentary on this treatise, see Jörg Baur, "Luther und die Philosophie," *NZSTh* 26 (1984): 13–28; and Enrico de Negri, *Offenbarung und Dialektik: Luthers Realtheologie* (Darmstadt: Wissenschaftliche Buchgesellschaft, 1973), 207–18.

88. *Confession concerning Christ's Supper*, in LW 37:252–53 (WA 26:379.27).

89. *Confession concerning Christ's Supper*, in LW 37:253 (WA 26:380.27–33).

90. *Confession concerning Christ's Supper*, in LW 37:295 (WA 26:439.6–7).

the law of contradiction and makes it problematic for reason to be able to affirm that bread simultaneously can be Christ's body. Luther noted that John Wycliffe (ca. 1330–84) solved the problem by affirming that bread remains bread while Christ's body is literally absent, while Aquinas maintained that Christ's body is literally present but the bread is absent. Luther responds, "Against all reason and hairsplitting logic I hold that two diverse substances may well be, in reality and in name, one substance."[91] Building his case, he provides examples of how two distinct beings can be one. The Trinity, for example, is a "natural union" of the three triune persons sharing the same essence. Likewise, Christ is one person with two natures, a "personal union." There is also a "union of effect" when angels are described in Scripture as winds and flames of fire. Similarly there is a "formal union" when the Holy Spirit is seen as a dove. All this makes plausible Luther's contention that there is a "sacramental union" in which bread can be Christ's body and wine can be Christ's blood. He chides Wycliffe's view of an absent Christ in the sacrament for prematurely applying logic and not taking into account the rules of grammar or the science of words.

> Logic rightly teaches that bread and body, dove and Spirit, God and man are diverse beings. But it should first seek the aid of grammar, which lays down a rule of expression applicable to all languages: when two diverse beings become one being, grammar embraces these two things in a single expression, and as it views the union of the two beings, it refers to the two in one term.[92]

Grammatically, Luther maintains that his examples are expressions of synecdoche. Hence, Luther concludes,

> No *identical* predication is even there; Wycliffe and the sophists only dream that it is. For even though body and bread are two distinct substances, each one existing by itself, and though neither is mistaken for the other where they are separated from each other, nevertheless where they are united and become a new, entire substance, they lose their difference so far as this new, unique substance is concerned.[93]

Hence we can see why, in the "Disputation on the Divinity and Humanity of Christ" (1541), Luther maintained that "it is certain that with regard to Christ [*in Christo*] all words receive a new signification, though the thing signified is

91. *Confession concerning Christ's Supper*, in LW 37:296 (WA 26:439.29–31).
92. *Confession concerning Christ's Supper*, in LW 37:301 (WA 26:443.12–16).
93. *Confession concerning Christ's Supper*, in LW 37:303 (WA 26:445.1–6; italics original).

the same."[94] He was building on his understanding of grammar as accountable to the narrative of Jesus Christ, who is the truth. In the old usage of language, "creature" signifies (causes us to think)[95] "a thing separated from divinity by infinite degrees," while in the new usage, "creature" "signifies a thing inseparably joined with divinity in the same person in an ineffable way."[96] Indeed, words like "man, humanity, suffered" and "everything that is said of Christ" are new words.[97] With Ingolf Dalferth, we can conclude that philosophy and theology deal not with different things but with the same things in different ways.[98]

Theology acknowledges a new signification for the same thing in Christ. In the old usage there can be no inclusion of the property of humanity in

94. "Disputation on the Divinity and Humanity of Christ," trans. Christopher B. Brown (http://www.leaderu.com/philosophy/luther-humanitychrist.html), thesis 20 (WA 39/2:94).

95. See Dennis Bielfeldt, "Luther's Late Trinitarian Disputations," in *The Substance of Faith: Luther's Doctrinal Theology for Today*, by Dennis Bielfeldt, Mickey Mattox, and Paul Hinlicky (Minneapolis: Fortress, 2008), 109.

96. "Disputation on the Divinity and Humanity of Christ," thesis 21 (WA 39/2:94.19–20).

97. "Disputation on the Divinity and Humanity of Christ," thesis 23 (WA 39/2:94.23–24).

98. Dalferth (*Theology and Philosophy*, 77) writes,

According to Luther, philosophy and theology are fundamentally different, yet they neither contradict nor complement each other (WA 39/2, 27, 31–2). Philosophy has the world for its field and whatever it talks about, even in metaphysics, must make itself felt in the present and experienced world. Theology, on the other hand, has "the invisible things as subject" (WA 39/2, 15, 8–9), i.e., those "which are believed, i.e., which are apprehended by faith" (WA 39/2, 6, 26–8). This looks like the traditional distinction between the knowable and the merely credible. But it is not. Philosophy and theology are neither different stages in our knowledge of things nor knowledge about different sorts of things. They are different kinds of knowledge of the same things, placed in different perspectives and different frames of reference: viz. the *coram mundo*-perspective of its relations to God. Both perspectives are necessary for an adequate understanding of reality; both allow for growth of knowledge and a perfecting of our understanding of God, world and human existence; but there is no transition from knowledge in the first perspective to knowledge in the second, and thus no direct combination of knowledge achieved in the one frame with knowledge achieved in the second. Confusion is bound to result from mixing philosophical discourse about things *coram mundo* with theological discourse about things *coram deo*; and precisely this mixing of discourses Luther diagnoses as having been the endemic evil of scholastic theology.

With respect to grammar, Risto Saarinen notes,

It can be observed that Luther distinguishes theological grammar from philosophical. However, theological grammar is for him by no means an esoteric code that has normal words and everyday phrases as its external manifestation. The difference between philosophical and theological grammar is, linguistically speaking, not primarily a syntactic but a *semantic* and a *pragmatic* difference. The specific art of theological grammar is determined by its subject matter, namely, by the *significata* of biblical language. The presence of the unique subject matter, the new entity (*nova res*), implies that even the way of understanding that new entity and the modes of speaking about its properties have to be unique, although these new ways and modes are, nevertheless, conveyed by normal, everyday words. ("The Word of God in Luther's Theology," *LQ* 4 [1990]: 39–40)

the property of God. But in the new, the property of the divine conjoins itself with the property of the human. Hence, the Sorbonne must be wrong in maintaining a univocal view of truth shared between philosophy and theology. It fails to acknowledge the newness of words transposed in Christ. This "eschatological" dimension[99]—for lack of a better term—of Christ the *novum* constitutes the old as old, but does not eliminate or dismiss it, instead allowing it to stand in its own unique temporality and likewise incorporating it in theology with its own intelligibility. As Luther notes, "We would act more correctly if we left dialectic and philosophy in their own area and learned to speak in a new language in the realm of faith apart from every sphere. Otherwise, it will turn out that, if we put the new wine in old wineskins, both of them will perish."[100]

The Semantics of the New Tongue

But this raises a question about Luther's theologically false syllogism, outlined above (p. 36): What semantic theory would allow (1) and (2) to be true but (3) false? Is it the case that new meanings of terms emerge within theological contexts, or is it the case that there is no real difference in meanings between the terms within the two languages, only a difference in the inferences permitted? It would seem that different rules govern theology and philosophy. Just as different rules apply in regions within philosophy, so too there are different rules operative between theology and philosophy. Dennis Bielfeldt has cogently argued that Luther should not be seen here as having employed standard Ockhamist supposition theory. Supposition is a semantic relation between the terms in a proposition and the things to which those terms refer (their extension).[101] Since Ockham rejected the existence of real universals or common natures, written and spoken terms must "primarily" signify individuals, "the things they can be truly predicated of." For example, in the proposition "'the cow is red' is true," the term "cow" supposits (refers to what it signifies) for the same individual for which the term "red" supposits. Late medieval supposition theory understood the truth conditions and the meaning of statements extensionally—that is, by whether they supposit for the same individual or individuals. By contrast, the *via antiqua* was more intensionalist. Bielfeldt argues:

99. Dalferth, *Theology and Philosophy*, 79.
100. "Disputation concerning the Passage: 'The Word Was Made Flesh,'" theses 40–41, in LW 38:242 (WA 39/2:5.35–38).
101. Bielfeldt, "Luther's Late Trinitarian Disputations," 111.

"All men are rational" is true if and only if "man" signifies (causes the mind to think about) a property inexorably instanced only if the property signified by "rational" is instanced. An intension of a predicate specifies all and only those properties a thing must have in order for the predicate truly to apply to it. An extension, on the other hand, is the class of things to which the predicate rightly applies. In an intensionalist semantics, the intension establishes the conditions by virtue of which extension is determined.[102]

Bielfeldt asks whether "God is man" is best understood in a nominalistic, extensional sense or in an intensionalist way. He answers that if "God is man" is construed intensionally, then the property of being God does not exclude the property of being a man. In theology, this is the truth of the incarnation. But this is impossible in philosophy. Here specification of the properties of God includes that of being infinite. But since human beings are not infinite, specification of God-making properties must include the property of not being a human being. Thus the conceptual rules by which theology proceeds must differ from philosophy, because terms such as "God" and "mother," for example, do not exclude predication by "man" and "virgin" respectively. Indeed, the terms "God" and "mother" have different significations in theology and philosophy respectively. They cause one to think about different things in philosophy and theology, as one would expect in signification theory.

The upshot of Bielfeldt's case is that theological truth cannot be reduced to that which can be said philosophically. Hence Luther refuses the notion that there could be one vast tree of Porphyry (or scale of being) in which only theology has access to some of the branches. Hence, with Christ, something new has emerged.[103] The semantics of the *via antiqua* can serve as a suitable vehicle of Christ the *novum*.

102. Ibid., 113.
103. Bielfeldt waxes lyrical in his positive assessment of the role of philosophy for theology: Just as old legalisms have been taken up in the grace of Christ's free justification, so too the old language of philosophy has been interrupted by the presence of something new. Just as the gospel is a new ingredient in the old mix of the law, so does the language that talks about the gospel possess a new ingredient in the old mix of philosophy. Just as the law cannot contain the gospel, so too does philosophical language not contain the good news about which theology speaks. The law, reason, and philosophy belong to God's left hand, while the gospel, faith, and theology concern His right. This intensionalist alternative fits well with the Lutheran notion of the infinite being available in the finite, for just as there is a real presence of Christ in the Lord's Supper, so too is there a "real presence" of the deepest theological truths in human philosophical language. Just as God's presence is mediated through the earthly elements of the sacraments, so too is the presence of the *nova lingua* of theology mediated through the old language of philosophy. Just as everyday earthly elements are retained yet transformed sacramentally, so too is the everyday language of philosophy retained yet transformed in theology. (ibid., 114–15)

Conclusion

The distinction between law and gospel governs Luther's approach to philosophy. Nominalism and realism are no longer alternatives for him because
their conclusions must each be evaluated in light of the law/gospel distinction.
Luther charts a new path beyond that philosophical debate. In Christ, men
and women are new creations, new beings, and they are not merely the set of
all who claim Christ as their own but instead share in the form of Christ and
so instantiate Christ himself in their service, which is similar to but not the
same as realism. Even so, his overall positioning of philosophy in relation to
theology has a nominalist contour. Philosophy is limited by the fact that it
knows nothing of the incarnation and is not able to accommodate its truth;
nor does philosophy have a sense of God's grace. But it does have its place
when restricted to this-worldly matters. Even so, Luther values syllogistic reasoning and uses it in theology when it is accountable to theological grammar.

Philosophy is no jump start that could impel us further along the ladder
of salvation. Instead, for Luther, philosophy becomes akin to law and can be
affirmed as appropriate for temporal matters, though not for eternal ones.
It can have a place in theology only as it is properly bathed. As such, it is
most helpful in establishing doctrinal truth that is beholden to Christ, who
as the *new*, having in his resurrection emerged from sin and the consequence
of sin, death, refigures human relationship with creation, indeed allows us
to accept our creatureliness under God and his goodness. Similar to other
medieval thinkers, Luther denies philosophy a stance by which it could set
the agenda for theology. More than anything, Luther would not want to see
philosophy misused to limit or stymie an active, risen Christ through whom
God favors sinners and imputes to them his righteousness. But Luther is ever
vigilant that genuine theology faithful to the gospel employs rigorous logic,
though only as faithful to the grammar of theology. Philosophy does not set
the agenda for theology.

Ultimately to understand beauty we cannot base its truth on analogies of
beauty in the world. Instead, it must be defined by and filtered through Christ
and his cross. Through that prism we will be able to distinguish the "love of
God," which "does not find, but creates, that which is pleasing to it," from the
"love of man," which "comes into being through that which is pleasing to it"[104]
and so understand God's beauty as inherently creative, albeit out of nothing.

---

104. *Heidelberg Disputation*, in LW 31:51 (WA 1:354.35).

>> 3 <<

Luther on Goodness

A study of Luther's view of beauty must examine the nature of goodness since medieval thinkers with whom Luther was conversant associated beauty with goodness. For instance, Aquinas claimed that the good and the beautiful differ in aspect only: the good "means that which simply pleases the appetite; while the beautiful is something pleasant to apprehend."[1] Medieval thinkers saw goodness as the nature of God.[2] Since God manifests his goodness as grace, a discussion of goodness should likewise explore the distinguishing features of grace in Luther and the medieval tradition. That tradition maintained that God is good because God satisfies humanity's deepest desire, which, whether or not humans are aware of it, is to be one with God. Goodness then is configured eudaimonistically as the self-fulfillment of humanity's potential for complete happiness. Humans can realize this potential since grace heals the wound of sin and elevates pilgrims (*viatores*) toward greater degrees of mimetic participation in God as they exercise the virtues of faith, love, and hope, and so reach their full potential in heaven.

Luther diverged from this tradition in important ways. The difference is not in that Luther recognized no teleological fulfillment for humanity. After all, he maintained that humanity was designed for a greater purpose than its vocation to tend and care for the earth (Gen. 2:15–17), important as that calling is. Humanity was created to "inhabit the celestial regions and to live an eternal life," as

1. Aquinas, *Summa theologiae* I-II, q. 27, a. 1 (trans. Fathers of the English Dominican Province [EDP] [Westminster, MD: Christian Classics, 1948], 2:707).
2. Aquinas, *Summa theologiae* III, q. 1, a. 1 (EDP, 4:2022).

43

indicated by humans' ability to think mathematically, which gives them insight into the eternal.[3] But, diverging from his contemporaries, the Reformer taught that God's goodness properly is God's *favor*, which forgives sinners for Jesus's sake and renews them so that they may become good.[4] A system of merit is not able to make humans good because, ironically, it undermines the goodness of "good works." In such a system, people do good things for their self-interest, securing their own salvation, and not solely for fostering the well-being of others.[5] God is loved not for his own sake but for the reward he offers. Thus human pride becomes inflated and human self-centeredness is reinforced.

For Luther, humans, whether prodigals or Pharisees, are made good when they shed their pride and self-centeredness, and trust that God's mercy in Christ is sufficient for them. Such trust secures humans' status in ultimate matters since it acknowledges that God regards sinners as his own children. Claiming sinners as his own, God imputes the righteousness of Christ to them. Through faith, repentant sinners claim nothing for themselves before God but instead receive God's favor as a gift, share in God's life, and so are led to cooperate with God in creation.[6] Having received of God's unmerited

3. See *Lectures on Genesis*, in LW 1:46 (WA 42:35.29–36.7):
   With the support of the mathematical disciplines—which no one can deny were divinely revealed—the human being, in his mind, soars high above the earth; and leaving behind those things that are on the earth, he concerns himself with heavenly things and explores them. Cows, pigs, and other beasts do not do this; it is man alone who does it. Therefore man is a creature created to inhabit the celestial regions and to live an eternal life when, after a while, he has left the earth. For this is the meaning of the fact that he can not only speak and form judgments (things which belong to dialectics and rhetoric) but also learns all the sciences thoroughly.

4. See *Against Latomus* (1521), in LW 32:227 (WA 8:106.6–15):
   The companion of this faith and righteousness is grace or mercy, the good will [favor] of God, against wrath which is the partner of sin, so that he who believes in Christ has a merciful God. For we would not be completely happy in this good of righteousness, and we would not highly esteem God's gift, if that was all there was, and it did not gain for us the grace of God. Here, as ought to be done, I take grace in the proper sense of the favor of God—not a quality of the soul, as is taught by our more recent writers. This grace truly produces peace of heart until finally a man is healed from his corruption and feels he has a gracious God. It is this which fattens the bones and gives joy, security, and fearlessness to the conscience so that one dares all, can do all and, in this trust in the grace of God, laughs even at death.

5. As Carter Lindberg notes, for many medieval ethicists God willed that there be poor in the world so that the rich would have an opportunity to atone for their sins. "Such perspectives created an obstacle to realistic understanding of poverty and its sources. . . . [Catherine] Lis and [Hugo] Soly suggest that this attitude toward poverty more than obscured the realities of misery; it perpetuated them and maintained both a labor market and social equilibrium" (*Beyond Charity: Reformation Initiatives for the Poor* [Minneapolis: Fortress, 1993], 32–33).

6. See *The Bondage of the Will* (1525), trans. J. I. Packer and O. R. Johnston (New York: Revell, 1957), 267–68 (WA 18:753.27–35):

generosity or "overflowing" goodness, unnatural (self-seeking, self-serving) desire as such must be extinguished.[7] Humans have a new status before God that affects their deepest core, their hearts, their very identity. Forgiven in Christ, sinners receive new and clean hearts and thus are reconstituted so as to love God from the heart and serve others for their own sake and not to attain merit.

Luther claimed that human goodness is established as sinners live trustingly as creatures (leaving ultimate matters in God's hands) and that such faith spontaneously expresses itself in acts of love to those in need and not for the sake of personal reward. Good works are spontaneous because recipients of generosity have the wherewithal and motivation to be generous themselves. A eudaimonistic approach such as Aristotle's fails to comprehend the nature of goodness. When desire is the defining feature of the self, then the self seeks itself in all things, wants the satisfaction of its own desire, and so is curved in on itself (*incurvatus in se*).[8] For Luther, more basic than desire is the question of trust: In what or whom do we place our confidence? Augustine had reenvisioned desire as a Neoplatonic transformation from *eros* to *caritas*, a conversion of desire from finding its good in earthly things to finding its good in heavenly things as humans are beckoned by divine love.[9] Even

---

What I assert and maintain is this: that where God works apart from the grace of His Spirit, He works all things in all men, even in the ungodly; for He alone moves, makes to act, and impels by the motion of His omnipotence, all those things which He alone created; they can neither avoid nor alter this movement, but necessarily follow and obey it, each thing according to the measure of its God-given power. Thus all things, even the ungodly, co-operate with God. And when God acts by the Spirit of His grace in those whom he has justified, that is, in His own kingdom, He moves and carries them along in like manner; and they, being a new creation, follow and co-operate with Him, or rather, as Paul says, are made to act by Him (Rom. 8.14).

7. See *Heidelberg Disputation* (1518), in LW 31:54 (WA 1:363.5–9]):
Thus also the desire for knowledge is not satisfied by the acquisition of wisdom but is stimulated that much more. Likewise the desire for glory is not satisfied by the acquisition of glory, nor the desire to rule satisfied by power and authority, nor is the desire for praise satisfied by praise, and so on, as Christ shows in John 4[:13], where he says, "Everyone who drinks of this water will thirst again." The remedy for curing desire does not lie in satisfying it, but in extinguishing it.

8. See *Lectures on Romans*, in LW 25:345 (WA 56:356.5).

9. "As Luigi Pizzolato points out, it is really an argument about the relation of nature to grace, and Augustine's 'synthesis' expresses his conviction that grace does not destroy nature, but perfects it. *Eros* and *agape* are not simply conflated in *caritas*: *eros* is elevated and transfigured by grace, not destroyed, but redeemed. '*Amor tuus migret*': 'Your love migrates,' says Augustine, and finds its focus in God. '*Venit Christus mutare amorem*': 'Christ came to transform love.' For Augustine, it is a matter of *dilectio ordinate*: love re-ordered by grace" (Robert Crouse, "*Paucis mutatis verbis*: St. Augustine's Platonism," in *Augustine and His Critics*, ed. Robert Dodaro and George Lawless [London: Routledge, 2000], 39). For Luther, merit based on human efforts will never help us achieve our ultimate fulfillment; faith alone in Christ alone right-wises us for that.

so, for Luther, in either case humans still find their confidence grounded in themselves, in their own efforts or dispositions. Such self-confidence subtly undermines the deity of God because it refuses to live solely from God's generosity. The Reformer believed that the agency of the law is to break down such self-confidence and the agency of the gospel is to remake humans so as to trust in God's generous mercy. Desire is then reconfigured away from an egocentrism that seeks benefits accruing from love of God and neighbor so that believers love God for God's own sake and humans for their own sakes. Indeed, the happiness of the other can be experienced as one's own.[10]

The gospel establishes God's mercy, but for Luther's opponents this leaves God's fairness in question. If no human agency is accorded some status with respect to God, then people are not responsible for their rejection of God, let alone their misdeeds. It would be unwarranted of God to punish sinners who had no choice but to sin in the first place. If God is omnipotent, as Luther maintained, then he would be a puppeteer who determines and manipulates everything, again reinforcing a view that humans are not ultimately accountable for their behavior. In contrast, for Luther sin is similar to what we nowadays call addiction.[11] In addiction, paradoxically, the disease controls addicts, but addicts are still held accountable for how they respond to their disease. Addicts "in recovery" can never use the disease as an excuse for their misbehavior or lack of trust in a "higher power." Between Christ's first and second advents, Luther is willing to live with cognitive dissonance between how God is merciful and how God is fair. That God is merciful is indisputable because of the work of Christ to save. Luther is convinced that God's fairness will be established eschatologically at the consummation of the world. In general, we can observe that reducing a relationship to fairness alone limits and cripples the freedom, and so the love, of any one in relationship to others. For Luther, predestination is not determinism. "It is not that God causes one to do this thing at this time but that whatever is chosen and done is under the inner dominance of God or the devil."[12] Luther distinguishes "matters above" from "matters below." Determinism would be to take matters below—chains of causality—and read them into matters above, an illicit move.

10. See Wilfried Härle, *Outline of Christian Doctrine: An Evangelical Dogmatics*, trans. Ruth Yules and Nicolas Sagovsky (Grand Rapids: Eerdmans, 2015), 201–2.
11. The analogy is taken from Gerhard Forde, *On Being a Theologian of the Cross: Reflections on Luther's Heidelberg Disputation, 1518* (Grand Rapids: Eerdmans, 1997), 15. Forde is quick to note that addiction is not meant to replace the category of sin but instead to help illustrate how sin holds sinners captive.
12. Kyle Pasewark, "Predestination as a Condition of Freedom," *LQ* 12 (1998): 63.

Brief Overview of Medieval Views of Goodness

In medieval thought goodness was a "transcendental," something that is proper to the structure of being and so common to all creatures, whose existence is due to their participation in being. Medieval thinkers debated which traits were to be included on the list of transcendentals, which were also seen as names for God. That list generally included being, oneness, and truth, along with goodness. Beauty was sometimes placed on that list, but its status was open to debate. Its status as a transcendental was questioned because medieval thinkers were not fully able to integrate the Platonic-Dionysian "metaphysics of the good," which prioritized goodness over being, with the Aristotelian-Avicennian "metaphysics of being," which prioritized being over goodness.[13] Nevertheless, most medieval thinkers associated beauty with goodness and so situated the nature of beauty within the context of goodness. For instance, Alexander of Hales (1185–1245) distinguished the good from the beautiful by designating the former as an expression of final causality and the latter as an expression of formal causality.[14] Aquinas claimed that the good preexists in God in a "more excellent way" than that of creatures and so causes goodness in creatures.[15] Hence, every creature participates in goodness to some degree or another.

With respect to divine goodness, all medieval thinkers were dependent on Pseudo-Dionysius the Areopagite, who saw God as the source (*archē*), goal (*telos*), and paradigm of goodness.[16] That is, God is good because all things come from him and are destined to return to him, and all things to one degree or another are patterned after God and should in their behavior increasingly conform to God. For Pseudo-Dionysius, God's goodness can be distinguished as light, beauty, and love.[17] Again, for Pseudo-Dionysius, to designate God as beauty is to reinforce his view of God as goodness as such. As beauty, God is the cause of "consonance and splendor" in all things. Likewise, God calls

---

13. Jan Aertsen, *Medieval Philosophy as Transcendental Thought: From Philip the Chancellor (ca. 1225) to Francisco Suárez* (Leiden: Brill, 2012), 176.

14. "Both the 'beautiful' and the 'good' express the disposition with respect to a cause: the 'good' with respect to the final cause, the 'beautiful' with respect to the formal cause. A sign that the beauty of a thing is derived from the form is the fact that we usually call that which is *speciosus* 'beautiful,' and the species is taken from the form" (ibid., 164).

15. Ibid., 166. "So when we say, God is good, the meaning is not, God is the cause of goodness, or, God is not evil; but the meaning is, whatever good we attribute to creatures, pre-exists in God, and in a more excellent and higher way. Hence it does not follow that God is good, because He causes goodness; but rather, on the contrary, He causes goodness in things because He is good" (Aquinas, *Summa theologiae* I, q. 13, a. 2 [EDP, 1:61]).

16. Aertsen, *Medieval Philosophy as Transcendental Thought*, 162.

17. Ibid., 161.

and gathers everything to himself.[18] In Dionysian terms, human goodness is conceived as conforming more and more to the divine life in its simplicity (oneness) and tranquility, and thereby humans can find fulfillment for their deepest desire, which ultimately is to be one with God. In sum, for medieval thinkers, God's goodness can be established metaphysically as a way to understand the nature of being as such. God's goodness is God's generosity expressing itself in creating a world, establishing itself as the pattern for how creatures are properly to live, and inviting creatures to return to God's life in order to find their own fulfillment. This view of goodness affects humanity in that humans are to find their good as they actualize their potential for self-fulfillment by actualizing their goal of becoming one with God through the exercise of virtue or spirituality.

Justification and Goodness

The Reformation is characterized as a conflict over many things, including the nature of salvation, the role of discipleship, the integrity of the church, the value of creaturely life, the basis for truth, and the relation between church and state, but seldom is it seen as a debate over the nature of goodness. But a case can be made that this is exactly what the Reformation, at least for Luther, is about. After all, Luther was convinced that no amount of good works can make one good. Instead, one must first be made good, and then good works will follow.[19] But this question of human regeneration, how one receives a new, clean heart, is closely associated with how God himself is good. It is God as goodness—as love[20]—who regenerates. The goodness of God has been a vexing problem in Luther research. Some scholars cannot reconcile God's hiddenness (*deus absconditus*), God seen as accuser, abandoner, or threat, with God's revealedness (*deus revelatus*), God received as sheer mercy granted in Christ. Some have accused Luther of Manichaean tendencies, advocating two gods, one bad, a monster of sheer indifferent power, and one good, the Christ of comfort, kindness, and love. Similarly, others, like Erasmus (1466–1536), have found Luther's view of an electing God as incompatible with a view of God as love. For Erasmus, Luther exaggerates the severity of the human

18. Ibid., 162.
19. See *The Freedom of a Christian* (1520), in LW 31:361 (WA 7:61.26–38).
20. Luther preached, "If I were to paint a picture of God I would so draw him that there would be nothing else in the depth of his divine nature than that fire and passion that is called love for people. Correspondingly, love is such a thing that is neither human nor angelic but rather divine, yes, even God himself" (WA 36:424.2–5; translation from Paul Althaus, *The Theology of Martin Luther*, trans. Robert C. Schultz [Philadelphia: Fortress, 1966], 115).

predicament. Humans do not need rescue, as Luther maintained, but instead require a program for moral improvement: things are bad, but not nearly as bad as Luther makes them.

For Luther, the proper understanding of the nature of goodness, how God is good and how sinners are made good, is understood through the article of justification by grace alone through faith alone. God's goodness is God's establishing his righteousness for sinners and granting them new life out of death, not on the basis of human worthiness or merit but on the basis of God's generous forgiveness made tangible in Christ's redemption. While the Reformer is aware of goodness as a transcendental,[21] God's goodness is established not metaphysically but instead on the basis of Christ's saving action. As definitive of God's being, God's proper work (*opus proprium*), Christ is the basis on which to affirm God's goodness and also to deliver God's goodness in proclamation so that sinners can actually take hold of this goodness. Luther developed his views on justification in the context of late medieval Scholasticism, particularly the theology of Gabriel Biel (1420/25–1495). The most important theological agenda of the young Luther (1513–21) was the nature of God's righteousness. Luther came to believe that righteousness is of two kinds, an active and a passive, and not merely one, as the tradition previously had assumed. The medieval tradition advocated only an active righteousness—that is, that we are saved by developing our potential to become godlike—although most theologians taught that grace must initiate the *viator* or pilgrim on the journey toward the beatific vision in which one becomes a *comprehensor*, finding ultimate fulfillment in God in heaven.

As described by R. Scott Clark, there was a broad consensus in medieval views of justification:

> One is ordinarily justified because and to the degree that one is intrinsically sanctified, whether as a necessity because of the divine nature (as in realism) or as a consequence of an apparently arbitrary divine will (as in voluntarism), whether from a strongly predestinarian standpoint (e.g., [Thomas] Bradwardine) or a Pelagianizing approach (e.g., Ockham). Justification was a process begun at baptism and ordinarily concluded only at the judgment. This process was described in different ways with differing degrees of emphasis on the nature and role of human cooperation, but, in virtually every pre-Reformation scheme,

---

21. "When in the beginning God created heaven and earth, the first trace of the Father was the substance of things. Later the form was added. In the third place, there was the goodness. . . . He who sees the use of a thing sees the Holy Spirit, he who discerns the form or beauty of a thing sees the Son, and he who considers the substance and continuing existence of things sees the Father. These three—substance, form, and goodness—cannot be separated" (*Lectures on Genesis*, in LW 4:195–96 [WA 43:276.33–36]).

God is said to have taken the initiative (*gratia praeveniens*) to infuse within the sinner divine grace. By all accounts, the sinner was obligated to cooperate with that grace toward final justification.[22]

Medieval views all affirmed that, while initially alien or external to the believer, righteousness must become proper to the believer through works of love. Faith itself along with love and hope was one of the three theological virtues.

Specifically, Gabriel Biel balanced God's initiative for salvation with human cooperation "by insisting that 'out of purely natural powers' (*ex puris naturalibus*) sinners could 'do what is in them' (*facere quod in se est*). By doing their best they could win 'congruent merit,' a worthiness or righteousness before God that is not truly worthy, but nonetheless accepted by God as the basis for receiving his grace."[23] This is the *pactum* or covenant that God provides for sinners. A problem with this account is its inability to offer a standard by which one can know or be certain that one has indeed done one's best. It is this feature that would lead Luther to reexamine the Scriptures, where in his intense study of Paul and the Psalms, he believed he had discovered a passive righteousness, salvation through trusting God's word of promise of forgiveness, which imparts a new status and, thereby, a new nature, a "clean heart," to the believer.

Such insights led Luther to an unthinkable move for the Scholastic theologians: distinguishing law from gospel. In this distinction, the law is not a manual that presents the steps on which to travel to eternal life, but a tormentor attacking any self-righteousness one seeks to bring before God. The gospel is not "new law," but a gift-word of promise that assures terrified consciences of God's mercy given only to sinners, a word that awakens the dead to new life. The reality of this new life is wholly defined by the promise and not by any behaviors or dispositions of the recipients. Luther's discovery of a passive righteousness allowed him to reframe active righteousness. Since righteousness can no longer be configured in terms of works that help us merit righteousness before God, but trust alone right-wises the sinner,[24] works take on a new meaning. God needs no works; the neighbor,

22. Clark, "*Iustitia Imputata Christi*: Alien or Proper to Luther's Doctrine of Justification," *CTQ* 70 (2006): 285.

23. Robert Kolb, *Martin Luther: Confessor of the Faith* (Oxford: Oxford University Press, 2009), 32.

24. Brian Gerrish notes that "the believer does not earn this divine imputation with his faith, neither is there any legal fiction: God counts the confidence of the heart as 'right' because that is what it is. Its rightness lives in the fact that faith, for its part, does not make God an idol but takes him for exactly what *he* is: the author and giver of every good, the precise counterpart

however, does. Luther's discovery of two kinds of righteousness was only possible through his breaking out of an Aristotelian anthropology, which depended on human action as the ultimate stabilizing factor in the world instead of starting with God, who in Christ stabilizes the world by bringing it peace.[25]

As Luther came to see it, the problem with sinners, old beings, is their inability to trust God to be God for them, to provide for and take care of them. Instead, old beings prefer to be "god" for themselves. This old being cannot be reformed. Indeed, the best that humanity has to offer—religion—simply aggravates the worst self-righteousness in old beings, as Luther himself experienced as a friar within the monastery. We are insecure with our status as creatures and seek to be our own self-creators. As Luther noted,

> Man, before he is created to be man, does and endeavors nothing towards his being made a creature, and when he is made a creature he does and endeavors nothing towards his continuance as a creature; both his creation and his continuance come to pass by the sole will of the omnipotent power and goodness of God, Who creates and preserves us without ourselves.[26]

Precisely stated, original sin is not trusting in God to be God but instead looking to oneself for one's good. We sinners need to become new beings, and this happens only by God's re-creative word. God's forensic word of judgment, which in fact kills old beings, is given in tandem with the word of absolution: your sins are forgiven you, for Jesus's sake. God's word does not merely provide information about God, the world, or the self, or establish directives for our behavior. Such information is encapsulated in God's law, whether heard in Scripture, sermon, or nature. Its accusation of sinners can only be stilled by the gospel promise.

In the word of absolution the sinner is embraced by God and in faith is reborn.[27] Hence, Luther noted, "grace actually means God's favor, or the good

---

of the believer's confidence. In a sense faith, by believing, is the 'creator of divinity' in us: it lets God be God" ("By Faith Alone," in *The Old Protestantism and the New: Essays on the Reformation Heritage* [Edinburgh: T&T Clark, 1982], 86).

25. Correspondence with Robert Kolb, summer 2014.

26. *Bondage of the Will*, 268 (WA 18:754.1–5).

27. "That the linguistic sign is itself the reality, that it represents not an absent but a present reality, was Luther's great hermeneutical discovery, his 'reformation discovery' in the strict sense. He made it first (1518) in reflection on the sacrament of penance. . . . The word of absolution is a speech-act that first establishes a state of affairs, first creates a relationship" (Oswald Bayer, "Luther as an Interpreter of Holy Scripture," trans. Mark Mattes, in *The Cambridge Companion to Luther*, ed. Donald McKim [Cambridge: Cambridge University Press, 2003], 76).

will which in himself he bears toward us, by which he is disposed to give us Christ and pour into us the Holy Spirit with his gifts. . . . The gifts and the Spirit increase in us every day, but they are not yet perfect since there remain in us the evil desires and sins that war against the Spirit."[28]

There is no question that for Luther the article of justification seeks to describe how God remakes sinners to be people of faith; an "effective" dimension of justification is inescapable, crucial, and decisive for Luther. However, this effective dimension of justification, like the forensic dimension, is something we passively undergo or receive.[29] Perhaps not too surprising for those who worship a crucified Jew, it takes the form or shape of death and resurrection—exactly what Christians claim to receive in the sacrament of holy baptism.

Robert Kolb describes Luther's view of justification as grounded in the etymology of the German word *rechtfertigen*:

"Justify" or "render righteous" . . . meant "to do justice to: that is to inflict punishment, 'judicially' on the basis of a conviction, and thus to execute the law's demands," or "to conduct a legal process as an activity of a judge," "to execute, to kill." From early on, Luther spoke of God's killing and making alive as he described justification, for he presumed that sinners must die (Rom. 6:23a) and be resurrected to life in Christ.[30]

28. "Prefaces to the New Testament," in LW 35:369 (WA DB 7:8.10–16). See also Kolb, *Martin Luther*, 108–9.

29. See Gerhard Forde, "Forensic Justification and the Christian Life: Triumph or Tragedy?," in *A More Radical Gospel: Essays on Eschatology, Authority, Atonement, and Ecumenism*, ed. Mark Mattes and Steven Paulson (Grand Rapids: Eerdmans, 2004), 114–36.

30. See Kolb, *Martin Luther*, 126. Kolb builds on the work of Werner Elert, who notes: When an accused person—in today's sense—justified himself we read that he "proves his innocence," or he "exonerates himself," or "he is able to prove himself innocent of the misdeed of which he is accused." The word "justification," on the other hand, which also occurred frequently, conveyed an entirely different meaning. It designated either the criminal law suit in which hide and hair or life and limb were at stake, or—and most frequently that—the execution of a sentence, especially a death sentence. For example, as late as the seventeenth century the Saxon penal code listed the hangman's fees and other expenses incidental to the execution of bodily punishment under the caption "*Unkosten der peinlichen Rechtfertigung*" (expenses incidental to penal justification). It speaks of the "*Körper der mit dem Schwert Gerechtfertigten*" (the body of the person justified by the sword). The same linguistic usage is found also in Hans Sachs. Thus it was not confined to the speech of jurists, which was foreign to the people in general. . . . Justification does not imply that man ex-culpates himself, but it means that the executioner "must mete out justice to the transgressor." Thus Luther conceives of it as the secular execution of punishment. (*The Christian Faith: An Outline of Lutheran Dogmatics*, trans. Martin H. Bertram and Walter R. Bouman [Columbus, OH: Lutheran Theological Seminary, 1974], 299–300) Elert concludes:

Our sin is nothing other than our own quest to be our own gods for ourselves (*ambitio divinitatis*).[31] Luther noted that we are humanized by God's judgment that evaluates us as sinners. Hence in his exposition of Psalm 5:3, Luther wrote, "Through the kingdom of his [Christ's] humanity, or (as the apostle says) through the kingdom of his flesh, occurring in faith, he conforms us to himself and crucifies us, by making out of unhappy and arrogant gods true men, i.e., miserable ones and sinners."[32] Luther's insight is that outside of sheer trust in God's mercy, doing virtuous acts or loving deeds, so valued by late medieval piety and theology as a basis for earning merit, is tantamount to self-righteousness, the opposite of goodness.

Luther's discovery, based on his study of Paul—in contrast to Scholastic theology—is that there are *two* kinds of righteousness, active and passive. Before God (*coram deo*) we are rendered passive, we suffer the death of the old being, so that God might be allowed to be our God and to redeem us in Christ. Before the world (*coram mundo*), faith lends itself to good works, to actively help our neighbors and the world, similar to how good fruit flourishes on a good tree. "This is our theology, by which we teach a precise distinction between these two kinds of righteousness, the active and the passive, so that morality and faith, works and grace, secular society and religion may not be confused. Both are necessary, but both must be kept within their limits. Christian righteousness applies to the new man, and the righteousness of the law applies to the old man."[33] Making this distinction is for the sake of establishing human goodness. The gospel creates and nurtures faith, makes human hearts clean, and reestablishes humans as creatures; thus they can live outside themselves, giving themselves as "Christs" to their neighbors.[34]

Justification by faith is judgment on "the old man." Justice has been done him. He receives death. That is the mortification carried out in repentance. And that is not to be understood figuratively, but very realistically. The man of faith is an other than the man of sin. To be sure, a final identity of the I remains. But it is the identity of the stalk of wheat with the seed-grain, which first had to be buried (John 12:24). As the sinner becomes a believing sinner, the enemy of God which he was but no longer is as soon as he receives forgiveness, dies. As our Confessions teach, justification is forgiveness of sin. However, forgiveness is not an exoneration for the "old" man. It is, rather, his end. The declaration of righteousness is his justification because he is receiving justice. It is death for the sinner and resurrection for the believing sinner. (305)

31. "Man is by nature unable to want God to be God. Indeed, he himself wants to be God, and does not want God to be God" ("Disputation against Scholastic Theology" [1517], thesis 17 [LW 31:10; WA 1:225.1–2]).

32. WA 5:128.39–129.4 (translation from Eberhard Jüngel, *The Freedom of a Christian: Luther's Significance for Contemporary Theology*, trans. Roy A. Harrisville [Minneapolis: Augsburg, 1988], 24).

33. *Lectures on Galatians* (1535), in LW 26:7 (WA 40/1:45.24–28).

34. See *The Freedom of a Christian*, in LW 31:367 (WA 7:66.3–4).

Omnipotence and Divine Goodness

The doctrine of justification bears on how God's goodness is to be understood. Unlike his contemporaries and forebears, Luther has no confidence in either metaphysics or mysticism to establish God's goodness, in spite of the fact that both approaches influenced his theological development. Luther's is a highly experiential theology—not that experience is a criterion for truth but that sinners can never detach emotionally when doing theology, and at some point in their lives all sinners will do theology. God's law as accusing resists being neutered. There is no cartography of divine truth that fails to bear on one's status with God. Indeed, the default mode of sinners is that of conflict and struggle with God. Even indifference to divine things constitutes a form of struggle: shrugging off divine threat as not imminent. For Luther, sinners' struggle with God is most manifest in their inability to avoid God since God is sheer will and omnipotent power hidden in all events and experiences. As Oswald Bayer notes, "God hides himself within the almighty power that works in life and death, love and hate, preserving life and removing life, fortune and misfortune, good and evil, in short, working everything in everyone, and we cannot extricate ourselves from having a relationship with him."[35] No one avoids this encounter, and Luther refuses to soften its impact: a sinner's initial encounter with God is with that of a devil. We encounter God as an accuser, tormenter, abandoner, and threat: "God cannot be God; to begin with he must become a devil."[36]

Acknowledging that outside of Christ-preached-for-our-salvation we encounter God as sheer power within all powers, seemingly indifferent to human plight, or at best good fortune, Luther in *De servo arbitrio* (*The Bondage of the Will*, 1525) distinguished God as hidden or "not preached" from God as revealed or "preached." Luther warned that we are to have nothing to do with the former, while regarding the latter Luther admonished that we are to cling to the promise as preached.

In his dispute over free will with Luther, Erasmus employed the ancient phrase "that which is above us is of no concern to us" (*quae supra nos nihil ad*

---

35. Bayer, *Martin Luther's Theology: A Contemporary Interpretation*, trans. Thomas Trapp (Grand Rapids: Eerdmans, 2008), 4.

36. See "Commentary on Psalm 117" (1530), in LW 14:31 (WA 31:249.20–250.2):
God's faithfulness and truth always must first become a great lie before it becomes truth. The world calls this truth heresy. And we, too, are constantly tempted to believe that God would abandon us and not keep His Word; and in our hearts He begins to become a liar. In short, God cannot be God unless He first becomes a devil. We cannot go to heaven unless we first go to hell. We cannot become God's children until we first become children of the devil. All that God speaks and does the devil has to speak and do first. And our flesh agrees. Therefore it is actually the Spirit who enlightens and teaches us in the Word to believe differently.

nos) in order to urge us to detach from the question of God's predestination, a strategy that Luther interpreted as a defense to preserve human free will *coram deo*. Erasmus sought to undermine the question of God's predestination by situating it as too remote of a concern for genuine faith, which ought instead to focus more on practical ethics and simple piety, matters seemingly doable to any sincere Christian. He connected this to his disdain for Luther's use of assertions and his own reliance on a magisterium to interpret the alleged murkiness of Scripture. In opposition to Erasmus, Luther turned this phrase on its head. Luther's distinction between God "not preached" and God "preached" reframes the entire discussion about "that which is above us is of no concern to us." For the Reformer, with respect to God "not preached," God in himself apart from Christ—the God of election—we are to have nothing to do. This is the God of absolute and unconditional power and sheer will who undermines any doing, agency, or autonomy before him.[37] We have nothing to do with this God, not because he is stingily prohibitive and closed-mindedly exclusive but because creaturely, human rapport with God as God is in himself is asymmetrical, just like clay is in the hands of a potter. It is the potter who molds the clay and not vice versa. Luther admonished:

> Now, God in His own nature and majesty is to be left alone; in this regard, we have nothing to do with Him, nor does he wish us to deal with Him. We have to do with Him as clothed and displayed in His Word, by which He presents Himself to us. That is His glory and beauty. . . . I say that the righteous God does not deplore the death of His people which he Himself works in them, but He deplores the death which he finds in his people and desires to remove from them. God preached works to the end that sin and death may be taken away, and we may be saved. . . . But God hidden in Majesty neither deplores nor takes away death, but works life, and death, and all in all; nor has He set bounds to Himself by His Word, but has kept Himself free over all things.[38]

37. Paul Zahl makes a strong case that a bound will is simply true to human nature:
   The point for theology is that we are not subjects; we are objects. We do not live; we are lived. To put it another way, our archaeology is our teleology. We are typically operating from drives and aspirations generated by our past. What ought to be free decisions in relation to love and service become un-free decisions anchored in retrospective deficits and grievances. This is the message of tragic literature. It is the message of diagnosis that sees into the animating engine of the unconscious. It is the scene in *The Exorcist*, when the possessed girl is spitting foul words at her mother, yet her mother and the nurse detect on her chest, dug into the little girl's skin, the words "Help me." That is it. We think the child is free, but she is under the thumb of a demon and there is someone there inside, crying to be heard and dying to be saved. She is an object in the only real sense of her destroyed humanity, but she is a subject to the degree that she is pleading. Her subjectivity lies in her need. (*Grace in Practice: A Theology of Everyday Life* [Grand Rapids: Eerdmans, 2007], 113)
38. *Bondage of the Will*, 170 (WA 18:685.14–24).

Outside of Christ (whom Luther here specified as *beauty*) one encounters God as sheer will, which cannot be controlled, bought off, manipulated, or bounded and so is indeed a threat to sinners' autonomy, security, and identity. If we wish to establish God as good and beautiful, it will not be on the basis of the hidden God. The hidden God will never be secured as goodness or beauty but will always have a question mark placed over him with respect to these attributes.

Schooled by his nominalist teachers in Erfurt, Luther affirmed that no definition of reason or goodness (or for that matter, beauty) establishes a priori perimeters for God's divinity:

> God is He for Whose will no cause or ground may be laid down as its rule and standard; for nothing is on a level with it or above it, but it is itself the rule for all things. If any rule or standard, or cause or ground, existed for it, it could no longer be the will of God. What God wills is not right because He ought, or was bound, so to will; on the contrary, what takes place must be right, because He so wills it. Causes and grounds are laid down for the will of the creature, but not for the will of the Creator—unless you set another Creator over him![39]

All this said, do we not confront a Manichaean tendency in Luther: God as devil and God as Christ? If God is a devil, how can God be good? If God is Christ, then how could he ever be a devil? The matter hinges on *perspective*: that of a sinner resisting God's accusation versus that of a sinner who knows of no other refuge in the face of the hidden God than that of Christ.

The matter of a contradiction between God as devil and as Christ, hidden and revealed, sheer will and goodness, must be seen in Luther's approach to the doctrine of God. Luther's use of nominalist language and logic regarding an unbounded God of sheer will is situated within his view of God as seen through law and gospel, of God's alien work (wrath) and God's proper work (mercy), and needs to be interpreted accordingly. The alien work exists for the sake of the proper; it is to break down defenses of old beings just so that they may receive God's mercy. There is nothing arbitrary about God's will in this regard.

> Luther's sustained defense of God's ordinance of salvation and damnation in *Bondage of the Will* is motivated by the need to defend the omnipotence of God. In its turn, God's omnipotence requires affirmation because only through omnipotence can we be certain that God's salvific aim for believers, that is, for me, cannot be frustrated no matter what occurs in the finite, worldly realm.

39. *Bondage of the Will*, 209 (WA 18:712.32–38).

> The Reformer's endorsement of predestination is intended in the first instance as a comfort to believers; *it is an existential pronouncement of faith's security before it is an objective affirmation.*[40]

In this light, we should challenge a contemporary critic of Luther, Michael Allen Gillespie. First, we should take issue when Gillespie asserts, "While Luther would like his God to be both omnipotent and good, in the end he is more concerned to preserve divine power than divine justice."[41] In spite of Luther's indebtedness to nominalism, we should interpret Luther as neither a nominalist (as Gillespie does) nor a realist (as some in the Mannermaa school do) but instead as forging his own new path independent of these two schools. In *De servo arbitrio* Luther does not employ nominalist distinctions such as *potentia absoluta* and *potentia ordinata*, even if such distinctions were formative for his development. Instead, sounding far more like Paul than his Scholastic forebears, he develops his own vocabulary of God "preached" and "not preached" and situates the doctrine of election and God's will as sheer power within that distinction. Clearly something is lacking in the older Scholastic terminology and so fails to convey the gospel as Luther understood it. What the nominalist *pactum* theology lacked, and what Luther advanced, was seeing the gospel as *promissio*, a word that when proclaimed defines reality every bit as much as did the creative word that effectuated the world out of nothing (*ex nihilo*). Luther makes it clear that we are to find God "when he [God] applies his Word and binds himself to it and promises: you are to find me here."[42] Unlike the nominalist *pactum* theology that highlighted the concept of covenant, Luther appealed to "testament" as a defining concept for human salvation precisely because a testament *gratuitously* delivers benefits to its recipients.[43]

Likewise, we should challenge Gillespie's assertion that "what Luther rejected was the soft, semi-Pelagian nominalism of Holcot and Biel, but in doing so he turned toward the harder, less compromising nominalism of Bradwardine, [Nicholas] d'Autrecourt, and Gregory of Rimini that emphasized the arbitrariness and unpredictability of God's absolute power."[44] True enough, outside of Christ—God "not preached"—God's absolute power comes across as arbitrary and unpredictable. Luther concedes as much by

40. Pasewark, "Predestination," 64 (italics original).
41. Gillespie, *The Theological Origins of Modernity* (Chicago: University of Chicago Press, 2008), 160.
42. *That These Words of Christ, "This Is My Body," etc., Still Stand Firm against the Fanatics* (1527), in LW 37:68 (WA 23:150.13–17).
43. *The Babylonian Captivity of the Church* (1520), in LW 36:38 (WA 6:513.24–33).
44. Gillespie, *Theological Origins of Modernity*, 131.

the "light of nature."[45] But the light of nature must be seen through the lens of the "light of grace," for which such power is anything but arbitrary or unpredictable. Just the opposite: it works in tandem with the accusing law to depotentiate sinners, rob them of their illusion of control, and allow them nothing other than the gospel (which is enough) as assurance for faith. Sinners are to look to nothing other than Christ alone in the face of everything that threatens, including God's sheer, apparently "indifferent" power. Robert Kolb summarizes the matter well:

> [Luther] defined God's essence not in terms of the Creator's fair treatment of human creatures according to their actions. Rather, he confessed that God is truly God *at his most Godly* when he shows mercy and bestows his love. Even his wrath betrays his desire to show mercy and goodness to those he wants to bring back to faith in himself, for whom he wants to restore truly human life.[46]

In order to ward off the kind of criticisms that Gillespie offers, Luther in his *Lectures on Genesis* clarified the rapport between God's sheer freedom and God's merciful goodness and provided a link between the two:

> If you believe in the revealed God and accept his Word, he will gradually also reveal the hidden God, for "he who sees me also sees the Father," as John 14:9 says. He who rejects the Son also loses the unrevealed God along with the revealed God. But if you cling to the revealed God with a firm faith, so that your heart is so minded that you will not lose Christ even if you are deprived of everything, then you are most assuredly predestined, and you will understand the hidden God. Indeed, you understand him even now if you acknowledge the Son and his will, namely, that he wants to reveal himself to you, that he wants to be your Lord and your Savior. Therefore you are sure that God is also your Lord and Father.[47]

To finish out the famous "three lights" (of nature, grace, and glory): only the light of glory will reveal that the God who is merciful to sinners is also just.[48]

Finally, Gillespie's charge that Luther's view of election is thoroughly Stoic needs to be challenged. Gillespie writes, "Luther's notion is thus not Manichean but closer to the Stoic notion of a divine logos or fate that determines all things. There is nothing that can be done to change this, and the only hope

---

45. *Bondage of the Will*, 317 (WA 18:785.26–27).
46. Kolb, *Bound Choice, Election, and the Wittenberg Theological Method* (Grand Rapids: Eerdmans, 2005), 34 (italics added).
47. Ibid., 37–38.
48. LW 33:292 (WA 18:785.28–38).

for individual human beings is that God will tear them away from Satan and unite them with this logos and this fate, making it their logos and their fate, thus liberating them from their slavery."[49] Now, Luther's gospel outwits any Stoic acquiescence to fate. Instead, as Luther insisted in his *Commentary on the Magnificat* (1521), the gospel opens a new horizon for sinners characterized by joy; indeed, "hearty love for Him is born. The heart overflows with gladness and goes leaping and dancing for the great pleasure it has found in God."[50] Set free from the law's accusations and secured in the goodness of God's "pure, fatherly, and divine goodness and mercy"[51] redeemed humans want to rejoice—even *leap* and *dance*—and rediscover the world no longer as threat but as discovery and adventure.

Discovery and adventure lead us to this creation that God sustains moment by moment. There are two ways of devaluing creatures with which Luther will have nothing to do. The first way is using others as ways to earn merit. The Middle Ages built poverty into the system of salvation since wealthy Christians needed the poor as recipients of alms given in order to achieve merit. For Luther, using others for securing one's own salvation is not good. Instead, giving because others are in need is. One does not need merit because human fulfillment is secure for each in Christ; or as Luther said to Dr. Justus Jonas about eternal reward: "as if your God has not provided it for you already."[52] Nor, however, does he have a place for a consumerist mentality that accumulates goods for the sake of social status and emotional stability and security. Such a "bourgeois" approach likewise undermines the openness to creation that Luther believes the gospel can set free. Note this table talk:

> [We] are presently in the dawn of the age to come, for we are beginning to acquire once again the knowledge of the creatures that we lost through Adam's fall. Now we can look at the creatures much more correctly, more than at any time under the papacy. But Erasmus is not interested in and is hardly concerned about how the fruit forms in the womb of the mother, how it is given shape and is made; he is also hardly concerned about the marriage relationship, as majestic as that is. But we begin, by the grace of God, to recognize his majestic works and wonders even within the little blossoms, when we reflect about how almighty and good God is. Therefore we praise and glorify him and thank him. We recognize the might of his Word in his creatures, how powerful it is. For he spoke and it came to be [Ps. 33:9]—even through a peach stone. Even though

49. Gillespie, *Theological Origins of Modernity*, 156.
50. LW 21:300 (WA 7:548.9).
51. The Small Catechism, in BC 354:2 (BSELK 870:15).
52. Bayer, *Martin Luther's Theology*, 96.

its outer shell is very hard, in its own proper time it must open up because of its soft center, which is inside. Erasmus passes over this artfully and looks at creatures the way the cow looks at a new [barn] door.[53]

The faith created by the gospel opens up an "enchanted view" of nature. God speaks not only in the Scriptures (where God's speech is most clear) but also in all creation. Each creature is full of wonder and mystery, not reducible to sheer mathematical measurement, because each, including a peach stone, is an expressive word of God. Indeed, we are God's poem; God himself is the Poet, and "we are the verses and songs that he makes and creates."[54] Christians renewed by God's mercy, liberated from incurvation, are open to creation as address, God's communication as threat but also as mercy and wonder to them. In the latter case, humans can become enchanted with creation, can have a "sense and taste for the finite" as Oswald Bayer (in opposition to Schleiermacher) puts it.[55]

Here it is clear that Luther departs from medieval metaphysical approaches to God's goodness. For Luther, divine goodness cannot fully be secured by natural reason even though natural reason has an awareness of it. It is only secured through Christ, through God "preached," through whom we can claim God as a Father. Luther noted in his *Lectures on Jonah* (1526):

And this feeling about a God the various cults of different men afterwards follow. As each one shapes a god for himself, so he also worships him, and the Divine Majesty is subject to the different opinions of men. Some think one way about God, others think another way. . . . We see the same thing here in the case of the sailors: they name the true God, but there was no certainty about form or conception. The only true form of God is for us to grasp Him by faith, namely, to learn that God is always a well-disposed Father and the Father of mercies. . . . All other opinions are idolatrous.[56]

Luther's view of justification as death to old beings and resurrection for new beings situates his view of God and is the basis for rejecting any alleged Manichaeism. God kills precisely in order to make alive. God's "alien work" of wrath exists for his "proper work" of mercy. God's alien work is a guise God wears just so to break down proud and idolatrous sinners so that they may be receptive to who he is in himself: love.

53. WA TR 1:574.8–19 (no. 1160) (trans. Bayer, *Martin Luther's Theology*, 108).
54. *Lectures on Genesis*, in LW 7:366 (WA 44:572.25–26). See also Bayer's discussion in *Martin Luther's Theology*, 16.
55. Bayer, *Martin Luther's Theology*, 169.
56. LW 19:11 (WA 13:246.10–19).

Sometimes Luther speaks as if there is struggle between justice and mercy within God himself: God against God.[57] Even so, such drama within the God-head itself is acknowledged because of an eschatological, ex post facto triumph of God's mercy over his wrath. God wrestles even with himself for the sake of claiming sinners as his own. God's definitive statement of himself is the gospel:

> Thus this gospel of God or New Testament is a good story and report, sounded forth into all the world through the apostles, telling of a true David who strove with sin, death, and the devil, and overcame them, and thereby rescued all those who were captive in sin, afflicted with death, and overpowered by the devil. Without any merit of their own he made them righteous, gave them life, and saved them, so that they were given peace and brought back to God. For this they sing, and thank and praise God, and are glad forever, if only they believe firmly and remain steadfast in faith.[58]

Hence, any distinction or opposition within God himself is not ultimately definitive of God but instead is defined by where the sinner stands with respect to God. For those who cling to their idolatries and injustices God will be an enemy. But to those who look to Christ in faith, God will be a "father."

Goodness as the Heart of God

The only way truly to know God is through Christ alone. Christ shows us the heart of God as giving humans all good things. In order to accentuate Christ as sheer mercy and gift, Luther retrieves the Augustinian distinction between Christ as sacrament (*sacramentum*) and Christ as example (*exemplum*). As sacrament Christ can be claimed by sinners as their own possession, a treasure that they can own and that can define them instead of their sin.

> This is so that you, when you look to him or hear that he does anything or suffers anything, will not doubt that he himself, Christ, is your own in those actions and sufferings and that you can trust in those actions just as much as if you had done them yourself, yes, as if you were this very Christ. See now, this is the gospel as recognized correctly, that is, as the unsurpassing goodness of God, which no prophet, no apostle, no angel has ever been able to assert, concerning which no heart can ever be astonished sufficiently and can comprehend. That is the great fire of the love of God for us.[59]

57. See *Operationes in Psalmos*, in WA 5:204.26–27.
58. "Prefaces to the New Testament," in LW 35:358–59.
59. "Ein Klein Unterricht, Kirchenpostille" (1522), in WA 10/I, 1:11.15–12.2 (trans. Bayer, *Martin Luther's Theology*, 64).

But the locus classicus highlighting God's goodness, written from the perspective not of the rebellious but the repentant sinner, is found in Luther's explanation of the first commandment—"You shall have no other gods"—in the Large Catechism. As is typical, Luther expounds the meaning of this commandment through the lens of both a threat and a promise. Because God's love is exclusive, humans who seek their well-being in something other than God, such as in money, or who believe they can earn their status with God and put God in our debt through "works of supererogation"[60]—such that God would owe fealty to us—practice idolatry and will encounter God's wrath. But for those who entrust themselves wholly into God's care, they will encounter God as sheer mercy and goodness since they are given everything by a God who owes them nothing.

Here Luther defines "god" as "the term for that to which we are to look for all good and in which we are to find refuge in all need. Therefore, to have a god is nothing else than to trust and believe in that one with your whole heart."[61] Such trust defines and situates one's being in its totality: "To cling to him [God] with your heart is nothing else than to entrust yourself to him completely."[62] Luther notes that "trust and faith of the heart alone" "make both God and an idol. If your faith and trust are right, then your God is the true one. Conversely, where your trust is false and wrong, there you do not have the true God. For these two belong together, faith and God. Anything on which your heart relies and depends, . . . that is really your God."[63] For Luther, God is "the one, eternal good" and wants to "lavish all good things upon you richly."[64] Incorrectly, but tellingly, Luther thinks the word "God" (Gott) is derived from the word "good" (gut), because "he is an eternal fountain who overflows with pure goodness and from whom pours forth all that is truly good."[65] God's goodness is centered on the fact that God gives humans "good things," "body, life, food, drink, nourishment, health, protection, peace, and all necessary temporal and eternal blessings. In addition, God protects us from misfortune and rescues and delivers us when any evil befalls us."[66] Luther notes that God's generosity is often mediated through other creatures: "Creatures are only the hands, channels, and means through which God bestows all blessings. For example, he gives to the mother breasts and milk for her infant or

60. The Large Catechism, in BC 389:22 (BSELK 938:2).
61. The Large Catechism, in BC 386:2 (BSELK 930:15–16).
62. The Large Catechism, in BC 387:10 (BSELK 934:1–2).
63. The Large Catechism, in BC 386:3 (BSELK 930:16–17).
64. The Large Catechism, in BC 388:15 (BSELK 934:22).
65. The Large Catechism, in BC 389:25 (BSELK 938:16).
66. The Large Catechism, in BC 389:24 (BSELK 938:10–12).

gives grain and all sorts of fruits from the earth for sustenance—things that no creature could produce by itself."[67]

Luther's trinitarian theology reinforces generosity as at the core of God's being. The Father gives humanity life together with all creatures. Human life, however, has become "darkened" through sin, and so the Son is given for human redemption and renewal. The Spirit gives the results of this redemption by granting humans a share in God's generosity.[68] Hence, God's truth is his fidelity to his promise, which raises Jesus Christ and all united with Christ in faith from the dead; his goodness is that he will be a God of mercy when the law would only condemn sinners to eternal death; his being is that he gives of himself sacrificially to establish his claim over his own in the face of opposition (even from his own law); his beauty is that he clothes sinners in the righteousness of Christ. Accordingly, these sinners cannot help but respond in gratitude and love toward God and want to reach out and help their neighbors in need.

In striking ways, Luther's description of divine goodness is indebted to his intense readings in German mysticism, such as the anonymous *Theologia Germanica*, a book that he edited and that served as his first publication. Of this little volume he claimed, "Next to the Bible and Saint Augustine no other book has come to my attention from which I have learned—and desired to learn—more concerning God, Christ, man, and what all things are."[69] Repeatedly, the *Theologia Germanica* names God as goodness: "God is goodness looked upon as goodness, not this or that particular form of good."[70] It sees the essence of sin as arrogating divine traits to oneself, as opposed to acknowledging them as belonging to God alone. Hence, the author says, "Note that when the creature assumes for itself some good thing, like being, life, knowledge, power—briefly, everything one might term good—as though the creature were indeed one of these goods, or as though the Good belongs to the creature—in such situations the creature is turning away from God."[71] Likewise, Adam's fall is decidedly "upwards":

> Man fancies himself to be what he is not. He fancies himself to be God, yet he is only nature, a created being. From within that illusion he begins to claim for himself the traits that are the marks of God. He does not claim only what

67. The Large Catechism, in BC 389:26 (BSELK 938:24–25).
68. *Confession concerning Christ's Supper* (1528), in LW 37:366 (WA 26:505.38–506.12).
69. *The Theologia Germanica of Martin Luther*, trans. Bengt R. Hoffman (New York: Paulist Press, 1980), 54.
70. *Theologia Germanica*, 102.
71. *Theologia Germanica*, 62.

is God's insofar as God becomes man or dwells in a divinized person. No, he claims what is the innermost of God, God's prime mark, namely the uncreated, eternal Being.[72]

The *Theologia Germanica* advocates the threefold process of purification, illumination, and union.[73] In Luther's overall theological approach this mysticism is reworked. "Purification" is not something we accomplish but instead is God's alien work to strip self-exalting sinners of their pride and defensiveness. "Illumination" likewise is the work of the Holy Spirit, who "has called me through the gospel, *enlightened* me with his gifts, made me holy and kept me in the true faith."[74] Finally, "union" is nothing other than Christ the groom marrying the sinner as his bride and exchanging his righteousness for the sinner's debt.

Luther's contribution to the discussion about the nature of divine goodness is that goodness is not established metaphysically on the basis of the convertibility of the transcendentals, that goodness is one with being and truth, as if truth, being, and goodness (let alone beauty) could be understood fully or exclusively apart from or outside of Jesus Christ. Hence, encountering God results in an attack on a human construal of goodness because humans are ever apt to try to place God in their debt, as evidenced, for example, in the *pactum* theology of Biel. Humans can never be claimants before God. Instead, God's goodness is established on the basis of God's action. God who is good displays his goodness as gift (apart from human merit or worthiness) and mercy, given in Christ and in all resources received in creation. Goodness opens creation as a horizon of delight—a place of beauty.

Comparison with Medieval Perspectives

Comparing Luther with the medieval perspectives on goodness outlined at the beginning of this chapter reveals profound similarities and differences. At the core of medieval thinking is desire, a kind of "erotic gravitational force"[75] within humans who thus must seek the good in order to gain self-fulfillment. This spirituality is decidedly teleological, focused on fulfillment, and eudaimonistic, focused on happiness as the natural payback for the exercise of virtue. Ultimately our happiness obtained through the exercise of the

72. *Theologia Germanica*, 115–16.
73. *Theologia Germanica*, 75.
74. BC 355:6 (BSELK 872:17–24).
75. Henry Paolucci, introduction to *The Enchiridion on Faith, Hope, and Love*, by Augustine (Chicago: Regnery, 1961), xiv.

theological virtues of faith, love, and hope will be our union with God in the beatific vision, seeing God face-to-face in heaven. Hence, this is the reason why for Alexander of Hales the good is the final cause. It is the goal of eternal life, which rewards the striving for godliness in this life. For Luther, that humans have an ultimate purpose to be fulfilled by God in heaven is spot on; that they can perfect their abilities to reach heaven in this life, though, is not.

Throughout his career Luther was convinced that one must "utterly despair" of oneself if one is to receive the grace of God.[76] Feeding desire as the path to unity with God is unable to surmount the apophaticism of a purely asymmetrical relationship between the infinite God and finite humanity. Sinners will feel painful disillusionment if they attempt to be their own "gods." But such pain is entirely creative. It unmasks the illusion that one's salvation ever could have been in one's own hands. It is in fact God's alien work to burn through and away such an illusion. Such an experience is painful, but ultimately it is good. Hence, goodness properly understood neither seeks nor avoids pain but recognizes that pain is not beyond God's creative work, even if it is an alien work. It reduces one to the nothingness out of which God can actually make something. It brings us to God's proper work where, as thesis 26 of the *Heidelberg Disputation* puts it, you "believe—and everything is already done,"[77] showing that God's goodness is nothing other than that salvation is placed outside of sinners' hands and put in the best of hands, God's. God's goodness is established not in that he is a judge who keeps score (though he is indeed that with respect to the law) but instead in that God is merciful and grants himself and his goodness to those who have nothing to offer—especially of their desire, which, as Luther put it, should be extinguished. This is not to say that for Luther there is no place for the notion that God fulfills us. But the fulfillment is granted now, in the *promissio*. When one has Christ, one has everything, "the love, the goodness, and the sweetness of God." Indeed, one has God's "wisdom, His power, and His majesty sweetened and mitigated to your ability to stand it."[78]

Luther thus reinterprets Pseudo-Dionysian categories of God as the *archē*, *telos*, and paradigm of goodness. With respect to the *archē*, God sustains all creatures moment by moment out of nothing. With respect to *telos*, God brings self-justifying sinners to their end and raises them as having the form of Christ himself. With respect to *paradigm*, Christ is first sacrament or gift, and only through him are sinners restored to God and given new, clean hearts. Guided

76. See *Heidelberg Disputation* (1518), thesis 18, in LW 31:40 (WA 1:354); and *Bondage of the Will*, 100 (WA 18:632.36–37).

77. *Heidelberg Disputation*, thesis 26, in LW 31:41 (WA 1:355).

78. *Lectures on Galatians*, in LW 26:30 (WA 40/1:79.18–19).

by Christ, sinners, free of their incurvation, are Christs in the world and assist their neighbors in need; this is Christ as example. The Reformer would challenge Aquinas's conviction that good preexists in God in a more excellent way because it assumes a greater sense of continuity between Creator and creature than what we could know apart from the gospel as promise. Both Aquinas and Luther affirm that God is goodness as such and that God's goodness is beyond human comprehension. Luther is wary of the creature claiming any goodness as a bargaining chip before God, and so he disavows any analogical reasoning from the creature to the Creator—at least outside of or independent from the gospel. This does not foreclose the possibility of analogies but simply the basis by which analogy would stand, which ultimately would be grounded christologically or in the *promissio*. Again, for him, to affirm that Christ alone secures God's goodness is a way of honoring the deity of God.

Conclusion

Luther was vitally concerned to address the question of God's goodness. It bears on salvation. His point was that people do not need merely an incentive and an example to be good. They need in fact to be made good from the core of their being, their hearts. Counterintuitively, God does this by granting sinners his favor and promising them new, eternal life in Christ. As believers' status with respect to God is changed, so is their identity. The law accuses old beings who seek to be their own gods for themselves and so control their lots and the lots of others to death. Humbled by the law, despairing of self, sinners can look to none other than Christ for salvation. In Christ they have a new identity and a new calling—to serve as Christ served in the world—and so to help especially those in need. The gospel promise unites believers with Christ, and Christ impels believers to serve their neighbors freely.

All this is grounded in God's own goodness. Outside of Christ, God is encountered as sheer power, a terror and threat to humans because such omnipotence jeopardizes sinners' own quest for power, status, and authority. But Luther admonishes sinners not to neutralize this power by harmonizing it with some modicum of human power, such as establishing a free will. Instead, only God has a free will (though humans indeed make choices with respect to temporal matters). If we are to see the content or center of God and find him as good, then we must cling to the gospel alone. It establishes God as wholly love and goodness, indeed overflowing generosity, and serves as a basis from which to affirm life and explore mystery in the world. Goodness can no longer be established as a transcendental through metaphysics.

Instead, goodness as a proper name for God and as a means by which every creature can participate in God is established only on the basis of how God acts in Christ, and that is to reconcile, redeem, and renew. Insofar as beauty is tied to goodness, it too will only be established through the gospel and not through metaphysics.

≫ 4 ≪

The Early Luther on Beauty

Luther wrote no treatise on the topic of beauty, but for that matter neither did he write a treatise devoted solely to the doctrine of justification (even though that was his intention).[1] Obviously the article of justification pervades Luther's thinking from early to late in his career. But what of beauty (*pulchritudo*, *decus*, *species*, or *forma*)? Is that topic—important to most humans—lost on Luther? While thousands of scholarly articles and books have been written about Luther, very little of this research deals with the theme of beauty in Luther, leading one to wonder if the Reformer had any interest in the topic or, if he did, whether his views contributed to his overall theological development. Luther's appreciation of music as "next to the Word of God" and deserving "highest praise"[2] is celebrated, and his collaboration with the artist Cranach is well known.[3] Obviously, Luther admired the arts. But is beauty a theme in Luther, and if it is, how important is it? One might surmise that with his emphasis on a hidden God (*deus absconditus*)—that is, what humans wrestle with outside of Christ is not God but the devil—Luther would have little to contribute to the discussion of beauty. What we will see is that beauty was a theme that helped shape his distinctive perspective on

1. Robin A. Leaver, "Luther on Music," in *The Pastoral Luther: Essays on Martin Luther's Practical Theology*, ed. Timothy J. Wengert (Grand Rapids: Eerdmans, 2009), 272. It was in his open letter "On Translating" (1530) that Luther expressed his intention to write a tract *On Justification*. See LW 35:198 (WA 30/2:643).

2. "Preface to Georg Rhau's *Symphoniae Iucundae*" (1538), in LW 53:323 (WA 50:371.1–2).

3. See Steven Ozment, *The Serpent and the Lamb: Cranach, Luther, and the Making of the Reformation* (New Haven: Yale University Press, 2011).

justification as both forensic and effective. Luther agrees with his medieval forebears that beauty is an attribute of God, appropriated by the Son, and that creation reflects God's beauty. Most importantly, the Reformer overturns the medieval criteria for beauty when he articulates the gospel: Christ who is beauty itself became ugly by identifying with sinners so that humans made ugly through sin might become beautiful in God's eyes. Thus the theme of beauty is critical if we want to understand Luther's conviction that justification entails God's alien work (*opus alienum*) of reducing sinners to nothing just so that he might do his proper work (*opus proprium*) of reestablishing them as new creations through faith. Luther affirmed aspects of ancient aesthetics *coram mundo* (before the world), but for him beauty *coram deo* (before God) is hidden and best understood paradoxically only by means of the fulcrum of Christ and his cross.

Unlike medieval thinkers, modern people tend to associate beauty with self-expressive creativity or an appreciation of nature. However, in the Middle Ages, beauty was understood not through the lens of what we call aesthetics, the study of how humans appreciate the world or the arts by means of their senses. As a discipline, aesthetics was not established until the mid-eighteenth century. Instead, for medieval theologians, the arts were a form of craftsmanship, and beauty was understood "intellectually"—that is, metaphysically. For medieval thinkers, beauty was a trait or attribute of God. All things share in God's beauty insofar as they participate in, are instances of, the divine. In short, medieval theologians saw the world pancalistically; that is, to one degree or another, all creatures are beautiful since they are either vestiges (nonhuman creatures) or images (human creatures) of God, who is beauty itself. In various ways, medieval thinkers built on the legacy of Plato and Neoplatonism as they developed pancalism.[4] However, the legacies of later Scholastics, such as Duns Scotus (1265–1308) and William of Ockham, whose teachings guided Luther's philosophy professors at Erfurt, Jodocus Trutvetter (ca. 1460–1519) and Bartholomäus Arnoldi von Usingen (1465–1532), did not focus their attention on beauty, and this may be one reason why Luther seldom deals with beauty directly in his treatises or later disputations.[5] However, the

---

4. These medieval thinkers included Robert Grosseteste (ca. 1175–1253), Bonaventure (1221–74), and Thomas Aquinas; they reworked the legacy of Plato (427–347 BC), Aristotle (384–322 BC), Plotinus (205–70), Augustine, and Pseudo-Dionysius the Areopagite.

5. Umberto Eco notes,

Late Scholasticism wreaked havoc upon the metaphysics of beauty. The mystics, who were the other philosophical and religious force of the age, were unable to rally or advance. The German and French mystics of the fourteenth and fifteenth centuries had some useful things to say about poetic creation, at least by way of analogy. . . . And they were always talking about the beauty which they experienced during their ecstasies. Yet

theme of beauty was important for monastic spirituality, as seen in the bridal mysticism of Bernard of Clairvaux (1090–1153), where the soul is attracted to Christ because he is beautiful, and Christ as bridegroom nurtures the soul. Such spirituality would, of course, have directly influenced Luther, though, as we shall see, in contrast to his forebears, he tends to draw out the forensic consequences for the soul in its marriage to Christ.

Where the theme of beauty comes to the fore in Luther's corpus is in his exegetical works, primarily in commentaries on the Psalms, such as Psalm 45, both early in his career (*Dictata super Psalterium*, 1513–15) and later in his career.[6] Luther's discussion of beauty is tied to his exegesis. But such exegesis would shape his entire polemical and doctrinal theology. While beauty is not a major theme in Luther's work, it is a crucial theme. It shapes the question of who God is, who Christ is, and who we are in Christ. Luther's views on beauty share common features with some medieval views but also depart from them in important ways. Medieval thinkers list proportion, color (brightness), and integrity as valid indicators of beauty, while Luther is apt to see such matters, at least *coram deo*, as hidden. God's beauty, Christ's beauty, and human beauty in Christ are not transparent, but are concealed to human eyes and grasped only by faith. Many medieval thinkers assert that beauty is a transcendental; that is, like being (*ens*), oneness (*unitas*), truth (*veritas*), and goodness (*bonitas*), it applies to the structure of all reality. For Luther, the chief problem in this way of thinking is that matters like divine goodness and beauty cannot be established on purely metaphysical grounds, independently of Scripture, because outside of Christ they are not certain. Luther at times appropriates the results of metaphysical inquiry, but he consistently rejects the method of such research—seeing it as a "work of man" in contrast to the work of God or as uncertain speculation.[7] For Luther, certainty in theology is best established through exegesis, and clarity about doctrine through logic. Undoubtedly, for Luther goodness and beauty are metaphysically real—God is the most real of all realities—but metaphysics is unable to establish decisively God's goodness or beauty. Only

---

they had nothing positive to say. Since God was ineffable, calling Him beautiful was like saying that He was good, or infinite: beauty was just a word used to describe the indescribable, so describing it by what it was not. Their experiences left them with the feeling that they had enjoyed the most intense delight, but a delight without feature or character. (*Art and Beauty in the Middle Ages*, trans. Hugh Bredin [New Haven: Yale University Press, 1986], 90)

6. For the *Dictata*, see LW 10 and 11 (WA 3 and 4); for his later work, see "Commentary on Psalm 45" (1532), in LW 12:197–300 (WA 40:472–610).

7. See *Heidelberg Disputation* (1518), theses 2, 3, 5, 8, 19, and esp. 22, in LW 31:39–40 (WA 1:353–55).

God himself can do that; and God does precisely that in Jesus Christ, who rescues humans from their own self-righteousness and the law that hounds humans to death. But it is faith alone and not speculation that grasps such gifts and can revel in the beauty that humanity can share in Christ. Finally, medieval thinkers view the world not first of all as raw material for human economic interests or consumption, but as symbolic, as testifying to God's reality and goodness. While the analogy of being is hardly operative in any definitive sense in Luther's thinking, Luther's alternative is that all creatures participate in God, specifically as masks or instruments[8] through which God speaks to humans and through which God orders human life through the three estates: the church (*ecclesia*), household (*oeconomia*), and civil government (*politia*). For Luther, God's utter transcendence (beyond either univocity or analogy) and his incarnation in Christ (deeper than analogy), as well as the human propensity to self-idolize through speculation, undermine both the (realist's) analogy and (nominalist's) univocity of being. Instead, for Luther God's being is self-subsisting and infinite, overflowing goodness that sustains all creatures.

This chapter will not be able to develop all these themes. Instead, we will limit ourselves primarily to the early Luther's view of beauty and how it helped him formulate the doctrine of justification. We will sketch the overall framework of medieval approaches to beauty, examine the early Luther's view of the beauty of Christ as hidden behind ugliness, and the Christian's beauty that likewise is hidden in Christ, and briefly assess the significance of Luther's views for today.

Proportionality, Light, and Desire

Medieval views on beauty incorporated and furthered the legacies of Greek and Roman perspectives on beauty. As noted above, medieval thinkers interpreted beauty through the lens of proportion and light. The root of interpreting beauty by means of proportion is found in Plato's appreciation of Pythagoras's (570–496 BC) view of mathematics as giving access to supersensible reality. Numbers are not only conventions by which to measure things but also windows to the eternal world of ideas. The mature Luther retains this appreciation of proportion, although with hyperbole, as he describes the

8. "Creatures are only the hands, channels, and means through which God bestows all blessings. For example, he gives to the mother breasts and milk for her infant or gives grain and all sorts of fruits from the earth for sustenance—things that no creature could produce by itself" (The Large Catechism, in BC 389:26 [BSELK 938:20]).

prelapsarian traits of Adam's soul and body.⁹ Likewise, the basis for appreciating color, particularly as light and brightness, is reminiscent of Plato's famous "allegory of the cave" in which people can be liberated from their ignorance, which is due to taking the shoddy world of the senses to be real, and through ascent beyond the sensible world into the supersensible world discover the true shape of reality as eternal verities—and ultimately truth itself.¹⁰ Pseudo-Dionysius, who was to have a wide impact on all medieval thinkers,¹¹ mediated this aesthetics of light for later thinkers.

Pseudo-Dionysius reveled in a "hidden divinity which transcends being" and sought an "understanding beyond being," advocating that we "look as far upward as the light of sacred scripture will allow, and, in our reverent awe of what is divine," urged readers to "be drawn together toward the divine splendor."¹² In the *Dictata*, Luther finds value in Pseudo-Dionysius as advocating the utter transcendence of God. "Therefore blessed Dionysius teaches that one must enter into anagogical darkness and ascend by way of denials,"¹³ and thereby Luther affirms apophatically that "God is hidden and beyond understanding."¹⁴ Even so, as early as the *Lectures on Romans* (1515–16) Luther rejected the overall trajectory of Pseudo-Dionysius because it omitted "all pictures of Christ's suffering" and wished "to hear and contemplate only the uncreated Word Himself, but not having first been justified and purged in the eyes of their heart through the incarnate Word."¹⁵ Luther often used mystical terminology such as "hiddenness" or Scholastic terminology such as "form" but disassociated these terms from the grammar and syntax in which they had been mediated and transposed them into a new, evangelical key. Hence, for Luther, God's hiddenness no longer is an invitation to mystical ascent beyond this world into the divine itself. Instead, outside of Christ we are apt

9. "Before sin Adam had the clearest eyes, the most delicate and delightful odor, and a body very well suited and obedient for procreation. But how our limbs today lack that vigor!" (*Lectures on Genesis*, in LW 1:100 [WA 42:76.16–17]).

10. Plato, *The Republic* 514a–520a. This allegory follows the "parable of the sun" (507b–509c), which compares the sun as the source that illuminates visible objects with the Form of the Good as the source that intellectually illuminates all Forms.

11. Very early in his career, Luther claimed that the Areopagite offered the "true cabala." See *Dictata super Psalterium*, in LW 10:313 (WA 3:372.16).

12. Pseudo-Dionysius, *The Divine Names*, in *Pseudo-Dionysius: The Complete Works*, trans. Colm Luibhéid (New York: Paulist Press, 1987), 49.

13. *Dictata super Psalterium*, in LW 10:119 (WA 3:124.32–33).

14. *Dictata super Psalterium*, in LW 10:120 (WA 3:124.33).

15. LW 25:287. Luther's repudiation of Pseudo-Dionysius is strongly accentuated in the *Antinomian Disputations*. See Holger Sonntag, ed. and trans., *Solus Decalogus est Aeternus: Martin Luther's Complete Antinomian Theses and Disputations* (Minneapolis: Lutheran Press, 2008), 89. For a slightly different reading of Luther's appropriation of Pseudo-Dionysius, see Knut Alfsvåg, "Luther as a Reader of Dionysius the Areopagite," *ST* 65 (2011): 101–14.

to encounter God not as an invitation to mystical ascent, but seemingly as untrustworthy or even as threatening. Hence, God's goodness (and beauty) is available only to faith that takes hold of Christ.

Medieval theologians were indebted to Plotinus's Neoplatonic approach to beauty. Plotinus furthered Plato's perspectives on proportion or light as he developed a specific metaphysical horizon for a theory of beauty. His thinking promotes an *exitus* and *reditus* scheme in which all things emerge (whether emanated or created) from the One and seek to find their ultimate end or good by means of returning to the One. For Plotinus, Goodness itself, the source of all sensible reality and to which all sensible reality wishes to return, is at the top of this great chain of being. All sensible things are motivated by *eros*, the desire to reunite with their original source, which is truly beautiful. As carried on by Augustine, the desire (*caritas*) of all earthly things to return to their heavenly source was to influence medieval spirituality and aesthetics.

In the *Symposium*, Plato's teacher, Socrates, explains that his understanding of desire or *eros* is informed by a wise and mysterious woman, Diotima of Mantinea, who, when he was a youth, explained to him the nature of *eros*. To various degrees, her perspective, as mediated through Plato, was to influence later thinkers. Diotima taught that *eros* is the offspring of Poverty and Resource. True to his mother's nature, *eros* lives with want. But true to his father's nature, he is resourceful and scheming for all that is "beautiful and good."[16] The goal of desire is to drive people to their true itinerary toward the heavenly good. Those who undertake this journey—and clearly in this life not all will—move from an attraction to bodies to that of the soul "and so estimate the body's beauty as a slight affair."[17] From the love of such particulars, one will ascend beyond to love of the soul, to the "final object" of love's earlier "toils." Diotima described this end as the ever-existent beauty that as such is not subject to perishability.

Over eight hundred years later, on the eve of his mother Monica's death, Augustine described a similar mystical itinerary. While in spiritual conversation about the nature of eternal life, Augustine wrote that he and Monica concluded that "no bodily pleasure, however great it might be and whatever earthly light might shed lustre upon it, was worthy of comparison" with eternal life. As the "flame of love burned stronger" in them, their thoughts ranged beyond the "whole compass of material things in their various degrees, up to

16. Plato, *Symposium* 203d (translation from *Plato: Lysis, Symposium, Gorgias*, trans. W. R. M. Lamb, LCL [Cambridge, MA: Harvard University Press, 1933], 181).
17. Plato, *Symposium* 210c (trans. Lamb, 203).

the heavens themselves" and higher still to the place where they "came" to their own "souls and passed beyond them to that place of everlasting plenty." "There life is that Wisdom by which all these things that we know are made, all things that ever have been and all that are yet to be. But that Wisdom is not made: it is as it has always been and as it will be for ever—or, rather, I should not say that it *has been* or *will be*, for it simply *is*, because eternity is not in the past or in the future." Augustine explained that "while we spoke of the eternal Wisdom, longing for it and straining for it with all the strength of our hearts, for one fleeting instant we reached out and touched it. Then with a sigh, leaving *our spiritual harvest* bound to it, we returned to the sound of our own speech . . . far, far different from your Word, our Lord, who abides in himself for ever."[18] Though his view has been challenged, Anders Nygren has shown that the pre-Christian Platonic vision of desire (*eros*) and the Augustinian vision of love (*caritas*) share important features.[19] Their common trajectory is up to the heavens and involves taking leave of the body and bodily pleasures. Both seek an ultimate self-fulfillment that is desirable to those seeking to be reunited with their heavenly origin and goal. In spite of their differences, since Plato has no notion of sin, which for Augustine is rebellious pride (*superbia*) and disordered desire (*concupiscentia*) fixated on earthly things, both Plato and Augustine think that human nature is best understood as desire for union with eternal, unchanging reality. In such expectation of union with the eternal, the human is defined and fulfilled. For Luther, in contrast, the core of human identity is found not in desire and its fulfillment but in faith. The center of humanity is defined by what the heart rests upon. This is not to deny any role for desire whatsoever. As we shall see, for the mature Luther there is a kind of restoration of desire, purged of eudaimonism, that desires what God desires.[20] Unlike eudaimonism, faith receives fulfillment as a gift and not as a reward for the exercise of virtue. In dying to the quest for egoistic fulfillment, humans can begin to love God from the heart.

For Augustine, what blinds us to God's beauty is sin, which he describes not only as a turning away from heavenly to earthly things but also occasionally as being turned toward self (at this juncture similar to Luther's *incurvatus in se*)

18. Augustine, *Confessions* 9.10 (trans. R. S. Pine-Coffin [Harmondsworth, UK: Penguin, 1961], 197–98; italics original).

19. See Anders Nygren, *Agape and Eros*, trans. Philip S. Watson (Chicago: University of Chicago Press, 1982). For Nygren's contrast between *eros* and *agapē*, see p. 210. Nygren's point is that *caritas* fails as a synthesis of *eros* and *agapē*. A reappropriation of *eros* on the basis of the gospel will be presented in chap. 8.

20. *Lectures on Genesis*, in LW 1:337 (WA 42:248.12–13).

and away from God.[21] For Augustine, God's goal is to make our souls beautiful.[22] However, Luther found even such desire as problematic and something to be "extinguished" (*extinguendo*),[23] since it too can be an attempt to claim status before God. This is not to say that Luther denied that the Christian should love God; after all, that is a command.[24] However, our humanity is structured around not desire but faith. Faith configures desire, not vice versa. Luther could appeal to other resources in Augustine in developing his view of beauty.

All Western medieval theologians in one way or another saw their work as an outgrowth of Augustine's legacy. In offering an aesthetics of proportionality, Augustine appeals to the apocryphal book of Wisdom (11:20), which extols God as having "arranged all things by measure, number and weight." God himself is "measure without measure, number without number, and weight without weight."[25] Even so, God is the author of proportionality in all created things, and proportion is a key by which to ascertain their beauty.[26] In the *City of God*, Augustine illustrates this in a vivid way: "Take the case of the

21. See Augustine, *City of God* 14.28 (trans. Gerald G. Walsh, SJ, et al., abridged by Vernon J. Bourke [New York: Doubleday, 1958], 321–22).

22. "If, then, the body, which is less than the soul and which the soul uses as a servant or a tool, is a sacrifice when it is used well and rightly for the service of God, how much more so is the soul when it offers itself to God so that, aflame in the fire of divine Love, and with the dross of worldly desire melted away, it is remolded into the unchangeable form of God and becomes beautiful in His sight by reason of the bounty of beauty which He has bestowed upon it" (Augustine, *City of God* 10.6 [trans. Walsh et al., 192–93]).

23. The desire for knowledge, glory, power, or praise is not satiated when such things are acquired, but is stimulated all the more.

> The remedy for curing desire does not lie in satisfying it, but in extinguishing it. In other words, he who wishes to become wise does not seek wisdom by progressing toward it but becomes a fool by retrogressing into seeking folly. Likewise he who wishes to have much power, honor, pleasure, satisfaction in all things must flee rather than seek power, honor, pleasure, and satisfaction in all things. This is the wisdom which is folly to the world. (*Heidelberg Disputation*, explanation to thesis 22, in LW 31:54 [WA 1:363.9–14])

24. We should fear, *love*, and trust God. See the Small Catechism, in BC 351:3.

25. Augustine, *Literal Commentary on Genesis* 4.3 (trans. John Hammon Taylor, ACW 41 [New York: Newman, 1982], 108): "It is a marvelous gift, granted to few persons, to go beyond all that can be measured and see the Measure without measure, to go beyond all numbers and see the Number without number, and to go beyond all that can be weighed and see the Weight without weight."

26. Monroe C. Beardsley notes that Augustine's view of proportionality is echoing Cicero (*Tusculanarum Disputationum* 4.13)

> almost word for word: "All bodily (corporeal) beauty consists in the proportion of the parts (*congruentia partium*), together with a certain agreeableness (*suavitas*) of color" (XXII, xix; cf. XI, xxii). But the Ciceronian formula has a good deal more meaning in St. Augustine, who, at various places in his works, sketches a highly formalistic account of the "congruence of parts," with ideas derived from Pythagoras, Plato, and Plotinus, as well as others, though combined in his own way. (*Aesthetics from Classical Greece to the Present: A Short History* [New York: Macmillan, 1966], 93)

beauty of the human form. Shave off one eyebrow and the loss to the mere mass of the body is insignificant. But what a blow to beauty! For, beauty is not a matter of bulk but of the symmetry and proportion of the members."[27] This is due to the fact that God designed the cosmos on the principle of numbers.[28] Indeed, Augustine notes that there "is in a man's body such a rhythm, poise, symmetry, and beauty that it is hard to decide whether it was the uses or the beauty of the body that the Creator had most in mind."[29] And if we do not find creation pleasing, it is because we fail to see it, so to speak, sub specie aeternitatis. "If the beauty of this order fails to delight us, it is because we ourselves, by reason of our mortality, are so enmeshed in this corner of the cosmos that we fail to perceive the beauty of a total pattern in which the particular parts, which seem ugly to us, blend in so harmonious and beautiful a way."[30] Proportionality factors into the nature of eternal life. For Augustine, the peace of the heavenly city "lies in a perfectly ordered and harmonious communion of those who find their joy in God and in one another in God. Peace, in its final sense, is the calm that comes of order. Order is an arrangement of like and unlike things whereby each of them is disposed in its proper place."[31]

Such perspectives are echoed in Luther's early *Dictata super Psalterium*, in which he writes,

> Thus the great Creator has created all things in wisdom, so that they may minister in such countless functions and services not only to the body, which, nevertheless, cannot grasp the wisdom in which they were created and which shines forth in them, but also to the soul, which can grasp the wisdom, as far as the mind and the heart are concerned. . . . Indeed, the more profoundly a created thing is recognized, the more wonders are seen in it, namely, how full it is of God's wisdom.[32]

Even late in his career, Luther would affirm, "He who knows God also knows, understands, and loves the creature, because there are traces of divinity (*divinitatis vestigia*) in the creature."[33] Additionally, with respect to the mature Luther, one has only to examine Luther's discussion of Adam's perfections in his *Lectures on Genesis* to see that the aesthetics of proportionality affected his thinking about beauty. Luther includes proportionality, at least *coram*

---

27. Augustine, *City of God* 11.22 (trans. Walsh et al., 229).
28. Augustine, *City of God* 12.19 (trans. Walsh et al., 260–61).
29. Augustine, *City of God* 22.24 (trans. Walsh et al., 528).
30. Augustine, *City of God* 12.4 (trans. Walsh et al., 249).
31. Augustine, *City of God* 19.13 (trans. Walsh et al., 456).
32. *Dictata super Psalterium*, in LW 11:15–16 (WA 3:534.3, 28–29).
33. *Lectures on Genesis*, in LW 4:195 (WA 4:276.28).

mundo, as a criterion for beauty in his assessment of the prelapsarian Adam. What Luther, early or late, will not accept is humans' ability to reason into God and ascertain his goodness or beauty as based on metaphysics, as he outlined in the *Heidelberg Disputation* (1518).

Beauty as a Transcendental

Many theologians of the High Middle Ages sought to establish being, oneness, goodness, truth, and beauty as transcendentals, meaning that all reality somehow is structured by these categories. To clarify, for medieval thinkers, beauty is a name for God (Augustine's "so ancient and so new"),[34] just like goodness.[35] The transcendentals can be conceptually distinguished by humans since each transcendental contributes something to human knowledge that the other transcendentals do not, but in truth they refer to the same reality. There was much precedence for this way of thinking from the Platonic and Aristotelian traditions. The latter tradition began the trajectory of thinking in terms of transcendentals by affirming the oneness of being and unity.[36] Pseudo-Dionysius would argue that the "Beautiful is therefore the same as the Good, for everything looks to the Beautiful and the Good as the cause of being, and there is nothing in the world without a share of the Beautiful and the Good."[37] As such he offers a pancalistic stance: "All being derives from, exists in, and is returned toward the Beautiful and the Good. Whatever there is, whatever comes to be, is there and has being on account of the Beautiful and the Good. All things look to it. All things are moved by it."[38] Franciscan theologians such as Alexander of Hales (ca. 1185–1245) and his colleagues connected goodness and beauty as transcendentals even while acknowledging their differences: "For beauty is a disposition of the good in so far as it pleases the apprehension, whereas the good strictly speaking has to do with the disposition in which it pleases our affections."[39] Hence, good is related to final causes, while beauty is related to formal causes. While Thomas Aquinas, a Dominican, did not specifically count beauty among the transcendentals, he closely associated it with goodness and thereby provided a threefold criterion

---

34. Augustine, *Confessions* 10.27.
35. In the Large Catechism, Luther describes God as goodness, specifically as an "eternal fountain who overflows with pure goodness and from whom pours forth all that is truly good" (BC 389:25 [BSELK 938:15]).
36. Aristotle, *Metaphysics* 1003b23.
37. Pseudo-Dionysius, *Divine Names*, 77.
38. Pseudo-Dionysius, *Divine Names*, 79.
39. Eco, *Art and Beauty in the Middle Ages*, 23.

for beauty.[40] In the *Summa theologiae* he builds his aesthetic right into his doctrine of the Trinity, in which eternity is ascribed to the Father, beauty is ascribed to the Son, and use or *usus* is ascribed to the Spirit. But even more importantly for our purposes, he situates beauty in the doctrine of Christ:

> According to the first point of consideration, whereby we consider God absolutely in His being, the appropriation mentioned by Hilary [of Poitiers] applies, according to which *eternity* is appropriated to the Father, *species* to the Son, *use* to the Holy Ghost. For *eternity* as meaning a being without a principle, has a likeness to the property of the Father, Who is *a principle without a principle.* Species or beauty has a likeness to the property of the Son. For beauty includes three conditions, *integrity* or *perfection*, since those things which are impaired are by the very fact ugly; due *proportion* or *harmony*; and lastly, *brightness*, or *clarity*, whence things are called beautiful which have a bright color.[41]

Beauty thus has three criteria: (1) *integritas sive perfectio*: nothing incomplete or insufficient is regarded as beautiful; (2) *proportio sive consonantia*: orderly proportion and harmony of the parts is required; (3) *claritas*: brightness in colors is generally seen as beautiful.[42] Defying these three criteria of beauty, Luther early and late emphasized that Christ in his earthly ministry was not physically handsome, having "no form or comeliness," and was also rejected and condemned by people.[43] For Luther, these three criteria either are appropriate for the beauty of creatures, or with respect to Christ himself and human life in Christ are hidden from the eyes of the world. Sinners who claim beauty for themselves are made ugly by God, and those made ugly by God can be remade as beautiful through belonging to Christ.

40. For an extensive study of Aquinas on beauty, see Umberto Eco, *The Aesthetics of Thomas Aquinas*, trans. Hugh Bredin (Cambridge, MA: Harvard University Press, 1988).

41. Aquinas, *Summa theologiae* I, q. 39, a. 8 (trans. Fathers of the English Dominican Province [Westminster, MD: Christian Classics, 1948], 1:201; italics original).

42. Miikka E. Anttila, *Luther's Theology of Music: Spiritual Beauty and Pleasure* (Berlin: de Gruyter, 2013), 55. Unlike Étienne Gilson and Jacques Maritain, philosopher Jan Aertsen claims that Aquinas never adds beauty (*pulcher*) to the list of the transcendentals because the place of the beautiful among the transcendentals is between the true and the good. For Aertsen, the beautiful adds a cognitive component to the good. When Aquinas defines the good as that which simply pleases the appetite, the beautiful is that which pleases when apprehended. Hence, to sense beauty is a cognitive act. In Aertsen's view, the beautiful is the connection between the true and the good, when truth is related to the intellectual and goodness to the appetitive. See Jan A. Aertsen, *Medieval Philosophy as Transcendental Thought: From Philip the Chancellor (ca. 1225) to Francisco Suárez* (Leiden: Brill, 2012), 168–76; see also Anttila, *Luther's Theology of Music*, 52–53.

43. Even so, Christ is *speciosus forma* (beautiful in form) since the beauty of God's redeeming love is manifest in the ugliness of Christ's death. See "Duo sermones de passione Christi, Sermo II. de passione" (WA 1:340.17–21, 26–33).

In comparison with Luther's work, we should note at the outset that Aquinas's christological aesthetic is based not primarily on the incarnate Word but on the Word as eternal. In his old age, Luther found such Scholastic terminology helpful, even though he did not employ the Scholastic method as such. He wrote, "Moreover, the use of a thing concerns the Holy Spirit. He who sees the use of a thing sees the Holy Spirit, he who discerns the form or beauty of a thing (*formam rei sive pulchritudinem*) sees the Son, and he who considers the substance and continuing existence of things sees the Father. These three—substance, form, and goodness—cannot be separated."[44] It would seem that like Aquinas, Luther had a sense for beauty as a transcendental or at least as a divine attribute and appropriated it to the identity of the eternal Son within the triune life. But while Luther employed such metaphysical terms he did not establish their truth in a metaphysical way. Instead he saw them as compatible with his exegesis of Genesis. The early Luther in the *Heidelberg Disputation* unmasked the task of metaphysics as seeking truth, beauty, and goodness outside of and independently of the cross, which should test all things (*crux probat omnia*), as an expression of the human love that is in opposition to God's love. While the later Luther approved of and utilized public disputations along with the rigor of logic, he continually eschewed the metaphysical enterprise and theological speculation in general as an impossibility, an attempt to domesticate the divine transcendence, human machinations seeking to establish a parity with God. Metaphysical terms can be helpful for doctrinal specificity and theological rigor, but they are not foundational. To put it baldly, the foundation for Luther's thinking—the very bedrock—is the Scriptures.

Beauty in the Theology of Humility

The early Luther was more concerned about the question of beauty—how God, Christ, and humans are beautiful—than most commentators realize. For instance, many have sought to interpret the significance of Luther's theology of the cross in his *Heidelberg Disputation*, but few have drawn out the implications of those theses for beauty. But the import for a theological aesthetics is present in this disputation. Consider the upshot of thesis 28: "The love of God does not find, but creates, that which is pleasing [*diligibile*] to it. The love of man comes into being through that which is pleasing to it."[45] Something is pleasing to someone because it is beautiful. Thesis 28 shows how humans

44. *Lectures on Genesis*, in LW 4:196 (WA 43:276.33–36).
45. LW 31:57 (WA 1:354.35).

and God have entirely different approaches to beauty. God does not find sinful humans to be beautiful but makes them to be beautiful, due solely to his generous self-giving love, whereas humans cannot love unless they first find the object of their love attractive. Luther sees the second sentence of the thesis as condemning Aristotle: "Thus it is also demonstrated that Aristotle's philosophy is contrary to theology since in all things it seeks those things which are its own and receives rather than gives something good."[46] Seeking one's own self-fulfillment and egocentrically receiving rather than altruistically giving something good are expressions of desire or *eros* embedded in the tradition as outlined above. Rooted in this early work, Luther's mature theology will reject an egocentric *eros*, which uses the beloved for one's own delight, precisely in order to affirm an original or renewed *eros*, which delights in the beloved's beatitude.[47] The clincher is the first sentence, which Luther explains: "The love of God which lives in man loves sinners, evil persons, fools, and weaklings in order to make them righteous, good, wise, and strong. Rather than seeking its own good, the love of God flows forth and bestows good. Therefore sinners are *attractive* (*pulchri*) because they are loved (*diliguntur*); they are not loved because they are attractive."[48] For Luther, God is sheer, one-sidedly *overflowing love* (a favorite divine name for Luther) and goodness—reaching out to those reduced to nothing, embracing them, and regenerating them. God finds nothing inherently attractive in the object of his love. But as reduced to nothing, having no obligatory claim over against God, this non-object can be the recipient of God's mercy. God *regards* (forensic justification) that which is nothing as the raw material on which he can build (effective justification). Unlike human desire, God's love does not need to receive anything in order to be generated or sustained; God is not eudaimonistic in any way. God loves the unlovely, regards the ugly as beautiful, and the sinner as just—all for which human love is not wired. Luther rejects the view of *eros*, and later *caritas*, in Plato and Augustine outlined above, as definitive ways to understand God's love.[49]

   Already within the *Dictata super Psalterium* Luther was developing thoughts about beauty that would lead him to make a distinction between human love as wholly egocentric and the love of God as wholly self-giving. In the *Dictata* we see the young professor as a highly energetic and creative mind constantly bringing to the fore ideas from Scholastic theology and mysticism and critically evaluating their ability to assist him in his quest properly to understand

46. LW 31:57 (WA 1:365.5–7).
47. For this wording, I am grateful to Paul Hinlicky, email correspondence, February 10, 2016.
48. LW 31:57 (italics added) (WA 1:365.8–12).
49. See chap. 8 for a case that *eros* can, in a sense, be redeemed or "liberated."

God's righteousness. The question that guides Luther in the *Dictata* is: How do we render God his due? We see the young Luther as a man constantly struggling with God: Have we sinners any claim or merit before God—some spirituality, goodness, or intelligence—by which God would be obliged to justify us? And our young exegete demolishes everything offered as a possibility for such an exchange of human merit for God's approval. This early stage of the Reformer's career has been called a "theology of humility" because for Luther humans are closest to God when they humble themselves before him or when God humbles them through crosses and trials. Increasingly in the *Dictata* and his *Lectures on Romans*, Luther moves toward a passive role for humanity in the presence of God and an active role for God as accuser or granter of mercy. Building on work in the *Dictata* and the *Lectures on Romans*, Luther in his *Lectures on Hebrews*[50] (1517) and several early sermons[51] articulates an alien work (*opus alienum*) of God, which reduces the sinner to nothing, and a proper work (*opus proprium*), which reestablishes the sinner through forgiveness. In spite of the differences between the *Dictata*'s theology of humility and Luther's mature stance of *solus Christus* (Christ alone) and *sola fide* (faith alone), we can see the seeds that germinate and blossom into Luther's mature theology, such as the rudiments of the theology of the cross, the distinction between law and gospel, and God's alien and proper works. At the core of this theology of humility is the conviction that humans justify God in his judgment against human pride—specifically, the assumption that we can offer something to God by which he would be obliged to us—when humans agree with God's judgment that they truly have nothing of their own to offer. At their core, humans both as created and as deformed by sin are nothing, not only in relation to God but also ontologically, at the core of their being, because human existence is wholly sustained by God. It is as if Luther's efforts are tantamount to a commentary on Paul's question: "What do you have that you did not receive?" (1 Cor. 4:7). Luther summarized his convictions: "Therefore God is not justified by anyone except the one who accuses and condemns and judges himself. For the righteous man is, first of all, one who is the accuser and condemner and judge of himself. Therefore he justifies God and causes Him to win out and to prevail."[52]

But this theology of humility has wide-reaching implications for a theology of beauty. Paradoxically, whoever is most ugly—that is, most self-accusatory and thus humble, making no claims before God but in fact accusing oneself

50. LW 29:135 (WA 57:128.14).
51. See "Sermon on St. Thomas' Day" on Ps. 19:1 (Dec. 21, 1516), in LW 51:18–19 (WA 1:111–12).
52. *Dictata super Psalterium*, in LW 10:236 (WA 3:288.30–32).

in agreement with God—is in fact the most beautiful, because such sinners are able to admit their sins due to God's illumination. Commenting on Psalm 51:4, Luther noted:

> Whoever is most beautiful [*pulcherrimus*] in the sight of God is the most ugly [*deformissimus*], and, vice versa, whoever is the ugliest is the most beautiful. . . . Therefore the one who is most attractive in the sight of God [*speciosissimus coram deo*] is not the one who seems most humble to himself, but the one who sees himself as most filthy and depraved. The reason is that he would never see his own filthiness, unless he had been enlightened in his inmost being with a holy light [*lumine sancto*]. But when he has such a light, he is attractive [*speciosus*], and the brighter the light, the more attractive he is. And the more brightly he has the light, the more he sees himself as ugly [*deformem*] and unworthy [*indignum*]. Therefore it is true: The one who is most depraved in his own eyes is the most handsome [*formosissimus*] before God and, on the contrary, the one who sees himself as handsome is thoroughly ugly before God, because he lacks the light with which to see himself.[53]

Clearly beauty here is influenced by an aesthetics of light due to the enlightenment of God. The corollary is that the more glory sinners claim for themselves the more they have lost beauty before God:

> But if you are beautiful [*pulcher*], righteous, strong, and good to yourself, this will already be a denial and vileness in you in the presence of God. For as long as you have removed confession, beauty refused to remain. For you have bent glory in on yourself, and therefore you have also lost beauty. Therefore give glory and confession to God, and this very glory will be your adornment, and the confession to God will be your beauty. But affirmation of yourself will be abasement of God, as far as you are concerned.[54]

Said pithily, "Whoever makes himself beautiful [*pulchrum*], is made ugly [*fedatur*]. On the contrary, he who makes himself ugly, is made beautiful."[55] Such paradoxical convictions about finding ugliness in human "beauty" and beauty in human ugliness is not without precedent in the tradition. In spite of Luther's implicit critique of *caritas*, we must take note of Augustine's christological approach to aesthetics: "Let that fairest one [Christ] alone, who loved the foul to make them fair, be all our desire."[56] Whether or not this

53. *Dictata super Psalterium*, in LW 10:239 (WA 3:290.23–291.3).
54. *Dictata super Psalterium*, in LW 11:262 (WA 4:110.21–26).
55. *Dictata super Psalterium*, in LW 11:263 (WA 4:111.7, 15).
56. Augustine, *Tractates on the Gospel of John* 10.13 (trans. John Gibb and James Innes, NPNF[1] 7:74).

Augustinian aesthetic had a direct bearing on Luther, a christological approach to aesthetics eventually took shape in Luther's hands as a twofold approach to divine hiddenness. God is not only hidden as the *deus absconditus*—God's backside (*posteriora dei*) to those seeking complete transparency with respect to his nature, which utterly transcends human thought or will—but God is also hidden as mercy in the ministry of and preaching of Jesus Christ.[57]

Such self-accusation takes away anything sinners might attempt to offer God and in fact gives God his due by agreeing with him in his accusing judgment on sinners. Made humble or, as Luther later puts it in the *Heidelberg Disputation*, "utterly despairing"[58] of themselves, sinners need Christ. Therefore, God forgives freely by not imputing sin.[59] Commenting on Psalm 45:2, Luther extolled Christ as "beautiful in form" (*speciosus forma*).[60] And the beauty of Christ is transferred to those of faith: "And thus this is the beautiful beauty of the King, that the inner man has beautiful eyes, beautiful ears, lips, cheeks, teeth, the whole face, hands, feet, belly, etc. all of which are in the spiritual man through grace and virtues."[61] Presumably, Luther here is saying that the "inner man" displays proper proportions and brightness with these features. However, just for the very fact that the proportionality and brightness is "inner" it is hidden and not exposed to sight.

The theology of humility has been characterized as a severe approach to faith since it incorporates self-hatred (*odium sui*) or self-reproach as a necessary feature. While that may be true, surely Luther's relishing of Christ as most beautiful and also beauty as imparted to the "spiritual man" ends severity and liberates the new person. In a word, it is the humble person forgoing all attempts at spiritual pride who can receive God's grace—and beauty. Luther appealed to 1 Peter 5:5, which says that God gives his grace to the humble, those who confess their sin and God's just judgment in condemning sinners. "Therefore, as long as confession remains in the heart, so long also beauty; as long as humility remains, so long also grace."[62] Ultimately such confession aligns or is congruent with God's own beauty:

> Similarly all are His [God's] beauty [*decor*], because they show Him to be splendid [*decorum*] and extremely beautiful [*pulcherrimum*]. But no one sees

57. See Brian Gerrish, "'To the Unknown God': Luther and Calvin on the Hiddenness of God," in *The Old Protestantism and the New: Essays on the Reformation Heritage* (Edinburgh: T&T Clark, 1982), 131–49.

58. Thesis 18, in LW 31:51 (WA 1:361.23).

59. *Dictata super Psalterium*, in LW 10:147 (WA 3:175.29).

60. *Dictata super Psalterium*, in LW 10:215 (WA 3:258.12).

61. *Dictata super Psalterium*, in LW 10:215 (WA 3:258.19–24).

62. *Dictata super Psalterium*, in LW 11:264 (WA 4:111.38).

this in things and creatures except he who inwardly has beauty and praise from the Spirit. But he does not have this, unless he first has self-denial and the humiliation of his own ugliness. Hence those who think themselves to be something think that there is much ugliness in things and that God neither is nor is beautiful. For they are not yet ugly and repudiated to themselves, *for all things are very beautiful* and rightly confessing God.[63]

In his own way, the early Luther affirms pancalism, but not by metaphysically defending the theological conviction that beauty is the same as goodness and that creatures are beautiful to one degree or another since they participate in beauty itself. The Luther of the *Heidelberg Disputation* would have found that approach to be a presumptuous theology of glory. To the point: even metaphysicians must be exposed to and expose their own inherent ugliness due to sin. To claim any divine trait or attribute, such as goodness, beauty, or freedom, for oneself is to take from God what is God's. The upshot: Christ alone is beauty—and the beauty of anything must find its place not in itself, which as such is nothing, but only as sustained by God. Commenting on Psalm 112:3–4, Luther wrote,

> "Beauty" [*Decor*] is every adornment in a person because of which he is honored and glorified. Therefore, when glory is without beauty, it is empty. But in Christ alone there is beauty. Therefore outside of Christ all glory is empty. He has "clothed Himself with beauty" (Ps. 93:1) and "is crowned with glory and honor" (Ps. 8:5). But it behooves us to be clothed with disgrace instead of glory, shame instead of honor, ugliness instead of beauty.[64]

More than anything, for the early Luther, it is our humanity, our status as *creatures* in opposition to self-deifying pride, that is at stake. "When you call God good, you must deny that you are good and confess that you are altogether evil. He will not suffer Himself and you to be called good together at the same time, for He wants to be regarded as God, but He wants you to be regarded as a *creature*."[65]

Beauty and the Question of Form

Already in Luther's early theology of humility we see the beginnings of what would be his unique approach to theology: God must kill us as sinners before

63. *Dictata super Psalterium*, on Ps. 104, in LW 11:317–18 (italics added) (WA 4:173.12–18).
64. *Dictata super Psalterium*, in LW 11:387 (WA 4:252.10–14).
65. *Dictata super Psalterium*, in LW 11:411 (italics added) (WA 4:278.37–279.2).

he makes us alive as new creatures,[66] ones with clean hearts. God forensically regards those who are nothing on the basis of their own merit as the raw material of his new creation. Luther's whole approach in the theology of humility is one increasingly governed by a forensic approach to the human relationship with God. That is, what counts in the human relationship with God is how God evaluates us. As we admit our nothingness, so are we embraced by God. Through his study of specific mystics, such as Johannes Tauler (ca. 1300–1361), Luther claimed that the core Christian identity before God—as all human identity—is one that is wholly passive. New creations are active with respect to their fellow creatures, their neighbors, by serving others in their need, but before God they know that they are entirely receivers. Hence, the humility of the earliest phase of Luther's theological career is transformed over time into a theology of the cross. Through various "trials and sufferings"[67] and the accusing voice of the law, God is crucifying the old Adam or Eve so that humans lose confidence in the old being's claims for its own self-deification and ability to control life. As a result, sinners put their trust in God's goodness—*and beauty*—granted in Jesus Christ. But such beauty is hidden. It is grasped by the eyes of faith alone. Smug sinners appear to their own thinking as beautiful but in fact *coram deo* are ugly. Accused by God's law, repentant Christians know their complete dependence on Christ, who before the world had "no form nor comeliness" (Isa. 53:2 KJV) but who grants them the beauty of his righteousness. Such beauty is trust in God's word, which as law reduces sinners to their nothingness and as gospel allows them to claim Christ's righteousness as their own. Thus, rid of self-justifying egocentrism as definitive of the core of their being, they live extrinsically, outside themselves, first in Christ in whom their confidence is centered, but also in their neighbor in whose service they now become "Christs."[68]

The *Lectures on Romans* (1515–16) continue the theme of struggling with God that we saw in the *Dictata*, here specifically a contest over truth, that God's truth accusing the sinner must prevail. "Therefore he who humbly repudiates his own righteousness and confesses that he is a sinner before God truly glorifies God, proclaiming that He alone is righteous."[69] Likewise, these lectures continue the theme of God making the self-secure who deem themselves beautiful to be ugly, but generously giving his beauty to those

66. For more on this theme, see Robert Kolb, "God Kills to Make Alive: Romans 6 and Luther's Understanding of Justification (1535)," *LQ* 12 (1998): 33–56.

67. *Lectures on Hebrews*, in LW 29:130 (WA 57/3:122.19).

68. "I will therefore give myself as a Christ to my neighbor, just as Christ offered himself to me" (*The Freedom of a Christian*, in LW 31:367 [WA 7:66.3–5]).

69. *Lectures on Romans*, in LW 25:200 (WA 56:215.5–7).

made ugly because their self-righteousness has been exposed as nothingness: "In the same way the righteousness of God is the more beautiful [*pulchrior*], the fouler [*fedior*] our unrighteousness is. But at this point the apostle is not referring to these ideas, because this is the internal and formal righteousness of God."[70] Likewise, "just as opposites show themselves to greater advantage when they are placed next to each other than when placed by themselves, so also His righteousness is the more beautiful, the fouler our unrighteousness is."[71]

Luther is concerned with weeding out not only humanity's worst but also humanity's best. He describes this as God destroying an "old form" and granting humans a "new form"; this new form is nothing other than the agency of Christ himself in believers. Christ secures the conscience and empowers humans for service. Following Aristotle, medieval thinkers identified a fourfold causality, the material (the stuff out of which something is made), formal (the pattern in which it is made), efficient (the agent who does the making), and final (the purpose for which something is made) causes. As noted earlier, medieval theologians associated the formal cause with beauty. Given Luther's radical proposal denying that the sinner retains something that can receive God's grace and on which God can build ("We are so entirely inclined to evil that no portion which is inclined toward the good remains in us"),[72] he proposes that God's regenerative work is to give humans a new form, since the old is so misshapen by sin. Appealing to the thinking of Gregorius Reisch (ca. 1467–1525), Luther writes:

> No one is exalted except the man who has been humbled, nothing is filled except that which is empty, that nothing is built except that which has been torn down. As the philosophers say: a thing is not brought into form unless there is first a lack of form or a change of previous form; again, a "potential idea" does not receive a form unless at its inception it has been stripped of all form and is like a tabula rasa.[73]

Luther's appeal to the use of the term "form" is not to provide an alternative theory of deification but to speak of our status *coram deo* as new creations. It eschews the Scholastic assumption of an entelechy, in which a thing has more goodness and beauty when it achieves a higher level of perfection of its form. Instead, God is about the business of making his creatures new. Believers are being conformed to the image of the crucified, which is effective justification.

70. *Lectures on Romans*, in LW 25:205 (WA 56:220.6–8).
71. *Lectures on Romans*, in LW 25:205 (WA 56:221.12–14).
72. *Lectures on Romans*, in LW 25:222 (WA 56:237.5–8).
73. *Lectures on Romans*, in LW 25:204 (WA 56:218.18–219.2).

They are not conformed to perfect order, or law, but to the form of Christ, which is ugly to us. As Luther's theology of the cross takes shape it is not done apart from a sense of beauty.

> In order that this may be more clearly understood, we must know what is meant by the work of God. It is nothing else but to create righteousness, peace, mercy, truth, patience, kindness, joy and health, inasmuch as the righteous, truthful, peaceful, kind, joyful, healthy, patient, merciful cannot do otherwise than act according to His nature. Therefore God creates righteous, peaceful, patient, merciful, truthful, kind, joyful, wise, healthy men. There are his handiwork, or his creations, as Ps. 111[:3] says, "Full of honor and majesty is his work." That is to say, praise and *comeliness*, or glory and *brightness* is the work of God. It is praiseworthy and very *beautiful* [*pulcherrimum*], without any blemish whatsoever, as Ps. 96[:6] says, "Honor and *beauty* [*pulchritudo*] are before him; strength and majesty are in his sanctuary," that is, in his church. The acts of God are therefore the righteous and the Christians; they are his new creation.[74]

God's alien work of breaking down self-righteousness and self-centeredness is bound to a creative purpose—to remake people anew.[75]

> Thus when a potter fashions a vessel out of clay, it is impossible for him to preserve the previous form of the clay and at the same time to fashion a vessel, since the previous form resists, and lacks the form of, a vessel, and, in general, as the philosophers say: "The evolvement of one thing is the destruction of another, and motion is from opposite to opposite." . . . Consequently, it is impossible for the natural state, the wisdom, prudence, purpose, or good intention of that man with whom and in whom God works to remain as it is or to move forward. For all these are the raw material and the unformed clay, as it were, which gives place to the direct opposite when God has begun to work.[76]

And the shape of this new life—a new creation—is that of a clean heart.[77] And the new form that is shaped within us by the agency of the word is nothing other than like Christ, the form of a servant.[78]

Finally, we should note that, with his focus on God's forensic regard of sinners, Luther reinterpreted bridal mysticism with its implicit affirmation of beauty, that Christ is beautiful and desirable to the soul and that the soul is

---

74. "Sermon on St. Thomas' Day" (December 21, 1516), in LW 51:18–19 (italics added) (WA 1:112.10–20).

75. *Lectures on Hebrews*, in LW 29:135 (WA 57:128.14–15).

76. *Lectures on Hebrews*, in LW 29:149 (WA 57:143.11–22).

77. *Lectures on Hebrews*, in LW 29:152 (WA 57:147.18–19).

78. "Two Kinds of Righteousness" (1519), in LW 31:301 (WA 2:148.15).

beautiful to Christ. Luther's bridal mysticism continues the forensic character established from the young Luther's earliest work appropriating beauty. That is, the bride comes into the relationship with debts and liabilities, "sins, death, and damnation."[79] But Christ as a bridegroom "must take upon himself the things which are his bride's and bestow upon her the things that are his. If he gives her his body and very self, how shall he not give her all that is his?"[80] Hence, Luther said that "here we have a most pleasing vision [*dulcissimum spectaculum*] not only of communion but of a blessed struggle and victory and salvation and redemption."[81] Christ absorbs these debts of his "wicked harlot."[82] She has a *right to* and *can claim* his status and properties even as he absorbs her debts. Once again, we have a kind of "forensic beauty" established. The "divine bridegroom Christ marries the poor, wicked harlot, redeems her from all her evil, and adorns [*ornans*] her [beautifies her] with all his good-ness [*omnibus suis bonis*]."[83] By "birthright" Christ is a king and a priest. Through marriage "the wife owns whatever belongs to the husband. Hence all of us who believe in Christ are priests and kings in Christ."[84] The happy exchange unites the soul with Christ, but not in such a way that the bride loses her sense of identity. Instead her identity is established on the basis of a relationship, and with all the rights, honors, and privileges accorded with marriage. It is the power of the word that effectuates this new relationship: the "word imparts its qualities to the soul . . . just as the heated iron glows like fire because of the union of fire with it."[85]

Conclusion

Beauty understood metaphysically was not an interest of Luther's. However, beauty seen as the truth hidden in Christ or the Christian was. As incarnate, the Son of God was made ugly just so that he might remake those uglified by sin beautiful to God. Moving further than Augustine, the early Luther stressed that God reduces to nothing pride-filled humans who claim beauty as something that they could exchange for God's righteousness. But that path

79. *The Freedom of a Christian*, in LW 31:351 (WA 7:55.1).
80. *The Freedom of a Christian*, in LW 31:351 (WA 7:55.5–6).
81. *The Freedom of a Christian*, in LW 31:351 (WA 7:55.7–8).
82. *The Freedom of a Christian*, in LW 31:352 (WA 7:55.26).
83. *The Freedom of a Christian*, in LW 31:352 (WA 7:55.26–27).
84. *The Freedom of a Christian*, in LW 31:354 (WA 7:56.35–38).
85. *The Freedom of a Christian*, in LW 31:349 (WA 7:53.27). See also Marc Lienhard, *Luther: Witness to Jesus Christ; Stages and Themes of the Reformer's Christology*, trans. Edwin H. Robertson (Minneapolis: Augsburg, 1982), 131–36.

will not work because God regards the lowly, who are "nothing" in the eyes of the world, as the raw material in which he will shape or form the beauty of Christ. That God has an alien work—indeed that God is even *deus abscon-ditus*, as we see in the mature Luther's work—is not incompatible with the assertion that God in his nature is beautiful or good. Luther's view of God is highly relational—the God with whom we deal shifts: if we come before God with pride, we will encounter God as menacing and threatening to our self-justification; if we come before God with repentance, we will encounter God as merciful for Jesus's sake. That God is sheer goodness is a truth to be established only eschatologically—with the light of glory, beyond the lights of nature and grace. Even so, Luther affirmed in his later commentary on Psalm 45, "This is a description or definition of God that is full of comfort: that in His *true form* God is a God who loves the afflicted, has mercy upon the humbled, forgives the fallen, and revives the drooping. How can any more pleasant picture be painted of God? Since God is truly this way, we have as much of Him as we believe."[86] Beauty is important to Luther—he shows us a Christ who forwent external beauty so that humans made ugly by sin could claim the beauty that God has for them as new creations.

---

86. LW 12:406 (italics added). Piotr J. Małysz notes,

> Luther's God whose *Allwirksamkeit* nothing can escape and, consequently, in whose power lies also human salvation, must appear as not only an arbitrarily predestining but also evil deity. This realization must fill one with dread. Yet the terror is ultimately meant to lead, as in the case of Luther's own anguish over God's justice, to "salutary . . . despair." Although God hidden in his majesty is the God who wields the power of salvation, he is not a different God from the God who veils himself in the weakness of the cross for the sake of the world's salvation. Rather, the purpose of his all-working hiddenness is to bring proud humans down to nothing, at which point they are no longer able to trust in themselves. . . . Thus the despair over God's *majestic* hiddenness gives way to an actual faith-full appreciation of his *salvific* hiddenness. ("Luther and Dionysius: Beyond Mere Negations," in *Re-thinking Dionysius the Areopagite*, ed. Sarah Coakley and Charles M. Stang [Oxford: Wiley-Blackwell, 2009], 156)

See also Robert Kolb, *Bound Choice, Election, and Wittenberg Theological Method: From Martin Luther to the Formula of Concord* (Grand Rapids: Eerdmans, 2005), 37–38.

» 5 «

The Mature Luther on Beauty

The mature Luther built upon and expanded the views of beauty (*pulchritudo*, *decus*, *species*, or *forma*) established in his earlier research in the *Dictata super Psalterium* (1513–15), the *Lectures on Romans* (1515–16), and the *Heidelberg Disputation* (1518). Following Augustine and Pseudo-Dionysius, Luther's medieval forebears believed that beauty is to be discerned in proper proportion and light. Likewise, they believed that all beautiful things actually participate not only in truth and goodness but also in beauty itself, a perspective called pancalism. Thomas Aquinas expanded the Augustinian and Pseudo-Dionysian criteria of proportion and light by adding a third criterion for beauty: completeness or perfection. By no means did Luther reject these three criteria for beauty, at least when beauty is seen not with respect to God's evaluation of sinful humans, but instead with respect to the evaluation of beauty as it exists in the world (*coram mundo*). As we shall see, these criteria are integral to the Reformer's view of the first humans' original righteousness (*iusticiae originalis*) as he portrayed it in his late *Lectures on Genesis*.[1] However, the Reformer broke with these criteria when examining beauty as claimed for sinners in the presence of God (*coram deo*). There the gospel subverts such standards: Christ who is beauty itself became ugly by identifying with sinners so that those made ugly through sin might become beautiful in God's eyes.

1. LW 1:164 (WA 42:123.37).

Luther's view requires a distinction between a law perspective and a gospel perspective on beauty. So he maintained that proportion, brightness, and completeness are appropriate standards *coram mundo* by which to assess beauty. But *coram deo* these criteria of beauty do not apply. Why? Unrepentant sinners view Christ as ugly because they are offended by his association with the lowly; they do not believe that they need his mercy. However, repentant sinners glory in Christ's beauty, which is his compassion, because they are hungry, even desperate, for God's forgiveness and mercy. Repentant sinners are adorned in Christ's beauty as a gift given externally to them. Forensically speaking, God judges the ugly to be beautiful for Jesus's sake. For Luther, in the words of the *Heidelberg Disputation* (1518), sinners are not loved because they are attractive (beauty as merit they could claim before God); instead, they are attractive because they are loved (God's love beautifies them by claiming them).[2] Luther thus subverts medieval views of beauty.

The early Luther ruled out any beauty in the sinner because, before God, sinners can claim nothing of either goodness or beauty for themselves, which, of course, is exactly what sinners want to do. Instead, such claims are shattered by God's accusing law. Instead of riding on their claims, sinners are placed wholly into God's hands. Medieval theologians appropriated beauty as the property or distinctive characteristic of the Second Person of the Trinity. In essence, Luther agrees here with his forebears: "He who sees the use of a thing sees the Holy Spirit, he who discerns the form or beauty of a thing sees the Son, and he who considers the substance and continuing existence of things sees the Father. These three—substance, form, and goodness—cannot be separated."[3] Christ as beauty, however, is not beautiful to sinners because he is a threat to their defense mechanisms. He makes those beautiful in their own eyes to be ugly, and those made ugly through the accusations of God's law he makes beautiful. Christ thereby subverts any and all systems governed by self-justification. As God's justifying word of forgiveness establishes new life within sinners, they more and more are conformed to the image of the crucified; that is, their fear, love, and trust in God above all things deepen.

A wider consequence of Luther's establishing beauty as an expression of God's overflowing love to accused sinners threatened by God's wrath is to extinguish the centrality of desire as the core of human identity. Instead, for Luther, faith in God or lack thereof (which is tantamount to faith in one-self) replaces desire as the key to human nature. But, no doubt, humans are

2. Consider the upshot of thesis 28: "The love of God does not find, but creates, that which is pleasing [*diligibile*] to it. The love of man comes into being through that which is pleasing to it" (LW 31:57 [WA 1:354.35]).

3. *Lectures on Genesis*, in LW 4:196 (WA 43:276.33–36).

creatures of desire, and ultimately their desire will be fulfilled in their future with God. Speaking of eternal life, Luther affirmed, "But in Him [God] all our needs and wants will be satisfied."[4] Desire in the first place is established in the faith of the heart. That to which the heart clings is the key to human desire. In this chapter, we will examine a few of Luther's later Psalms lectures (1530s and 1540s), the *Lectures on Galatians* (1535), and the *Lectures on Genesis* (1535 and following years) to see how Luther developed his mature outlook on beauty, specifically the beauty of Christ who rescues sinners, the beauty of the new life that God establishes for those of faith, and the sheer, unblemished beauty of prelapsarian humanity.

Beauty *Sub Contrario* in Selected Psalms (1530s)

Luther's early perspectives on beauty came to the fore by means of his exegesis of the Psalter in the *Dictata super Psalterium*. The book of Psalms often claims that both God and the Messiah are beautiful and hence trustworthy and desirable. Luther's early exegesis of Psalms 45, 51, and 112 made him think about the nature of beauty and its application to how humans should render God his due. At this early stage of the Reformer's career, his perspective has been designated a "theology of humility," because for Luther those closest to God are those who actively humble themselves before God or who are passively humbled through various crosses and trials. Increasingly in the *Dictata* and his *Lectures on Romans* (1515–16) Luther moved toward this passive role for humanity *coram deo* and, conversely, an active role of God as accuser or granter of mercy. The upshot of his work with respect to beauty is a paradoxical approach: "Whoever makes himself beautiful [*pulchrum*], is made ugly [*fedatur*]. On the contrary, he who makes himself ugly, is made beautiful."[5] It is to the humble that God gives his grace. For any human to claim any divine trait, name, or attribute for oneself, such as goodness, beauty, or freedom, is to take from God what properly belongs to God.

As Luther moved away from a theology of humility and toward a theology of the cross in which humans' active role in humbling themselves before God is consistently exchanged for a passive role of being humbled by God through the accusations of the law, such paradoxical themes about beauty are reinforced. God kills sinners just so that he can make them alive through the risen Christ. But such a dynamic sets up a discrepancy between appearance and reality. Christ appears ugly, if not physically, then in his person, at least to sinners,

---

4. *Commentary on 1 Corinthians 15* (1532–33), in LW 28:144 (WA 36:596.25).
5. *Dictata super Psalterium* (1513–15), in LW 11:263 (WA 4:111.7, 15).

who detest his mercy because they trust in their self-sufficiency before God; in reality Christ is beautiful—indeed beauty itself. Similarly, sinners appear beautiful to themselves but in reality are ugly to God, whose judgment instead of sinners' ugliness is definitive and final. Finally, Christians are in no position to claim beauty for themselves; rather, they can claim beauty only as it is *imputed* to them by Christ. These themes are set forth and expanded in the mature Luther's commentaries on various psalms in the 1530s and 1540s. Most importantly, righteousness by faith, in the Reformer's judgment, is simply an expression of God's beauty. God's beauty is an expression of his righteousness. *Coram deo*, justification is beauty and God's imputed beauty (Christ himself) is justification. With respect to the imputation of beauty: the beauty outside the eye of the beholder is created by the eye of the beholder. That is the nature of God's beholding.[6]

The most pertinent material about beauty in Luther's later Psalm commentaries is found in his remarks on Psalms 8 and 45. The commentary on Psalm 8 is a sermon that Luther preached on November 1, 1537. In addressing Psalm 8:5, the Reformer asserts God's vindication of Jesus Christ as the true and faithful witness in the face of opposition and adversity. Based on the description in Isaiah (53:2) of the suffering servant (Christ) having "no form nor comeliness,"[7] Luther both early and late acknowledged Christ's "ugliness" as due either to the fact that Christ was not actually physically handsome or to the fact that sinners are simply hardwired to see him as ugly. Here the assessment of Christ's ugliness is repeated, particularly in relation to his rejection by his opponents. Luther assails Christ's opponents, who include all unrepentant sinners. However, he also comforts repentant sinners who align themselves with Christ's sufferings and who, with Christ, share in persecution when they confess the gospel. The Reformer develops a theme related to that of persecution, which ties beauty to the eschatological consummation of God's purpose for his people. Thus Luther provides hope for those undergoing adversity, as Luther himself and many evangelical Christians had been.

> Him [Christ] whom no one will support, who is forsaken by God and the whole world, Him thou [God] wilt snatch from suffering to peace, from anguish to consolation and joy. Because of the contempt, mockery, and shame He has endured Thou wilt adorn [*zieren*] Him with honor. Because of the ugly form [*hesliche Gestalt*] He had on earth Thou wilt dress [*kleiden*] Him preciously, so that He will be dressed, adorned, and crowned on all sides. Not only will He be beautiful [*schoen*] in body and soul for His own person, full of eternal

6. Insight received from Robert Kolb, correspondence in spring 2014.
7. See, for example, "Commentary on Psalm 45" (1532), in LW 12:208 (WA 40/2:487.9).

salvation, wisdom, power, and might, full of heavenly majesty and deity, so that all creatures will regard and adore Him; He will also be gloriously adorned and decorated with His Christians and believers on earth and with the elect angels in heaven, in this world and in the world to come.[8]

At its core, this passage accentuates the distinction between appearance and reality with respect to beauty, the paradox that constitutes the core of Christ's beauty and subverts the medieval affirmation of beauty as perfection, proportion, and light. As rejected by sinners, Christ's beauty is hidden, is not apparent, and thus is not available for any to see. Nevertheless, Christ, along with his faithful, will be vindicated and honored by God. This assuring theme, which eschatologically ties beauty to hope, is repeated later in Luther's *Lectures on Genesis*:

> These reproaches she [the church] endures; they are her beautiful precious stones [*schöne Edlestein*] which she wears on earth, her jewels and golden chain. These are her gems and her most beautiful and precious [*pulcherrima et preciosissima*] jewels, with which God adorns [*ornat*] her in this life. So in this example a picture is drawn of how God tempts us privately and the whole church according to the example of Jacob. For He wrestles with her and conducts Himself like an adversary and enemy who wishes to forsake, cast away, and indeed destroy her.[9]

Appealing to comfort that martyrs long to hear, Luther claims that persecution is not to be avoided, for through such suffering God will establish the very marks of Christ's identity in believers who constitute his church. Human reproach does not define the church's identity, but instead God's assessment of one's fidelity to Christ is on trial. Steadfast while under assault, Christians will grow more in their faith and look less to themselves and so become more like Christ, who is the epitome of beauty itself. For Luther, behind such adversity God himself is present—albeit hidden—so that, again, in time of need believers may learn to flee to Christ.

Based on lectures given in 1532, Luther's commentary on Psalm 45 clarifies that Christ's beauty is to be looked for not in his physical but in his spiritual traits. This bears on gospel beauty: if beauty is a spiritual trait—for example, faithfulness—then beauty is found not in an Aristotelian golden mean but in God's own self-giving and in trust in God's promise. The Reformer repeats his conviction originally forged in the early theology of humility that sinners

8. "Commentary on Psalm 8" (1537), in LW 12:128 (WA 45:241.35–242.10).
9. LW 6:147 (WA 44:110.6–11).

who claim beauty for themselves ignore their own ugliness *coram deo*. Again, the appearance of beauty, with its boastful attempt to claim merit before God, results in an ugliness before God and is ever at work in sinners' lives. Sinful humans are blind to such ugliness and, even worse, to the beauty of Christ. Elsewhere, Luther notes that sinners can only see their nothingness *coram deo* through the Holy Spirit's enlightenment. It is Christ alone who is truly beautiful.

> It could perhaps be that some were fairer in form than Christ, for we do not read that the Jews especially admired His form. We are not concerned here with His natural and essential form, but with His spiritual form. That is such that He is simply the fairest in form among the sons of men, so that finally He alone is finely formed [*solus formosus*] and beautiful. All the rest are disfigured, defiled, and corrupted by an evil will, by weakness in their resistance to sin, and by other vices that cling to us by nature. This ugliness of man [*turpitudines*] is not apparent to the eyes; it makes no impression on the eyes, just as spiritual beauty makes no visual impression. Since we are flesh and blood, we are moved only by the substantial form and beauty that the eyes see. If we had spiritual eyes, we could see what a great disgrace it is that man's will should be turned from God.[10]

But what makes up Christ's beauty? Is it that, unlike sinners, he is truly righteous on the basis of the law? The Reformer does not indicate this. On the contrary, he claims that Christ's beauty is his identifying and becoming one with sinners, all for the sake of helping and saving them. Christ "did not keep company with the holy, powerful, and wise, but with despicable and miserable sinners, with those ruined by misfortune, with men weighed down by painful and incurable diseases; these He healed, comforted, raised up, helped. And at last he even died for sinners."[11] So, what makes Christ beautiful simply violates the standard medieval criteria of proportion, clarity, and perfection. In aligning himself with sinners of all sorts, Christ associates with the disproportionate, the dark, and the imperfect, and he himself becomes all this ugliness. Hence, Christ's beauty is one which is "hidden under the opposite appearance" (*sub contraria specie*).[12]

10. "Commentary on Psalm 45" (1532), in LW 12:207 (WA 40/2:485.5–11).
11. "Commentary on Psalm 45," in LW 12:208 (WA 40/2:486.11–12).
12. "Commentary on Psalm 45," in LW 12:208 (WA 40/2:487.26). That beauty is "hidden under the opposite appearance" would influence Luther's later preaching:
> The world cannot and does not want Christ in the way He shows Himself, in the cross and an offensive form, not bringing what they desire: the power, honor, riches, glory, and praise for their own wisdom and holiness, etc. The world is completely sunk and drowned in its own desires and love for earthly goods. If it does not see and find such

Instead of the three standard criteria of beauty as applying to Christ, Luther's new criterion for beauty is Christ's compassionate, self-originating love that reaches out to the lost and outcast, those who do not register as important, mighty, or valuable on the scale of law. Indeed, those in power, those with proportion, clarity, and perfection, threatened by such compassion, can only reject Christ and deem him ugly. It would seem then that the medieval criteria for beauty are constituted by law, not gospel. Luther's quest then is to resituate beauty as gospel, if any beauty is to be had *coram deo*. Speaking of the righteous upholders of the law, the Pharisees, and their rejection of Christ, Luther notes:

> [The Pharisees and priests] were so inflamed with hatred for Christ that they could not even bear to look at Him. While He was present and speaking among them, there still proceeded from His mouth rays—in fact, suns—of wisdom, and from His hands beams of divine power, and from his entire body suns of love and every virtue. But whatever of His beauty [*pulchritudinum*] He showed them was nauseating and an abomination to them, not through Christ's fault but through their own.[13]

In Jesus Christ, God gives his beauty as compassion and his compassion as beauty to those oppressed by law, but such a gift threatens the power structures sustaining human self-righteousness. "That is the manner and nature of the world; it judges this King to be shameful beyond all the sons of men, and it holds His most beautiful gifts and virtues to be diabolical villainy and malice. We encounter the same thing today."[14]

Divine beauty can appear only under the sign of its opposite (*sub contrario*) because it is a threat to human power, which insists on assigning people value based on what they offer or contribute to defend social order or growth. In contrast, God's beauty is compassion, which makes no such distinctions between those worthy and those unworthy, and in fact undermines and destroys all such distinctions, at least with respect to God. Hence, a paradoxical approach to beauty is unavoidable: those who claim their own beauty are in fact

---

things, then it understands, sees, and knows nothing further, and its desire and love, hope and comfort cease; moreover, it cannot have the desire to be in danger of being robbed of such goods. But it especially cannot tolerate that its praise and glory for high gifts—its wisdom, virtue, and holiness—should be taken away and become sin and shame before God.
See "Gospel for Pentecost Sunday [John 14:23–31]" (1544), in LW 77:352 (paragraph 67) (WA 21:466.8–17).
   13. "Commentary on Psalm 45," in LW 12:208 (WA 40/2:487.15–20).
   14. "Commentary on Psalm 45," in LW 12:208 (WA 40/2:487.22–25).

ugly before God, while those who are ugly before other humans are in fact endeared to God. Jesus Christ, who is God's beauty, is ugly to sinners and put to death by them because he is a threat to their ways of maintaining power and their own defense structures. For that reason, sinners are condemned and in need of mercy. In summary, Luther writes,

> This King is hidden under the opposite appearance: in spirit He is more beautiful [*pulcher*] than the sons of men; but in the flesh all the sons of men are more beautiful than He, and only this King is ugly, as He is described in Isaiah 53:2, 3. . . . Therefore we see that delightful and pleasant things are stated of this King in the Psalm, but they are enveloped and overshadowed by the external form of the cross. The world does not possess or admire these gifts; rather it persecutes them because it does not believe. These things are spoken to us, however, to let us know that we have such a king. All men are damned. Their beauty [*pulchritudinem*] is nothing in God's eyes. Their righteousness is sin. Their strength is nothing either. All we do, think, and say by ourselves is damnable and deserving of eternal death. We must be conformed to the image of this King.[15]

If humans are to have a beauty *coram deo*, they must receive it forensically and externally as a gift from God. Only as other than nature can grace permit nature to be nature, restore humans to nature. "Then you are beautiful [*decora*] not by your own beauty, but by the beauty of the King, who has adorned [*ornavit*] you with His Word, who has granted you His righteousness, His holiness, truth, strength, and all gifts of the Holy Spirit."[16] In other words, for the Reformer, beauty *coram deo* is another way of saying righteousness *coram deo*, and it is quite consistent to say that God's righteousness is likewise beauty. Justification by faith alone is God imparting his beauty to sinners, clothing them in his beauty. To be justified by faith is to be made beautiful. In Christ humans are made both "lovely" and "acceptable to God."

> Our beauty [*pulchritudinem*] does not consist in our own virtues nor even in the gifts we have received from God, by which we exercise our virtues and do everything that pertains to the life of the Law. It consists in this, that if we apprehend Christ [*Christum apprehendamus*] and believe in Him, we are truly lovely [*vere formosi*], and Christ looks at that beauty [*decorum*] alone and at nothing besides. Therefore it is nothing to teach that we should try to be beautiful by our own chosen religiousness and our own righteousness. To

15. "Commentary on Psalm 45," in LW 12:208–9 (WA 40/2:487.26–39).
16. "Commentary on Psalm 45," in LW 12:278 (WA 40/2:580.28–30).

be sure, among men and at the courts of the wise these things are brilliant, but in God's courts we must have another beauty [*aliam pulchritudinem*]. There this is the one and only beauty [*sola pulchritudo*]—to believe in the Lord Jesus Christ.[17]

Defined not by law but by Christ, sinners are deemed beautiful. Perhaps to be consistent, we must say they are simultaneously beautiful and ugly, just as they are *simul iustus et peccator* (simultaneously just and sinful).

Beauty in the *Lectures on Galatians* (1535)

Unlike the later commentaries on the Psalms, which deal directly with Luther's view of beauty, the *Lectures on Galatians* (1535) do not directly broach the theme of beauty. Even so, there are important challenges to the medieval view that proportion, clarity, and perfection apply to beauty *coram deo*. Likewise, a critique of these three factors *coram deo* can help clarify passages to which the late Tuomo Mannermaa has appealed in support of his view that human justification before God is a result of God's indwelling believers, seen as divinization or *theosis*, instead of a forensic approach to justification as is traditionally maintained. And it is this latter task that we will attend to first. A passage in dispute is the following:

> Such are the dreams of the scholastics. But where they speak of love, we speak of faith. And while they say that faith is the mere outline but love is its living colors and completion [*vivos colores et plenitudinem ipsam*], we say in opposition that faith takes hold of Christ and that He is the form [*forma*] that adorns and informs [*ornat et informat*] faith as color does the wall. Therefore Christian faith is not an idle quality or an empty husk in the heart, which may exist in a state of mortal sin until love comes along to make it alive. But if it is true faith, it is a sure trust and firm acceptance in the heart. It takes hold of Christ [*Christus apprehenditur*] in such a way that Christ is the object of faith [*obietum fidei*], or rather not the object but, so to speak, the One who is present in the faith itself. Thus faith is a sort of knowledge or darkness that nothing can see. Yet the Christ of whom faith takes hold is sitting in this darkness as God sat in the midst of darkness on Sinai and in the temple. Therefore our "formal righteousness" is not a love that informs faith; but it is faith itself, a cloud [*nebula*] in our hearts, that is, trust in a thing we do not see, in Christ, who is present especially when He cannot be seen.[18]

17. "Commentary on Psalm 45," in LW 12:280 (WA 40/2:583.19–27).
18. *Lectures on Galatians* (1535), in LW 26:129–30 (WA 40/1:228.27–229.21).

Luther offered an alternative to the Scholastic position that love is the form of faith. Catholic opponents feared that for Luther faith meant sheer intellectual assent alone; therefore, they reaffirmed the Scholastic conviction that faith must be formed or shaped as works of love that help one attain merit before God. Luther made it clear that faith is not reducible to intellectual assent alone. Instead, Christ is the form of faith.

Christ as the form of faith bears on beauty and vice versa in a number of important ways. Since we are dealing with a matter of "form," we are dealing with something that medieval thinkers associated with beauty. For Alexander of Hales (ca. 1185–1245) and subsequent thinkers, "truth and beauty were then both defined in terms of form: truth was the disposition of form in relation to the internal character of a thing; beauty was the disposition of form in relation to its external character. In this way, beauty was given a new foundation, for the true, the good, and the beautiful were convertible. They differed only *ratione*—conceptually, logically."[19] More specifically, with respect to the difference between goodness and beauty, matters of goodness deal with final causality or affection while matters of beauty deal with formal causality or *apprehension*.[20] We need not conjecture that Luther maintained the convertibility of the transcendentals in any metaphysical way. That would be inconsistent on his part, since from early to late in his career, Luther resists metaphysics as a comprehensive enterprise. If Luther were to maintain a convertibility between truth, beauty, and goodness, it is because Christ is all three and defines all three. It is through Christ that we experience God as truthful, beautiful, and good. It would seem that this position is exactly what he maintained.

To get to the heart of the argument in this passage, Luther notes that when Scholastic theologians maintain that love is faith's "living colors and completion," these theologians appealed to two medieval criteria of beauty: brightness and perfection. As we have seen, Luther rules out such criteria for beauty *coram deo* and instead maintains the paradox that Christ made ugly through sinners' rejection is, as God's compassion or overflowing goodness and mercy, the true beauty that transforms sinful humans apart from and

---

19. Umberto Eco, *Art and Beauty in the Middle Ages*, trans. Hugh Bredin (New Haven: Yale University Press, 1986), 23–24.

20. Eco writes the following regarding John of La Rochelle (ca. 1200–1245):

[He] simply took it for granted that the good and the beautiful were identical in objects themselves, and subscribed to the Augustinian view that honor or nobility (*honestum*) belonged in the realm of intelligible beauty. None the less, the good and the beautiful were different, "For beauty is a disposition of the good in so far as it pleases the apprehension, whereas the good strictly speaking has to do with the disposition in which it pleases our affections." He goes on to add that God is related to final causes, beauty to formal causes. (ibid., 23)

independent of proportion, brightness, or perfection. It is not human effort that reflects the true brightness of beauty *coram deo*, but Christ himself, who as beauty is the "color" that informs, indeed "adorns," faith.

Likewise, Luther's appeal to Christ as the "form of faith" undermines the Scholastic assumption of an entelechy in which acts of love generate more goodness and beauty and thus achieve a higher level of perfection of its form. However, such thinking saturates the theology of divinization. In contrast, the Reformer builds on his earlier work in the *Lectures on Romans* where he indicates that God destroys an "old form" and grants humans a "new form," which is nothing other than the agency of Christ himself in believers, of Christ who secures the conscience but also empowers the faithful for service.[21] Without a sense of entelechic growth, it is awkward if not inaccurate to speak of this passage as advocating deification. Indeed, if such a text were viewed as advocating deification, then Luther would be contradicting what he later indicates in the *Lectures on Galatians*, where he writes that those attempting to "keep the law" are striving for their own deification:

> They not only do not keep it, but they also deny the first Commandment, the promises of God, and the blessing promised to Abraham. They deny faith and try to bless themselves by their own works, that is, to justify themselves, to set themselves free from sin and death, to overcome the devil, and to capture heaven by force—which is to deny God and *to set oneself up in place of God*. For all these are exclusively works of the Divine Majesty, not of any creature, whether angelic or human.[22]

No doubt, the language of "form" indicates that Christ is no mere object of one's apprehension but indeed is the agent of faith itself in believers' lives. But this would seem to be hardly different from his earlier perspective in *The Freedom of a Christian* (1520), where he maintained that a Christian is a perfectly free lord over all, subject to none, and a perfectly dutiful servant, subject to all.[23] Christ as the form of faith naturally includes both of his natures as divine *and human*. So on the one hand, Christians as kings and priests are elevated to a divine status of lordship, but on the other hand, Christians as servants are fitted for humble service to those in need. In a sense, the paradox that exists in Christ who is lord and servant, divine and human,

---

21. *Lectures on Romans* (1515–16), in LW 25:204 (WA 56:218.18–219.2).
22. *Lectures on Galatians*, in LW 26:257–58 (italics added) (WA 40/1:404–5). See also the "Disputation against Scholastic Theology" (1517), thesis 17 (LW 31:10; WA 1:225), his exposition on Ps. 5:3 (WA 5:128.39–129.4), and the *Treatise on Good Works* (LW 44:32; WA 6:211) for his argument that the heart of sin is tantamount to self-deification.
23. LW 31:344 (WA 7:49.22–25).

is duplicated in that of his disciples. Regarding Luther's occasional use of the idiom "deification," William F. Schumacher notes:

> [It] is not so much a term to describe the believer's restored and renewed relationship to God, but rather refers to the resultant relationship to other people, expressed by a zeal to help the neighbor and pray for him. . . . For Luther the Christians' vocation in the world, far from being a distraction or an obstacle to their spiritual life, is precisely the place where they show themselves to be truly spiritual and "*vergottet*."[24]

Hence, in the *Lectures on Galatians* Luther describes faith itself as the "divinity of works [*divinitatis operum*], diffused throughout the works in the same way that the divinity is throughout the humanity of Christ."[25]

When Luther uses the term "apprehension" (e.g., in *Christus apprehenditur*), here as elsewhere he is not indicating that faith is an exercise in seeking understanding, as the Augustinian and Anselmian traditions would have it. Its context instead is that of a guilty sinner harassed by the accusations of the law and needing freedom from both sin itself and God's accusation, or that of a dead person needing new life. It is not a mere intellectual exercise, but something upon which one's whole being and salvation rest. This is not to say there is no intellectual dimension to faith. Instead, it is to acknowledge that *notitia* (information) is enveloped in an overall portrait of faith as trust. In this Galatians commentary and elsewhere, Luther repeatedly urges those oppressed by sin and harassed by God's accusing law to take hold of or apprehend Christ. One can do this because God makes himself to be a graspable God. The Reformer's language is designed to help sinners undergoing *Anfechtungen* (spiritual attacks) to find relief from such harassment by clinging to Christ and finding reconciliation with God and attendant tranquility in him. In his "Commentary on Psalm 45" (1532), Luther illustrates this by presenting Christ as one who rescues such a guilty and harassed sinner: "It is like a man who has fallen into the middle of a stream. He catches the branch of a tree somehow to support himself above the water and be saved. So in the midst of sins, death, and anxieties we, too, lay hold on Christ with a weak faith. Yet this faith, tiny though it may be, still preserves us and rules over death and treads the devil and everything under foot."[26]

24. Schumacher, *Who Do I Say That You Are? Anthropology and the Theology of* Theosis *in the Finnish School of Tuomo Mannermaa* (Eugene, OR: Wipf & Stock, 2010), 124–25. *Vergottet* is the German term for "divinized."
    25. *Lectures on Galatians*, in LW 26:266 (WA 40/1:417.15–17).
    26. "Commentary on Psalm 45," in LW 12:262 (WA 40/2:559.37–560.2 and 560.15–19).

With respect to the medieval criterion of brightness, Christ himself is the brightness of faith; that is, he establishes color for faith, but faith itself must be content with nothing other than a "darkness," an apprehending of Christ in the "clouds." Sinful humans can claim no brightness or color of their own. It must be granted them externally. Indeed, in this world human apprehension or "knowledge" or sight is beset by darkness. A clue for Luther's way of thinking can be found in his earlier *Commentary on the Magnificat* (1521), where he advocates a tripartite view of human life: spirit, soul, and body. While we need not maintain that this tripartite view of human nature is Luther's definitive perspective, it underscores his understanding of how we know God—specifically, how we know that God is for us. Of "spirit," Luther writes that it, "the first part," "is the highest, deepest, and noblest part of man. By it he is enabled to lay hold on things incomprehensible, invisible, and eternal. It is, in brief, the dwelling place of faith and the Word of God."[27] In other words, apart from faith in God's word we can have no apprehension or knowledge of God or know God's disposition toward us. We have no Christ or gospel apart from its proclamation. That our faith is a "cloud in our hearts" harkens all the way back to the *Dictata super Psalterium* (1513–15). The Psalter often presents the clouds as an abode of God's presence or a symbol of how God comes to humans. In the *Dictata*, Luther noted, "For who sees Christ in His preachers and believers? No one, but He is believed to be in them and is understood by the light of the words and works which He sends through them as from the cloud. Hence He is in the cloud, that is, in the dim recognition of Him, by which He is recognized to be in others."[28]

In a word, this passage in the *Lectures on Galatians* acknowledges Christ himself as truly beautiful for sinners in contrast to any good or beautiful deeds that sinners may wish to contribute to God. It urges repentant sinners to apprehend Christ and thus to know God's mercy. Such apprehension is an expression of faith. It is "knowledge" because Christ as the "form" of faith and not sin or self-justification is the truth granted externally to the believer's life. Faith itself is a "darkness" because it clings to the invisible (though audible, preached) Christ and not to its own visible works. But such apprehension implies that prior to it there must be one who mediates Christ: a preacher. Christian faith implies that the self is by no means a mediation of oneself by means of oneself, as an existentialist might put it; it claims that Christ himself takes over the core of a person through the word of God and that, thus, every Christian "self" is in reality not merely "decentered" but in fact is dead and

27. *Commentary on the Magnificat* (1521), in LW 21:303 (WA 8:550.28–31).
28. *Dictata super Psalterium*, on Ps. 104, in LW 11:321 (WA 4:175.33–35).

buried with Christ. Indeed, in faith Christ himself is the proper agent in the Christian's activities. The passage upon which we are commenting is about how a Christian is united with Christ. Such unity is established not by means of a continuous self-absorption into the divine, as many mystics would have it,[29] but through the self's being co-opted by Christ, who himself takes up his alien residency and agency within the believer. Again, with faith ascending into the darkness[30] and having Christ in the cloud we deal with a beauty *sub contrario*, not one established in transparency or luminosity.

The early Luther affirmed that God is beauty and that all things are beautiful.[31] However, in light of his overall theology we must qualify such metaphysical statements. In the *Lectures on Galatians* it is clear that a metaphysical approach to God as beauty is foreign to Luther. Indeed, the Reformer indicates that God is not beautiful outside of Christ and indeed is a threat. As he says,

> For as in His own nature God is immense, incomprehensible, and infinite, so to man's nature he is intolerable. Therefore if you want to be safe and out of danger to your conscience and your salvation, put a check on this speculative spirit. . . . Therefore begin where Christ began—in the Virgin's womb, in the manger, and at His mother's breasts. For this purpose he came down, was born, lived among men, suffered, was crucified, and died, so that in every possible way He might present Himself to our sight. He wanted us to fix the gaze of our hearts upon Himself and thus to prevent us from clambering into heaven and speculating about the Divine Majesty.[32]

The project of metaphysics fails as a road that grants access into God's being independently of God's self-giving in Jesus Christ. Luther rules out a metaphysical approach to divine beauty because it provides no security. Reason is capable of generating many machinations when it is not tethered to the Scriptures. Hence, contemplation is no journey beyond faith or other than faith. Instead, we are called to fix our gaze on Christ as he is presented in the preached word. Christ alone bridges God's utter transcendence, which is insurmountable by either human thinking or doing. So Luther admonishes us

---

29. "This is not an ontological absorption into the other, as some medieval mystics envisioned salvation, but a union as mysterious as husband and wife becoming 'one flesh' . . . in which each preserves his/her own identity and delights in the other being different from oneself. In this kind of union self-seeking disappears into mutual commitment and devotion to the other" (Robert Kolb, *Martin Luther: Confessor of the Faith* [Oxford: Oxford University Press, 2009], 79).

30. *Lectures on Galatians* (1535), in LW 26:113 (WA 40/2:204.5).

31. *Dictata super Psalterium*, in LW 11:317–18 (WA 4:173.12–18).

32. *Lectures on Galatians*, in LW 26:29 (WA 40/2:77.20–78.13).

to "take hold of Him [Christ]; cling to Him with all your heart, and spurn all speculation about the Divine Majesty; for whoever investigates the majesty of God will be consumed by His glory."[33] Like Moses, outside of Christ we are given only the backside of God. Luther supposes that metaphysics assumes a safe, neutral, scientific stance but that it proves to be an illusion. The more one attempts to dissect God, the more one ends up becoming dissected by God. Hence, the metaphysical path offers no assurance with respect to divine beauty but instead creates just its opposite. Its way grants no tranquility; that would be found in the promise alone. This is not to say that there are no metaphysical implications to Christology; instead it is to say that such metaphysical implications are guided by the grammar of Scripture and not vice versa.

Finally, that Christ is the bridge between God and humans rather than reason or law is reinforced through Luther's designation of Christ as the "jewel" and faith as the "ring" that encircles and encloses this jewel: "Faith takes hold of Christ and has Him present, enclosing Him as the ring encloses the gem. And whoever is found having this faith in the Christ who is grasped in the heart, him God accounts as righteous."[34] This metaphor reinforces the importance of beauty because a jewel is something that is rare, precious, and desirable. Christ is desirable for those completely laid low and brought to nothingness. No longer looking to or counting on their own resources, nor seeking to affirm their own goodness or beauty, they can see Christ for the beauty that he is. Sinners reduced to nothing are in a position to receive Christ as their being, life, or identity. To be clear, however, this alien righteousness that justifies a person before God is due to the fact that "God accepts you or accounts you righteous only on account of Christ, in whom you believe," and not because Christ indwells the Christian.[35] Indeed, his beauty is apprehended just in the fact that he rescues sinners. Hence, Luther describes those justified by faith as able to bear all things easily since "everything within is sweet and pleasant" (*suavia et dulcia*).[36]

Lectures on Genesis (1535 and Following)

Luther's commentary on the creation of humans and their "original righteousness" (*iusticiae originalis*) has extensive references to beauty. While

33. *Lectures on Galatians*, in LW 26:29 (WA 40/2:78.16–17).
34. *Lectures on Galatians*, in LW 26:132 (WA 40/2:233.17–19).
35. *Lectures on Galatians*, in LW 26:132 (WA 40/2:233.22–24).
36. *Lectures on Galatians*, in LW 26:133 (WA 40/2:234.27).

his paradoxical understanding of Christ, who appears ugly but is in truth beautiful, and of people, who appear beautiful to themselves but are in fact ugly, undermines the medieval criteria for beauty as proportion, clarity, and completeness, these criteria that are excluded *coram deo* find a place *coram mundo* as Luther presents the fitness of human ability to care for creation as it originally comes directly from God's hand. For this reason, we can draw a distinction between beauty associated with the gospel and beauty associated with the law. The former is not apparent to reason or the senses. Instead, it is claimed only on the basis of God's imputing Christ's righteousness to sinners. The latter has a place for these three medieval criteria. If anything, for Luther, when we deal with the creation of Adam, the problem with the medieval criteria *coram mundo* is that they say far too little. Indeed, the Reformer's overall perspective on Adam's qualities is similar to Albert the Great's (ca. 1193–1280) view of beauty as "resplendence of form":

> Just as corporeal beauty requires a due proportion of its members and splendid colours . . . so it is the nature of universal beauty to demand that there be mutual proportions among all things and their elements and principles, and that they should be resplendent with the clarity of form.[37]

It is hard not to view Luther's portrait of the prelapsarian Adam's physical and mental traits as hyperbolic. Speaking of the image of God in Adam, and using the Augustinian trio of memory, intellect, and will, Luther notes:

> Both his inner and his outer sensations were all of the purest kind. His intellect was the clearest, his memory was the best, and his will was the most straightforward—all in the most beautiful tranquility of mind [*pulcherrima securitate*], without any fear of death and without any anxiety. To these inner qualities came also those most beautiful and superb [*pulcherrima et excellentissima*] qualities of body and of all the limbs, qualities in which he surpassed all the remaining living creatures. I am fully convinced that before Adam's sin his eyes were so sharp and clear that they surpassed those of the lynx and eagle. He was stronger than the lions and the bears, whose strength is very great; and he handled them the way we handle puppies. Both the loveliness and the quality of the fruits he used as food were also far superior to what they are now.[38]

No doubt Luther accentuated the sufficiency of Adam's physical and mental prowess to serve as a just lord over the other creatures in Eden. Likewise, Luther heightened the contrast between humanity in a state of integrity and

---

37. Eco, *Art and Beauty in the Middle Ages*, 25.
38. *Lectures on Genesis*, in LW 1:62 (WA 42:46.18–27).

fallen humanity. Pivotal to this contrast is the peace of mind and security that the prelapsarian Adam experiences, unlike the postlapsarian Adam, who fears death. The prelapsarian Adam wholly living in filial fear, love, and trust in God, and thus in right relationship with God, has nothing to fear of death, or anything else for that matter. Hence, "before sin Adam had the clearest eyes, the most delicate and delightful odor, and a body very well suited and obedient for procreation. But how our limbs today lack that vigor!"[39] Even stronger, the Reformer notes that through the fall, humans have lost

> a most beautifully enlightened reason [*pulcherrime illuminatam rationem*] and a will in agreement with the Word and will of God. We have also lost the glory of our bodies, so that now it is a matter of the utmost disgrace to be seen naked, whereas at that time it was something most beautiful and the unique prerogative [*pulcherrimum et singularis praerogativa*] of the human race over all the other animals. The most serious loss consists in this, that not only were those benefits lost, but man's will turned away from God.[40]

In fact, for Luther, due to the pervasiveness and perversion of sin, we are not able to comprehend the nature of the *imago dei*, the image of God in humans. For Augustine and the Scholastics, the image of God consisted of (1) memory, which should blossom in hope in God; (2) intellect, which should lead to faith in God; and (3) will, which should exercise itself in loving God. Indeed, God's image would be perfected by means of humans exercising the gracious gifts of hope, faith, and love.[41] For Luther, the definitive traits ascribed to the image of God—memory, intellect, and will—are presently "utterly leprous and unclean"[42] due to sin. However, such convictions serve not just to chastise human disobedience but to accentuate the beauty and power of humans in their state of original righteousness. It is clear that the proportions of Adam's members were commensurate with his needs and the task of taking care of Eden, "a garden of delight and joy" (*deliciarum et voluptatis*),[43] and thus his sight stood superior to that of eagles or lynxes while his strength was greater than that of lions and bears. Luther makes it clear that in Eden, Adam and the other animals were not competitors for food or, least of all, planning to make a meal out of one another. Instead, Adam and the beasts ate from a

39. *Lectures on Genesis*, in LW 1:100 (WA 42:76.15–18).
40. *Lectures on Genesis*, in LW 1:141 (WA 42:106.12–17).
41. *Lectures on Genesis*, in LW 1:60 (WA 42:45.11–17).
42. *Lectures on Genesis*, in LW 1:61 (WA 42:46.7).
43. "The world was most beautiful [*pulcherrimus*] from the beginning; Eden was truly a garden of delight and joy" (*Lectures on Genesis*, in LW 1:90 [WA 42:68.35–36]).

"common table," and would have lived on rye, wheat, and other products of nature had there been no sin.[44]

No doubt the human in original righteousness is complete or perfect in every way. It is only the criterion of color that Luther passes over—strange, since the name "Adam" in Hebrew seems to imply the redness of the soil out of which he was taken. While the Reformer does not examine the applicability of light as a criterion of beauty with respect to Adam and Eve, he had earlier described the creation of light as the most beautiful adornment of creation[45] and the sun and moon as "most beautiful."[46] Even so, his overall portrait of Adam's creation seems to reinforce medieval standards of beauty and make them to be viable criteria for evaluating the beauty of created things.

The affirmation of proportion (at least *coram mundo*) is likewise reinforced in the *Lectures on Genesis* as Luther agrees with Peter Lombard (ca. 1100–1160) that humans were "created for a better life in the future than this physical life would have been, even if our nature had remained unimpaired." Repeatedly the Reformer states that "at a predetermined time, after the number of saints had become full, these physical activities would have come to an end; and Adam, together with his descendants, would have been translated to the eternal and spiritual life."[47] Indebted at this point to Augustine and the Pythagorean tradition in which Augustine stood, which so highly valued mathematics as the key to unlocking the meaning of reality, the cosmos, human nature, as well as the criterion of beauty itself, Luther writes,

> When the body has gained strength, and mind and reason are fully developed in a sound body—only then does there come a gleam of the life of the intellect, which does not exist in other earthly creatures. With the support of the mathematical disciplines—which no one can deny were divinely revealed—the human being, in his mind, soars high above the earth; and leaving behind those things that are on the earth, he concerns himself with heavenly things and explores them. Cows, pigs, and other beasts do not do this; it is man alone who does it. Therefore man is a creature created to inhabit the celestial regions [*terra coelestia*] and to live an eternal life when, after a while, he has left the earth. For this is the meaning of the fact that he can not only speak and form judgments (things which belong to dialectics and rhetoric) but also learns all the sciences thoroughly.[48]

44. *Lectures on Genesis*, in LW 1:38 (WA 42:29.4).
45. *Lectures on Genesis*, in LW 1:39 (WA 42:29.25–26).
46. *Lectures on Genesis*, in LW 1:40 (WA 42:30.16).
47. *Lectures on Genesis*, in LW 1:56 (WA 42:42.24–27).
48. *Lectures on Genesis*, in LW 1:46 (WA 42:34.37–35.7).

For Luther, the human ability to do mathematics, which in terms of harmony and rhythm of course includes music, indicates human destiny, which is more than physical—and indeed is properly spiritual. Humanity's eternal destiny most certainly involves thought and contemplation. Presently sinners "have become deaf toward what Pythagoras aptly terms this wonderful and most lovely music coming from the harmony of the motions that are in the celestial spheres. But because men continually hear this music, they become deaf to it, just as the people who live at the cataracts of the Nile are not affected by the noise and roar of the water which they hear continually."[49]

Finally, the beauty of Adam and Eve's original righteousness indicates that nature and grace were not external to each other, as they are since the fall, but instead interpenetrated each other.

> Let us rather maintain that righteousness was not a gift which came from without, separate from man's nature, but that it was truly part of his nature, so that it was Adam's nature to love God, to believe God, to know God, etc. These things were just as natural for Adam as it is natural for the eyes to receive light. But because you may correctly say that nature has been damaged if you render an eye defective by inflicting a wound, so, after man has fallen from righteousness into sin, it is correct and truthful to say that our natural endowments are not perfect but are corrupted by sin [*non integra sed corrupta*]. For just as it is the nature of the eye to see, so it was the nature of reason and will in Adam to know God, to trust God, and to fear God. Since it is a fact that this has now been lost, who is so foolish as to say that our natural endowments are still perfect?[50]

Certainly such a characterization of the relation between nature and grace indicates the depth of beauty, the "resplendence of form," with which Adam and Eve were created. Adam's nature as such was graced so that he lived in harmony with God, his wife, Eve, and his fellow creatures. It was *natural* for him to love God. Indeed, similar to a metaphor of Augustine's, that God "fills us to the brim,"[51] Luther's Adam was "intoxicated with rejoicing toward God."[52] It is into such a state that God's people and the world are being renewed. In his commentary on 1 Corinthians 15, Luther repeatedly indicates that the resurrection body will be beautiful.[53] And, recalling his description of

49. *Lectures on Genesis*, in LW 1:126 (WA 42:94.33–37).
50. *Lectures on Genesis*, in LW 1:165 (WA 42:124.4–13).
51. Augustine, *Confessions* 1.5.
52. *Lectures on Genesis*, in LW 1:94 (WA 42:71.31).
53. Luther writes of the resurrection life, "You will always be strong and vigorous, healthy and happy, also brighter and more beautiful than sun and moon, so that all the garments and the gold bedecking a king or emperor will be sheer dirt in comparison with us when we are illumined by but a divine glance" (LW 28:142; WA 36:593.34–38); and he notes, "This will make

the happy exchange in *The Freedom of a Christian*, we find the same metaphor of intoxication to describe the properties of Christ shared by the Christian:

> Since these promises of God are holy, true, righteous, free, and peaceful words, full of goodness, the soul which clings to them with a firm faith will be so closely united with them and altogether absorbed by them that it not only will share in all their power but will be saturated and intoxicated by them. If a touch of Christ healed, how much more will this most tender spiritual touch, this absorbing of the Word, communicate to the soul all things that belong to the Word.[54]

Comparing this passage with that of the Genesis passage immediately above, it is clear that grace restores human nature to its original righteousness. The promise of God is able to intoxicate the soul, making it love God, in a way that is reminiscent of original righteousness. In other words, nature needs not a self-driven perfection, but liberation. Through such liberation God will bring humans to their fulfillment. Healing the wounds of sin inflicted on the intellect and will and elevating them by means of a superadded gift of the Holy Spirit are insufficient for human need in light of sin. Instead, God remakes believers to be new creations. The upshot is: "In this life we lay hold of this goal [the likeness of God] in ever so weak a manner; but in the future life we shall attain it fully."[55] In other words, as our salvation, God is leading his people toward beauty.

Conclusion

What can be said of beauty in the mature Luther? In a word, beauty is not an insignificant concept in Luther's thinking—unless one regards the doctrine of justification as insignificant. In fact, not only can one not understand Luther's view of beauty apart from his doctrine of justification as God's imputed righteousness to believers, which also calls them from death to life, it would seem that one also cannot fully understand God's justification apart from beauty. God's beauty in its most proper form is revealed as mercy granted in Christ. To assume that the topic of beauty is insignificant to Luther is to go against Luther's own conviction that the question of beauty is crucial to human life with God: God loves sinners not because they are beautiful, but they are beautiful because they are loved.

---

the whole body so beautiful, vigorous, and healthy, indeed, so light and agile, that we will soar along like a little spark, yes, just like the sun which runs its course in the heavens" (LW 28:143; WA 36:494.40–495.1).

54. *The Freedom of a Christian*, in LW 31:349 (WA 7:53.15–20).

55. *Lectures on Genesis*, in LW 1:131 (WA 42:98.22–24).

Now, obviously, Luther's predecessors did not make the distinction between God's accusing and killing law and God's promising and life-imparting gospel. For them, beauty remains on a continuum: God is beauty itself, and all created things are beautiful to some degree by participating in this beauty. Luther cannot affirm this view of beauty as it stands, and this is where he distinguishes himself from his predecessors. He certainly acknowledges that God and his creatures are beautiful. But he notes that sinful creatures are apt to claim matters like goodness or beauty (and freedom too)—which properly are names or traits belonging to God and not to creatures—for themselves. Indeed, ultimately they claim such traits so that they might claim righteousness in the presence of God. Thus they do not think they need God's generosity or mercy, but instead believe they are entitled to God's grace. Luther will have none of that and ends up distinguishing a creation beauty from a gospel beauty. Beauties in creation do not exist for securing one's status *coram deo*. They do not serve as stepping-stones on which one can jump on the way to establishing eternal life. But that sinners would misuse creatures in no way jeopardizes creatures' beauty. It is the gospel that allows sinners to drop their guards and appreciate the wonder, mystery, and dignity of creation as a gift from God.

The creation beauty, which is appropriate as a way to evaluate creaturely things as creaturely, includes the traditional medieval standards for beauty such as proportion, brightness, and perfection or integrity, even though they are hardly adequate for assessing beauty in creation. But these criteria are inappropriate when acknowledging the beauty of Christ. His beauty is instead compassion, mercy, and forgiveness, and it is hidden to the eyes of sinners because they refuse to live by God's mercy alone. They want their own righteousness; indeed, they want to establish themselves as gods and to be done altogether with God's divinity in their lives. So Christ is seen not as beautiful to them, but as ugly. And God's law exposes human emptiness *coram deo*—sinners have no "beauty" that they can offer to God. Instead, as sinners they are ugly. The only beauty they can claim is to be clothed or adorned in Christ's righteousness, given to them from without. The beauty of Christ is imputed to them and that is their righteousness *coram deo*. It is the basis for their identity as Christians: God's children who are loved not because they are beautiful but instead are beautiful because they are loved.

In a sense, Luther affirms the pancalism of his predecessors, but not on the basis of establishing the convertibility of the transcendentals of goodness and beauty on metaphysical grounds. Indeed, God is hidden because what humans experience is often not God's beauty, but what appears to be God's indifference or downright antagonism. If there is to be any certainty with respect to beauty, it will be had in Christ alone. Christ is goodness and beauty, and through Christ humans can understand and appreciate the world as creation, as gift and as God's communication to us. In other words, the gospel opens creation as beautiful and confirms the human intuition of its beauty, again, not on the basis of an intellectual argument but because faith resituates humanity away from its tendency to claim some divine status for itself and toward a childlike trust that receives the goodness of creation as it comes to humanity from the Creator.

Briefly, it needs to be said that the fact that Luther's view of beauty *coram deo* is paradoxical does not entail that it is ambiguous. All too often, theologians misread Luther's use of paradox to think that it undermines clarity of doctrine. Such is not the case at all. A parallel case would be when Christ tells us that whoever would save their life must lose it and whoever loses their life for his sake will find it (Mark 8:35). There is no ambiguity involved here whatsoever. With respect to Luther it is simply the fact that sinners invariably claim a status of divinity for themselves—such as claiming their own beauty or freedom, which are themselves properly divine names—and that they will be opposed by God's law and will experience death. Yet it is to such nothings that God, who properly as Creator is to create *ex nihilo*, calls them into new life through trusting Christ Jesus. Far from implying ambiguity, Luther's paradoxical approach to beauty reinforces his conception of original sin and God's activity as Creator.

Finally, how might human life be different in light of Luther's views of beauty? Very simply, that sinners are clothed with an alien righteousness that makes them beautiful is a trait that they can claim before both God and the world. Believers have a new identity in Christ—beauty. Likewise, enjoying this beauty in Christ, they can be open to the beauty with which God surrounds them in the world and thus "thank, praise, serve, and obey" God.[56] In a word, parents always think of their children as beautiful, even more so in the case of God. And children are struck with awe and wonder at all sorts of things that they perceive as beautiful, things that adults have learned to take for granted. How much more then should men and women of faith be open to that beauty that God has fashioned in the world.[57]

56. BC 355 (BSELK: 870:16–18).
57. Again, I am grateful to Robert Kolb for this insight.

≫6≪

Luther on the Theology and Beauty of Music

I t is well known that Luther highly valued music. This valuation indicates the importance of beauty for Luther: if any earthly activity presents beauty, it is music. Of polyphonic vocal music Luther wrote that "there exists nothing more wonderful and beautiful."[1] Luther summarized his encomium on music thusly: "Music is an endowment and gift of God, not a gift of men. . . . I place music next to theology and give it the highest praise."[2] No study of Luther's view of beauty can ignore or dismiss the importance that he attributed to music, in spite of the fact that Luther was not able to finish a systematic study on the nature of music as he had intended.[3] We can learn about Luther's view of music from his correspondence, table talks, prefaces to hymnals and other writings on music, and unfinished sketches. Although it is underdeveloped, Luther's view of music is compelling and evocative. While his systematic inquiry into music is limited, it testifies to how he believed that music's beauty is yoked to the gospel. Music consists of free variations expressed as polyphonic voices dancing around a theme, the *cantus firmus*, which winds its way through a musical piece; likewise, the gospel liberates sinners and establishes them in a new life defined by spontaneous gratitude to God and good deeds to the neighbor.

1. See *Praefatio d. M. Lutheri in Harmonias de Passione Christi*, E, Opera Latina, VII, 551–54; St. Louis ed., XIV, 428–31; quoted by Walter Buszin, "Luther on Music," *MQ* 32 (1947): 81.
2. WA TR 6:348.23; translated in Ewald Plass, *What Luther Says: A Practical In-Home Anthology for the Active Christian* (St. Louis: Concordia, 1959), 980 (no. 3091).
3. See Robin Leaver, *Luther's Liturgical Music: Principles and Implications* (Grand Rapids: Eerdmans, 2007), 86.

The very nature of music itself is analogous to the gospel. How so? Music is a complex interchange between order and freedom. Order in music is based on the numerical patterns of rhythm as well as the numerical ratios within harmony. For early medieval thinkers influenced by Pythagoras[4] and Augustine, numerical ratios within harmony testified to the mathematical nature of the cosmos, and, indeed, beauty is composed of such ratios. But music also "has another aspect, that of movement, sometimes called liberty. Music has a freedom that makes it what it is."[5] It is this latter dimension that Luther highlighted and that he saw as effectively able to resituate human dispositions, and thereby human life. For Luther, music is the spontaneous and native response to the gospel that liberates the conscience. It is tied to the newness of life that the gospel effectuates by establishing new men and women in Christ. In short, music not only is doxological but also proclaims the gospel.

Music as a Creation and Gift of God

Few theologians have valued music to the degree that Luther did. For Luther, music is a creation and gift of God. In his "Preface to Georg Rhau's *Symphoniae Iucundae*" (1538), Luther wrote, "I would certainly like to praise music with all my heart as the excellent gift of God which it is and to commend it to everyone. . . . And you, my young friend, let this noble, wholesome, and cheerful creation of God be commended to you. . . . At the same time you may by this creation accustom yourself to recognize and praise the Creator."[6] Luther had little patience with those who turn a deaf ear to music: "But any who remain unaffected are unmusical indeed and deserve to hear a certain filth poet or the music of the pigs."[7] Nor is it solely the text of music that Luther praised. Indeed, the *notes* factor in as precisely God's good gifts.

> The book of Psalms is a sweet and delightful song because it sings of and proclaims the Messiah even when a person does not sing the notes but merely recites and pronounces the words. And yet the music, or the notes, which are a wonderful creation and gift of God, help materially in this, especially when the people sing along and reverently participate.[8]

4. See Albert Seay, *Music in the Medieval World* (Englewood Cliffs, NJ: Prentice-Hall, 1965), 20–21.
5. See Theodore Hoelty-Nickel, "Luther and Music," in *Luther and Culture*, by George Wolfgang Forell, Harold J. Grimm, and Theodore Hoelty-Nickel, Martin Luther Lectures 4 (Decorah, IA: Luther College Press, 1960), 151.
6. LW 53:321, 324 (WA 50:368.17–18; 373.20–23).
7. LW 53:324 (WA 50:373.5–6).
8. *The Last Words of David* (1543), in LW 15:273–74 (WA 54:33).

Repeatedly, Luther defined music in theological terms as "the creation and gift of God." Hence, he saw music not primarily as an art, which was the view of the late Middle Ages, nor as a science, which was the dominant view of the early Middle Ages, though the study of music includes both. Instead, for Luther, music is a creation of God and as such is something whereby God shapes humans. As a gift, it is something that humans neither earn nor deserve but instead are given gratuitously. The gift is given precisely for human enjoyment, an "innocent pleasure," as he put it; yet only a theological understanding of music specifying how God uses music to reshape human life can adequately approach its significance.

Music cannot be reduced to a merely secular endeavor. Instead, it is a means whereby God forms and reforms humans, through both the texts that enlighten the intellect and the notes that stimulate the affects. Music touches the whole person. Obviously, music is a human creation—insofar as it is crafted, rehearsed, practiced, and performed. But for Luther the human production of music is completely dependent on the fact that God has provided it as a gift with the power to reshape and resituate human life. That music is a divine gift ties it to the doctrine of justification by grace alone through faith alone. As Robin Leaver notes:

> That music comes from God as a gift means that it has dimensions of meaning, power and effectiveness that far exceed any human art or science. Music is not an *inventio*, a work of humankind, but a *creatura*, a work of God. Again there are parallels here with the doctrine of justification. In the same way as justification is God's gift of grace rather than the reward for human effort, so music is in essence God's gift of creation rather than a human achievement.[9]

Indeed, music affords a glimpse into God's wisdom: "When [musical] learning is added to all this and artistic music which corrects, develops, and refines the natural music, then at last it is possible to taste with wonder (yet not to comprehend) God's absolute and perfect wisdom in his wondrous work of music."[10] Outside the gospel, it would seem that music is a way to experience God within creation. Even more importantly, music is a way in which the gospel can be sung, and so internalized in believers' hearts and homes, thus sanctifying human life.[11]

9. Leaver, *Luther's Liturgical Music*, 89.
10. "Preface to Georg Rhau's *Symphoniae Iucundae*," in LW 53:324 (WA 50:372.11–13).
11. For an extended discussion, see Christopher Boyd Brown, *Singing the Gospel: Lutheran Hymns and the Success of the Reformation* (Cambridge, MA: Harvard University Press, 2005).

Luther's Response to the Ancient Church's Mixed Reception of Music

Given the fact that music is a hallmark of Christian worship, it is surprising to see that it has had a mixed reception in the Christian tradition. While Christians have honored music, particularly singing, for its ability to make truth more memorable and potent, many have worried that music makes worship too emotional—that the sounds will not enhance the words but instead detract from them and so take people away from a genuine worship of God. By emboldening the lower passions, music could lead people away from God—who, with respect to human faculties, is (in a Platonic bias) more akin to reason than the emotions. A brief survey of such concerns is pertinent. Justin Martyr (ca. 100–165) critiqued music performed for Roman holidays as lascivious: "Your [pagan] public assemblies I have come to hate. For there are excessive banquets and subtle flutes that provoke people to lustful movements."[12] Likewise, Clement of Alexandria (ca. 150–215) wrote:

> If people occupy their time with pipes, psalteries, choirs, dances, Egyptian clapping of hands, and such disorderly frivolities, they become quite immodest. . . . Let the pipe be resigned to the shepherds, and the flute to the superstitious ones who are engrossed in idolatry. For, in truth, such instruments are to be banished from the temperate banquet. . . . Man is truly a peaceful instrument. However, if you investigate, you will find other instruments to be warlike, inflaming to lusts, kindling up passion, or rousing wrath.

In spite of these reservations, Clement is able to put a charitable construction on the use of instrumental music, if even only metaphorically:

> The Spirit, distinguishing the divine service from such revelry, says, "Praise Him with the sound of trumpet." For with the sound of the trumpet, He will raise the dead. "Praise him on the psaltery." For the tongue is the psaltery of the Lord. "And praise him on the lyre." By the lyre is meant the mouth struck by the Spirit.[13]

Again, for Clement, the criterion of distinguishing permissible from impermissible music is temperance: "Temperate harmonies are to be allowed. But we are to banish as far as possible from our robust mind those liquid harmonies. For, through pernicious arts in the modulations of tones, they lead persons to effeminacy and indecency."[14] So, for Clement, music has a place in moral

12. Justin Martyr, *The Discourse to the Greeks* 4 (*ANF* 1:272).
13. Clement of Alexandria, *The Instructor* 2.4 (*ANF* 2:248).
14. Clement of Alexandria, *The Instructor* 2.4 (*ANF* 2:249).

development and etiquette: "Music . . . is to be studied for the sake of the embellishment and composure of manners. For instance, at a banquet, we pledge each other while the music is playing. By song, we soothe the eagerness of our desires, and we glorify God for the copious gift of human enjoyments."[15]

Reservations about music are likewise echoed by Cyprian (ca. 200–258): "God also gave man a voice. Yet, love songs and indecent things are not to be sung merely on that account."[16] Here Luther would earn Cyprian's displeasure or even anger, since he relaxed with his table companions singing not only motets of Josquin des Prez (1450/55–1521) but also on occasion popular love ballads.[17] Indeed, quite different from Luther's perspective, music for Cyprian can be an instrument of the devil leading people away from disciplined Christian living: "[Satan] presents to the eyes seductive forms and easy pleasures, by the sight of which he might destroy chastity. He tempts the ears with harmonious music, so that by the hearing of sweet sounds, he may relax and weaken Christian vigor."[18] For Luther, music, as we shall see, drives the devil away and resituates the disposition of music makers from sadness to gladness, from solitariness to fellowship.

In his *Confessions*, Augustine summarized the reservations about music with which Luther would have been most familiar when he wrote that "sometimes" he felt that he treated music "with more honour than it deserves." Augustine acknowledged that when hymnody is sung or Scripture chanted, "these sacred words stir my mind to greater religious fervour and kindle in me a more ardent flame of piety than they would if they were not sung." His reservation, similar to that of Justin, Clement, and Cyprian, is that "I ought not to allow my mind to be paralysed by the gratification of my senses, which often leads it astray. For the senses are not content to take second place. Simply because I allow them their due, as adjuncts to reason, they attempt to take precedence and forge ahead of it, with the result that I sometimes sin in this way but am not aware of it until later." Nevertheless, he acknowledged the role of music in his conversion. The sweetness of singing in the Christian assembly had moved him as a seeker toward accepting the faith.

> So I waver between the danger that lies in gratifying the senses and the benefits which, as I know from experience, can accrue from singing. Without committing myself to an irrevocable opinion, I am inclined to approve of the custom

15. Clement of Alexandria, *The Stromata, or Miscellanies* 7.40 (ANF 2:500).

16. Cyprian, *Treatise* 2, chap. 11 (ANF 5:433).

17. See the charming description of relaxation through singing after supper in the Luther household in Paul Nettl, *Luther and Music*, trans. Frida Best and Ralph Wood (Philadelphia: Muhlenberg, 1948), 13–14.

18. Cyprian, *Treatise* 10, chap. 1 (*ANF* 5:491).

of singing in church, in order that by indulging the ears weaker spirits may be inspired with feelings of devotion. Yet when I find the singing itself more moving than the truth which it conveys, I confess that this is a grievous sin, and at those times I would prefer not to hear the singer.[19]

Luther did not share Augustine's scruples in this regard. Commenting on this passage, Luther wrote, "St. Augustine was afflicted with scruples of conscience whenever he discovered that he had derived pleasure from music and had been made happy thereby; he was of the opinion that such joy is unrighteous and sinful. He was a fine pious man; however, if he were living today, he would hold with us."[20] If anything, for Luther, music leads one out of and not into sin. He certainly does not play "base" emotion against "elevated" reason.

But the question raised by Augustine and early church fathers merits attention in our era, which so highly values the emotional side of faith, often at the expense of the intellectual side. Our time revels in the release of human emotions in worship at the expense of focusing on the centrality of God and his saving efficacy. How might Luther respond to such worship today, seemingly governed by a *Schwärmerei* mentality, which celebrates the inner life in sharp contrast to the external word at the heart of worship? A clue can be found in the fact that several of Luther's own hymns were distinctively catechetical, focusing on the Ten Commandments, the Lord's Prayer, and the creed. Likewise, Luther's other hymns center not on subjective experience but on God's objective presence and care: "A Mighty Fortress," "Dear Christians One and All Rejoice," "Out of the Depths," and "Lord, Keep Us Steadfast." Luther's own tendency is not to revel in his own feelings or subjectivity but instead to allow both the words and the notes to move him outside of himself and into Christ and the neighbor on the basis of the truth of God's own objective promise.

Luther's Response to Reformed Reservations about Music

During the Reformation, the question of music's ability to corrupt believers by moving their base passions instead of stimulating their reason was brought to the fore among the Reformed and the Anabaptists. First in line was Andreas Bodenstein von Karlstadt (1486–1541), Luther's colleague who led an iconoclastic charge in Wittenberg while Luther was sequestered at the Wartburg and translating the New Testament. Not only did Karlstadt

19. Augustine, *Confessions* 10.33 (trans. R. S. Pine-Coffin [Harmondsworth, UK: Penguin, 1961], 238–39).
20. *Tischreden*, no. 2641; quoted by Buszin, "Luther on Music," 89.

oppose images in churches as idols, but he also claimed that "organs belong only to theatrical exhibitions and princes' palaces."[21] Ulrich Zwingli, who could play several instruments and had set two of his own songs to four-part music, insisted that music potentially distracted the congregation from attention to the Word. As is well known, Zwingli "cold-bloodedly allowed the organ in Zurich to be hacked to pieces, while the organist stood by, helpless and weeping."[22] John Calvin (1509–64) likewise "excluded from worship the use of organs, part-singing and all songs except 'psalms from the Bible and psalms only.'"[23] His biblical justification for terminating or limiting the use of instrumental music and choir singing was that rituals permissible in the Old Testament have now been superseded and fulfilled in Christ. Commenting on 1 Samuel 18, he wrote:

> It would be a too ridiculous and inept imitation of papistry to decorate the churches and to believe oneself to be offering God a more noble service in using organs. . . . All that is needed is a simple and pure singing of the divine praises, coming from heart and mouth, and in the vulgar tongue. . . . Instrumental music was tolerated in the time of the law because the people were then in infancy.[24]

Similar to the ancient church fathers such as Clement of Alexandria, Calvin did recover a place for music:

> Music of itself cannot be condemned; but for as much as the world almost always abuses it, we ought to be so much the more circumspect. . . . The Spirit of God condemns . . . the vanities that are committed in music . . . because men delight too much in them: and when they set their delight and pleasure in these base and earthly things, they think not a whit upon God.[25]

The inner logic for such reservations about music both within the ancient church and among the Reformed is a latent Platonism, which insists on subordinating the passions to reason. In the *Republic* Plato argued that the way to establish morality in the community was to develop an appropriate harmony or balance among the three classes that should make up the ideal community—craftsmen, auxiliaries (the police), and guardians or philosopher-kings—with

21. Ernest G. Schwiebert, *Luther and His Times* (St. Louis: Concordia, 1950), 536.
22. Nettl, *Luther and Music*, 4–5.
23. Kurt J. Eggert, "Martin Luther, God's Music Man," Wisconsin Lutheran Seminary Essay File, http://www.wlsessays.net/bitstream/handle/123456789/1274/EggertLuther.pdf.
24. See Robert M. Stevenson, *Patterns of Protestant Church Music* (Durham, NC: Duke University Press, 1953), 14.
25. Ibid., 17.

each fulfilling their own appropriate role.[26] Philosopher-kings are to govern the craftsmen and auxiliaries since they are best able to establish reason over passion and so govern well. For Plato, the individual with his or her appetites, spirit, and reason correlates with the community. Establishing ethics in community bears on ethics in the individual. Like the community, individuals are tripartite. The individual's appetite corresponds with the community's craftsmen; the individual's spirit with the auxiliaries; and his or her reason with the philosopher-king. In any case, whether speaking of individuals or the community, reason has precedence over emotions.[27] Deeper issues than merely matters of taste differentiate Lutherans from the Reformed. There is a kind of intellectualizing of the faith latent in the Reformed heritage that hearkens back to Plato and is not shared by the Lutheran Reformers. Indeed, Birgit Stolt nicely indicates that for Luther *intellectus* (understanding) is balanced by *affectus* (emotions) and vice versa.[28] Luther does not disdain the senses, let alone hold them suspect.

In general, the Reformed tradition's tendency is to pit a specific "biblical" pattern of worship against the rituals that had accrued in the medieval catholic heritage. Hence, the question of worship is no mere "external" matter over which Christians need not see eye to eye provided that the gospel is proclaimed. Instead, it is a matter of fidelity to the pattern found in the Bible. Luther looked less to Scripture as providing a specific pattern for worship and instead accepted those aspects of the medieval tradition of the Mass that did not conflict with Scripture. Additionally, such iconoclasm is fed by the Reformed conviction in Christology that the "finite is not capable of bearing the infinite" (*finitum non capax infiniti*). Hence, sacraments are not means of grace per se but, instead, symbols of grace. Physical things such as water or bread and wine as embodied or audible words do not mediate grace but instead only testify to or witness to such grace beyond them.[29] For Luther, in contrast, such physicality grants both objectivity and tangibility

---

26. Plato, *The Republic* 434d.

27. In Plato's *Philebus* (28c), reason is described as "the king of heaven and earth."

28. Stolt, "Joy, Love and Trust—Basic Ingredients in Luther's Theology of the Faith of the Heart," *SRR* 4 (2002): 37.

29. On the physicality of baptism, Luther writes,

Now, these people are so foolish as to separate faith from the object to which faith is attached and secured, all on the grounds that the object is something external. Yes, it must be external so that it can be perceived and grasped by the senses and thus brought into the heat, just as the entire gospel is an external, oral proclamation. In short, whatever God does and effects in us he desires to accomplish through such an external ordinance. No matter where he speaks—indeed, no matter for what purpose or through what means he speaks—there faith must look and to it faith must hold on. (The Large Catechism, in BC 460:30 [BSELK 1118:5])

to grace that allows one in faith to apprehend the promise attached to the word. For Luther, the incarnation is the basis for affirming that "the finite is capable of bearing the infinite" (*finitum capax infiniti*) and thus that Christ is really present in the Lord's Supper.

This integration of *intellectus* and *affectus* grew out of Luther's experiences both in the monastery with its focus on the affects and in the university with its focus on the intellect. Oswald Bayer has helpfully situated the development of Luther's theology of *promissio* within these two institutions.[30] Luther praised reason as God's "greatest gift," but as is well known he constantly chided reason as the "devil's whore" when reason sought to overstep its bounds and establish the conditions for salvation. The thought that music could lower human nature or even be an instrument of the devil never seemed to occur to Luther. Just the opposite: music was an antidote to evil. While he was sequestered at the Coburg castle in 1530, Luther wrote to the musician Ludwig Senfl (ca. 1486–1542): "Except for theology [music] alone produces what otherwise only theology can do, namely, a calm and joyful disposition. Manifest proof [of this is the fact] that the devil, the creator of saddening cares and disquieting worries, takes flight at the sound of music almost as he takes flight at the word of theology."[31] For Luther, music was a crucial resource for combating *Anfechtungen* (spiritual tribulations). Indeed, he found music to be a resource for pastoral counsel of those suffering similar *Anfechtungen*. He advised Mathias Weller, an organist in Freiberg,

> When you are sad, say to yourself, "Come! I will strike up a song to my Lord Jesus Christ on the regal [a small portable organ], be it *Te Deum Laudamus* or *Benedictus*, for the Scriptures teach me that He rejoices in glad song and the sound of the strings." So with renewed spirit reach for the claves [keys] and sing until your sad thoughts are driven away, as did David and Elisha.[32]

Limiting as he did the scope of reason in matters of faith, Luther's anthropology is less beholden to Plato's favoring of reason over emotion than that of the Reformed. Reason has its place in human life—as a way to solve matters

---

30. "Luther holds that the 'monastic' aspect of theology with its liturgical spirituality grounded in the divine service is constitutive, in that this provides theology with its content. On the other hand, he says that its 'scholastic' academic aspect is purely regulative in that it orders, analyzes, and reflects on the content of theology and makes the necessary distinctions and connections. These two sides of theology are kept united in a special way by meditation (*meditatio*)" (Bayer, *Theology the Lutheran Way*, trans. Jeff Silcock and Mark Mattes [Grand Rapids: Eerdmans, 2007], 83).

31. LW 49:428 (WA BR 5:639.12–16).

32. *Luther: Letters of Spiritual Counsel*, trans. and ed. Theodore G. Tappert (Philadelphia: Westminster, 1955), 96–97 (WA BR 7:104–5).

pertaining to this world and in theology only as it is beholden to the grammar of faith.[33] As a human faculty, reason is enfolded within the core identity of the human, designated as the heart. As such, it is beholden to God's word, which ought to reign in the heart. The heart is geared toward what it can trust. Unfortunately it is often prone to trust in idols of its own making (and control) instead of God (over whom it has no control).

The Affectivity of Music as Embodied Word

As noted, Luther claimed that musical notes and not just the words are wonderful creations and gifts of God. Given Luther's sacramental approach to the gospel promise as a gift-word coming to humans through physical means such as the waters of Holy Baptism and the bread and wine of the Lord's Supper, we can affirm that just as God's word comes to sinners through embodied or physical means, so words come wrapped in notes. Proclamation always is given by such physical means—such as the tongue, larynx, and vocal folds—which craft exhalation into meaningful words. Similarly, as a response to the gospel, music is natural, native, and spontaneous. While it would be unwise to establish the rapport between words and music as a matter of principle (since obviously God's word can come apart from singing), the fact of a connection between proclamation and music must still be recognized. Luther noted that of the four disciplines in the *quadrivium* (mathematics, geometry, astronomy, and music), it was music through which the prophets conveyed their message.[34] Embodiment is an important dimension of Luther's approach to the gospel, and it is not lost on his view of music.

Why such an emphasis on embodiment? With respect to the sacrament of the Lord's Supper, bread and wine are given "that our human nature can lay hold of God more certainly and fasten onto one sign by which it can grab hold of him, so that we do not go back and forth in endless speculation."[35] Likewise,

33. See chap. 2 above and Mark Mattes, "A Contemporary View of Faith and Reason in Luther," in *Propter Christum: Christ at the Center; Essays in Honor of Daniel Preus* (St. Louis: Luther Academy, 2013), 145–68.
34. See LW 49:427–28 (WA BR 5:639):
  I plainly judge, and do not hesitate to affirm, that except for theology there is no art that could be put on the same level with music, since except for theology [music] alone produces what otherwise only theology can do, namely, a calm and joyful disposition. . . . This is the reason why the prophets did not make use of any art except music; when setting forth their theology they did it not as geometry, not as arithmetic, not as astronomy, but as music, so that they held theology and music most tightly connected, and proclaimed truth through Psalms and songs.
35. "Sermo de testamento Christi" (1520), in WA 9:448.34–36 (trans. Bayer, *Theology the Lutheran Way*, 46).

when plagued by *Anfechtungen*—spiritual attacks—the human heart is better anchored and secured in God's word when that word is sung. As a result, its truth becomes etched into the human heart and made available for daily appropriation.

Luther thus was concerned with how music moves the heart. This he expressed in a sketch for a treatise on music that he never completed:[36]

> I love music.
> Its censure by fanatics does not please me
> For
> 1. [Music] is a gift of God and not of man
> 2. For it creates joyful hearts
> 3. For it drives away the devil
> 4. For it creates innocent delight, destroying wrath, unchastity, and other excesses.
> I place music next to theology.
> This is well known from the example of
> David and all the prophets, who all
> produced poetry and songs.
> 5. For [music] reigns in times of peace.
> It will be difficult to keep this delightful skill after us.
> The Dukes of Bavaria are to be praised in this, that they honor music.
> Among our Saxon [Dukes] weapons and cannons are esteemed.

Repeatedly Luther focused on what music can do: create joyful hearts, drive away the devil, and incite innocent joy. His emphasis was on how music renews and rejuvenates life. Indeed, for the Reformer, music has the power to influence all the emotions:

> For whether you wish to comfort the sad, to terrify the happy, to encourage the despairing, to humble the proud, to calm the passionate, or to appease those full of hate—and who could number all these masters of the human heart, namely, the emotions, inclinations, and affections that impel men to evil or good?—what more effective means than music could you find?[37]

For Luther, a natural response of a human whom the gospel has transformed is spontaneously to express gratitude and joy. For example, in the *Treatise on Good Works* (1520), Luther noted,

> Next to faith the second work is the work of the second commandment, that we shall honor God's name and not take it in vain. This, like all the other works,

---

36. WA 30/2:696; translated in Leaver, *Luther's Liturgical Music*, 86.
37. "Preface to Georg Rhau's *Symphoniae Iucundae*," in LW 53:323 (WA 50:371.5–9).

cannot be done without faith. However, if it is done without faith, it is simply sham and show. After faith we can do no greater work than to praise, preach, sing, and in every way laud and magnify God's glory, honor, and name.[38]

We see this emphasis throughout his corpus.[39] As the angel referred to in the children's Christmas hymn "From Heaven Above" puts it: "Glad tidings of great joy I bring / To all the world, and gladly sing: / To you this night is born a child."[40]

Luther's focus on how music affects the human emotions shows how he was in step with a broader movement late in the Middle Ages advocated by Jean Gerson (1363–1439) and Johannes Tinctoris (ca. 1435–1511), which redefined music as a practical art and no longer saw it as a speculative science. This is not to say that no "science" is involved with music. Instead, it is to note that for these thinkers music is no longer tied to a cosmological ("harmony of the spheres") or mathematical basis ("sounding number") to ground its truth. Instead, the tendency of music theorists in the later Middle Ages was to honor music's ability to touch human affectivity. Similarly, it saw music primarily as an art and not a science per se.

The speculative approach to music looked back to Pythagoras, who, as we noted earlier, interpreted harmony within music as an expression of numerical ratio. He also claimed that sound was more beautiful to the degree that the numerical ratio involved was simpler. Indeed, this view was adopted by Augustine and Boethius (ca. 480–524), and their work on music was to influence the entire medieval era. Of this perspective, Albert Seay notes, "Music demonstrates in sound the pure world of number and derives its beauty from that world."[41] In this Pythagorean and Augustinian perspective, performed

---

38. *Treatise on Good Works*, in LW 44:39 (WA 6:217.11).

39. In his commentary on 1 Cor. 15, Luther wrote, "And now St. Paul appropriately concludes with a song which he sings: 'Thanks and praise be to God, who gave us such a victory!' We can join in that song and in that way always celebrate Easter, praising and extolling God for a victory that was not won or achieved in battle by us . . . but was presented and given to us by the mercy of God" (LW 28:213; WA 36:695.30–35). Commenting on Ps. 45:17, Luther noted, "This is the single outstanding worship of the New Testament—to celebrate and praise this Son of God with singing, writing, and preaching" (LW 12:300; WA 40/2:909.29–31). In his lectures on Isaiah, commenting on Isa. 12:2 ("Behold, God is my salvation"), Luther noted, "This is a description of the peace that comes after the forgiveness of sins has been received. Thus the heart stands firm, and this is proclaimed. Now I have someone on whom I may rely and in whom I may trust, to whom I may look, namely, God, who no longer is angry and punishes but saves from every danger and evil." Hence, "I have no one to sing and chant about but Christ, in whom alone I have everything. Him alone I proclaim, in Him alone I glory, for *He has become my Salvation*, that is, my victory" (LW 16:129; WA 31/2:92.22–24).

40. LBW, no. 51.

41. Seay, *Music in the Medieval World*, 20.

music was on a lower level than the study of music. This was not least of all due to the fact that the Pythagorean tradition espoused the notion of "the music of the spheres," according to which the celestial orbs, as they circle the earth, create harmonious vibrations that, though not audible to the ear, are audible to the inner senses. In this perspective, the beauty of all things is due to the fact that everything is dependent upon numbers. Hence, "the most beautiful thing is God and the world is but a reflection of God's beauty, just as man's beauty is a reflection of that of the world. All of these beauties may then be expressed as forms of numerical ratio, ratio that has been made easily sensed by the ear in music. Thus it is that music stands as a way of depicting the beauty and perfection of God and his creations, the world and man."[42] This way of thinking was not lost on Luther:

> We do not marvel at the countless other gifts of creation, for we have become deaf toward what Pythagoras aptly terms this wonderful and most lovely music coming from the harmony of the motions that are in the celestial spheres. But because men continually hear this music, they become deaf to it, just as the people who live at the cataracts of the Nile are not affected by the noise and roar of the water which they hear continually, although it is unbearable to others who are not accustomed to it.[43]

Likewise this aspect is built into Luther's view of music since he upholds a cosmic dimension to music. Music is

> instilled and implanted in all creatures, individually and collectively. For nothing is without sound or harmony. Even the air which is invisible and imperceptible to all our senses, and which, since it lacks both voice and speech, is the least musical of all things, becomes sonorous, audible, and comprehensible when it is set in motion.[44]

In other words, music is an inescapable dimension of creation. Repeatedly, for Luther, the echo of this cosmic dimension of music is vocalized through the birds and their singing, which is bound to evoke wonder in any thoughtful person.

Though important, this cosmic dimension is not Luther's primary approach to music. Instead, his view reflects more the later medieval view, which highlighted music as a practical art and not an intellectual science, and which even went so far as to deny altogether the theory of the music of the spheres. This newer view emphasized the power of music to move the heart

42. Ibid., 21.
43. *Lectures on Genesis*, in LW 1:126 (WA 42:94.32–37).
44. "Preface to Georg Rhau's *Symphoniae Iucundae*," in LW 53:322 (WA 50:369.23).

and mind—exactly the emphasis we see repeatedly in Luther's insistence that music can replace negative human dispositions with liberating joy.

The move to understand music less in speculative terms and more as an art clearly was influenced by several factors. For one, Bernard of Clairvaux highlighted experience as the way to attain knowledge of God, understood as union between the soul as the bride and Christ as the Bridegroom. For Bernard, music is language of experience.[45] Similarly, for Thomas Aquinas, everything that can help the human *affectus* to move toward God is useful to Christian worship and, most importantly, "it is evident that the human soul is moved in various ways according to the various melodies of sound."[46] When in *De laude musica* Jean Gerson praised music, he appealed to factors indicating the emotional power of music that Luther was to echo a century later. For Gerson, music refreshes the spirit, drives away cares, soothes ennui, and is a congenial companion to the pilgrims whom it upholds: "Through the midst of snows and through [blazing] suns, in reliance on song I shall go, patient in hope, happy, eager and cheerful. For miserable cares flee [the sound of] a song . . . and every hostile plague that might lie in wait is dispelled."[47]

Criteria for Beauty in Music

With this new appreciation for music as affective and not cosmological, the criterion of beauty in music also changes. The earlier Middle Ages singled out numerical ratio as music's criterion of beauty. By contrast, Luther—true to the newer perspectives of Gerson—would identify the criterion of music's beauty as the interplay between simplicity (*simplicitas*) and sweetness (*suavitas*). Commenting in a 1538 table talk on a motet by Antoine de Févin (ca. 1470–1511/12), Luther raised these two criteria for beauty. He found the four parts of polyphony in the de Févin motet to be a "marvel of sweetness and simplicity."[48]

45. See Miikka E. Anttila, *Luther's Theology of Music: Spiritual Beauty and Pleasure* (Berlin: de Gruyter, 2013), 37–38.
46. *Summa theologiae* II-II, q. 91, a. 2 (trans. Fathers of the English Dominican Province [Westminster, MD: Christian Classics, 1948], 3:1584).
47. Anttila, *Luther's Theology of Music*, 47.
48. WA TR 4:216.1–2 (no. 4316) (see Leaver, *Luther's Liturgical Music*, 56). As others have noted, here there would seem to be a parallel between Glarean's aesthetics and Luther:
The humanist Henricus Glareanus, one of the first theoreticians of the *musica reservata*, published his *Dodekachordon* in 1547, a year after Luther's death. It actually belongs, according to its contents, to the year 1510, and is thus contemporary with both Luther and Josquin. Almost exclusively did he take Josquin's compositions as a material basis for his theories, neglecting altogether the contemporary Italian music. According to Glarean,

As mentioned earlier, in widest terms, music expresses an interplay between order and freedom. The older Pythagorean and Augustinian approach highlighted order at the expense of freedom: it based beauty in music only on numerical ratios; it ignored the creative, unpredictable, surprising, and captivating element of harmonious exchange of the polyphony dancing around the *cantus firmus*. But this latter feature, in contrast, is exactly what Luther accentuated and delighted in. The simplicity or order to which Luther alludes is no longer defined by numerical ratio. Instead, it is the *cantus firmus* itself, the central theme running sometimes stronger, sometimes more subdued, throughout the entire piece of music. It is the thread that holds the polyphony together, providing coherence and enabling the other parts to flourish, and it allows counterpoint to be "developed to its limits."[49]

What grabbed Luther's attention was the exuberant "ever-varying art and tuneful sound" of the four or five other voices that sing around this *cantus firmus*. This is the freedom that music expresses and that, for Luther, is akin to the freedom that the Christian has in Christ. For Luther, such musical freedom, more than any other earthly reality, is analogous to the freedom that the gospel grants and that is to be celebrated. Thus the gospel is the *cantus firmus* of the polyphonic Christian life. Luther—like contemporary musicologists—acknowledged Josquin as the leader who brought such creativity to the forefront of music.[50] As John Caldwell notes, Josquin's "creation of the paraphrase Mass . . . freed composers from the tyranny of the *cantus firmus* and enabled them to fashion an independent structure from given material. . . . There was a new attention to the overall spirit of the words: this, and not their

---

a work of art requires two prerequisites: *ars* [skilled craft] and *ingenium* [innate talent]. *Ars* he interprets as the laws and rules of music that can be taught and learned. *Ingenium* to him means the original and creative impulse of the musician, which is purely a gift. Where *ars* and *ingenium* meet in the process of composing, there will necessarily ensue a perfect work of art. *Ars* alone is not sufficient, and *ingenium* alone is despicable, since it places itself above all musical order, and by denying the validity of the *ars* draws music into impossible subjective situations. (Music must always be a manifestation of objective situations to be found in the *ars musica*.) Therefore the *ingenium* must accept the *ars* as the criterion of its creative process, and it must respect the objective limits dictated by the rules and regulations of the *ars*. (Hoelty-Nickel, "Luther and Music," 147–48)

49. See Jeremy Begbie, "Theology and Music," in *The Modern Theologians*, ed. David Ford (Oxford: Blackwell, 2005), 726. Begbie here is describing Dietrich Bonhoeffer's approach to theology, which included appropriating the metaphor of the *cantus firmus*. See also H. Gaylon Barker, *The Cross of Reality: Luther's* Theologia Crucis *and Bonhoeffer's Christology* (Minneapolis: Fortress, 2015), 119–20.

50. For more on Josquin, see Howard Mayer Brown and Louise K. Stein, *Music in the Renaissance* (Upper Saddle River, NJ: Prentice Hall, 1999), 103–33; and Patrick Macey and Jeremy Noble, "Josquin des Prez," in *New Grove Dictionary of Music and Musicians*, ed. Stanley Sadie and John Tyrrell, 2nd ed. (Oxford: Oxford University Press, 2001), 13:220–66.

outward form, should be the composer's guide."[51] Indeed, "in his lament on the death of Ockeghem, which occurred in 1495, Josquin abandons his Latin *cantus firmus* in the second half (though it is no great constraint in the first) and calls on his contemporaries to weep for their master in simple but affecting phrase."[52] No wonder that Luther described Josquin as the master of the notes in contrast to other musicians who were instead mastered by the notes.

For Luther, the sweetness of musical polyphonic innovation is akin to evangelical liberty. That Luther fought for the freedom of a Christian was a hallmark of his career. But what did he mean by evangelical liberty? Clearly his Catholic predecessors and opponents likewise believed that they too were striving for evangelical freedom. For them, freedom meant preservation from the temptations incited by the devil, the world, and even our own bodies. This was to lead to the liberation of the righteousness of a new spiritual life. Luther in contrast saw freedom as the freedom of conscience from the law, which results in a spontaneous willingness to love God and neighbor. Good works flow naturally out of the gift of salvation. Because Christ's righteousness is reckoned as our own (*imputatio*) as an alien righteousness, we can accept ourselves as sinful but also see ourselves with new eyes through Christ's righteousness.[53] We are free lords subject to none, no longer owing fealty to the law, and also dutiful servants subject to all, willing to offer our service freely to those in need. The beauty established in music hearkens to this very freedom. Christian freedom and service are polyphonic ("perfectly free lords of all, subject to none," "perfectly dutiful servants of all, subject to all") inasmuch as they are grounded in the *cantus firmus* of the gospel, which frees for such service. It is not that we need freedom from the *cantus firmus* (as Josquin suggests) as much as it is that Christ himself, the one who frees, is this *cantus firmus*, and he opens the polyphony of Christian existence as both freedom and service. Indeed, both sides of Christian existence, freedom and service—only function if the gospel is this *cantus firmus*.

Poetic Summary of Luther's View of Music

The truth of such evangelical freedom is summarized in Luther's charming poetic introduction "A Preface for All Good Hymnals" (1538). This preface

51. Caldwell, *Medieval Music* (Bloomington: Indiana University Press, 1978), 255. The paraphrase Mass was a musical setting of the ordinary of the Mass, employing as its basis an elaborated *cantus firmus* chosen from plainsong or another sacred source.
52. Ibid., 256.
53. See Berndt Hamm, *The Early Luther: Stages in a Reformation Reorientation*, trans. Martin J. Lohrmann (Grand Rapids: Eerdmans, 2014), 154–71.

was written for Johann Walther's rhymed encomium, "Glory and Praise of the Laudable Art of Music," in which Walther developed a theology of music based on Luther's scattered remarks about music.[54] Luther put his words on the lips of Dame Music, who likely is no mere personification of music but reflects instead the very cosmic dimension that Luther accords music, as mentioned above.[55]

> Of all the joys upon this earth
> None has for men a greater worth
> Than what I give with my ringing
> And with voices sweetly singing.
> There cannot be an evil mood
> Where there are singing fellows good,
> There is no envy, hate, nor ire,
> Gone are through me all sorrows dire;
> Greed, care, and lonely heaviness
> No more do they the heart oppress.
> Each man can in his mirth be free
> Since such a joy no sin can be.
> But God in me more pleasure finds
> Than in all joys of earthly minds.
> Through my bright power the devil shirks
> His sinful, murderous, evil works.
> Of this King David's deeds do tell
> Who pacified King Saul so well
> By sweetly playing on the lyre
> And thus escaped his murderous ire.
> For truth divine and God's own rede
> The heart of humble faith shall lead;
> Such did Elisha once propound
> When harping he the Spirit found.
> The best time of the year is mine
> When all the birds are singing fine.
> Heaven and earth their voices fill
> With right good song and tuneful trill.
> And, queen of all, the nightingale
> Men's hearts will merrily regale
> With music so charmingly gay;
> For which be thanks to her for aye.
> But thanks be first to God, our Lord,

54. See LW 53:319–20 (WA 35:483–84).
55. Leaver, *Luther's Liturgical Music*, 89.

Who created her by his Word
To be his own beloved songstress
And of *musica* a mistress.
For our dear Lord she sings her song
In praise of him the whole day long;
To him I give my melody
And thanks in all eternity.

In this rhyme Luther creatively summarized his understanding of how music conveys beauty. His emphasis drew on the practical consequences of music's ability to alter moods from despair to hope and alter behavior from competitive jealousy and spitefulness to cooperative goodwill and wholesome collegiality. In a sense, the effect of music, like the gospel, is to remake sinners curved in on themselves into liberated children of God who live outside themselves in Christ and in the neighbor. Latent within the word "give" in the third line is forensic justification. When Luther explains the first article of the creed in the Small Catechism, he associates God's creative work with giving. "I believe that God has *created* me together with all that exists. God has *given* me and still preserves." And this work of creation is tied to that of redemption: "All this is done out of pure, fatherly, and divine goodness and mercy, without any merit or worthiness of mine at all!"[56] That is, our creation (out of nothing) is not based on our ability to achieve merit through good works; instead, it comes entirely as a gift. Nor is it based on our worthiness, such as worthiness to be admitted to the Lord's Table, but instead is given solely as a gift.

But such forensic justification leads to effective justification, a change or renewal of our hearts such that "each man can in his mirth be free." No longer are sinners oppressed by God's judgment or the consequences of their sin; instead, with their defenses down they have their senses opened by the word dwelling within and thus experience more of the world. New beings in Christ are no longer curved in on themselves but instead are oriented to an external word and neighbor's needs. Enjoying conviviality established through forgiveness for Christ's sake, one can be open to the needs of one's neighbor. Unlike various church fathers, Luther here has no sense of music leading to immoral, irrational excitement of passion. Instead, music is able to calm the troubled soul and liberate one's humanity—akin to the liberation evoked by the gospel.

In line 14 of Luther's rhyme, the reference to "earthly minds" reaffirms, contrary to much of the tradition, Luther's equalizing of intellect and affect, his not favoring intellect over affect, but allowing both to enjoy their specific

56. The Small Catechism, in BC 354:2 (BSELK 870:10).

traits. Likewise, noting that the devil shirks his works at music's power, the theme of exorcism seen earlier is repeated. Finally, the reference to the "nightingale" is no mere literary allusion but instead is a metonym of the Christian. For it is the Christian "created . . . by [God's] Word" who lives freely to God's glory and constantly praises God. The Christian is truly renewed by the Word, established as a new person in Christ. As Luther explains it in the *Lectures on Galatians* (1535),

> A new creation is a work of the Holy Spirit, who implants a new intellect and will and confers the power to curb the flesh and to flee the righteousness and wisdom of the world. This is not a sham or merely a new outward appearance, but something really happens. A new attitude and a new judgment, namely, a spiritual one, actually come into being, and they now detest what they once admired.[57]

Luther says that such renovation in the heart leads to a "renewal of the senses,"

> for when the heart acquires new light, a new judgment, and new motivation through the Gospel, this also brings about a renewal of the senses. The ears long to hear the Word of God instead of listening any longer to human traditions and notions. The lips and the tongue do not boast of their own works, righteousness, and monastic rule; but joyfully they proclaim nothing but the mercy of God, disclosed in Christ. These changes are, so to speak, not verbal; they are real. They produce a new mind, a new will, new senses, and even new actions by the flesh, so that the eyes, the ears, the lips, and the tongue not only see, hear, and speak otherwise than they used to, but the mind itself evaluates things and acts upon them differently.[58]

The justifying word that claims sinners as God's own for Jesus's sake renews a person's whole being; God quickens and regenerates people by creating faith. Such renewal bears upon how one lives. Of course, we must keep in mind that for Luther Christian life is ever that of saint and sinner—*simul iustus et peccator*. So it is the word that does it all in Christian life; claiming sinners, it remakes them to be people of faith. Those who are new in Christ allow the word to do as it wills in their lives, but invariably it lends itself to a greater hunger for God's word and an attendant renewal of the senses. It expresses itself in music because musical texts establish the mind on God's generosity and goodness while the notes stimulate the affects, moving one from sadness to mirth and from solitariness to community.

57. LW 27:140 (WA 42/2:178.21–25).
58. LW 27:140 (WA 42/2:178.32–179.15).

Conclusion

For Luther, music expresses beauty. Participating in music, we are vessels of beauty, which is, for him, in a sense synonymous with the gospel itself. The beauty of music happens in the interplay between order and freedom, "simplicity" and "sweetness," which as Luther understood it is at the core of music. Music is best seen when understood in relation to the doctrine of justification by grace alone through faith alone because claimed sinners, when liberated from sin and the concomitant accusations of the law, can do nothing other than express grateful joy with the voice and tongue.

But music is more than a vehicle of our gratitude to God. It likewise is a metaphor for new life in Christ. Living from the word of the gospel, Christians have clean hearts and spontaneously want to express love for God and for neighbor. Music is an expression of that renewal but, as a creation and gift of God, it also shapes that renewal. Unlike many of his predecessors and contemporaries, Luther had no suspicions about the merit or worthiness of music. In his view, music also does something positive since it creates joy, drives away the devil, and establishes an innocent delight. Nevertheless, he honored a didactic or catechetical aspect to music. Musical texts should focus on the objectivity of God's actions for human welfare and not the subjectivity of religious or mystical experience. That truth might serve as a criterion for our evaluation of the appropriateness of hymns or songs in contemporary worship life. As an innocent delight, music beckons Christians to enjoy this good creation. Luther's stance on music complements his conviction that God's word comes through earthly, physical, and bodily means. It refuses any Manichaean separation of earthly as bad and heavenly as good. Instead, it reinforces Luther's deeply christological approach to theology and life: the finite is capable of bearing the infinite; bodily and earthly things can be channels of grace when appropriated by the word.

≫ 7 ≪

Luther on Visual Imaging

Luther's valuation of the visual arts seems to be more tangential and less explicit than his appreciation of music. But if we examine what Luther has to say about the wider category of imaging, either as word or craftsmanship, then we can get a sense for how he configures the relation between theology and the visual arts. For Luther, imaging not only is at the core of what the human heart does, whether concocting idols or honoring God, but it is also how the proclaimed word portrays or pictures Christ primarily as a gift (and secondarily as an example) to believers who thereby receive God's favor. Hence, imaging not only is a central category for theological anthropology but also is the means by which the gospel is conveyed, precisely as it pictures Jesus Christ as benefit for sinners. Unlike his brief comments on music from which we can discern specific criteria for evaluating the beauty of music, Luther offered no such specificity for judging beauty in the visual arts, other than their ability to convey the liberating Christ in contrast to the self-righteousness generated either by icon veneration or icon smashing. This lack of specificity may simply be due to the fact that Luther "accepted and approved" art while "music he lived and breathed."[1] Even so, unlike the aniconism of both the Anabaptists and the Reformed, Luther asserted his approval of artistic expression in church life. Criticizing iconoclasts, he wrote, "Nor am I of the opinion that the gospel should destroy and blight all the arts [*alle Kuenste*], as some of the pseudo-religious claim. But I would like

1. See John Tonkin, "Word and Image: Luther and the Arts," *Colloq* 17 (1985): 52.

to see all the arts, especially music, used in the service of Him who gave and made them."[2] Here "arts" refers not just to the liberal arts, of which music was one, but also to artistic expression in general, because the context is dealing not with the core curriculum of a sound education but with public worship. Together with the Reformed and other Christians, Lutherans applaud art in daily life. But counter to the iconoclasm of either the Reformed (Zwingli) or the enthusiasts (Karlstadt), Luther affirmed a role for the visual arts in public worship.

Luther's view of the visual arts has been described as "utilitarian," at best educative, portraying scriptural personalities or events for spiritual edification, but not valuing art for its own sake.[3] But this interpretation is too simplistic. Obviously, the modern concept of valuing art for its own sake finds no advocate in Luther. But the Reformer thought that the visual arts have an important role to play in presenting the gospel, which as an image-saturated word regenerates and transforms human imaginations and so alters sinners' hearts and minds. Such images reorient and govern Christian imaginations, enlighten thought and will, secure one's identity in Christ, and thus assist one in honoring God above all things and serving neighbors as a Christ to them. For Luther, if any criterion surfaces explicitly for discerning beauty in the visual arts, it is none other than the word itself, which evaluates all human activity. Luther's failure to itemize more specific criteria for judging beauty in the visual arts, such as those employed in the *Lectures on Genesis*, where Adam's traits conform to or even surpass Augustinian *proportio*, Dionysian color or light, and Thomistic integrity or perfection, in no way diminishes the value of the visual arts for Christian worship. Luther's friendship with the painter Lucas Cranach the Elder, godparent to his children,[4] and his opposition to the iconoclasts who sought to purify Wittenberg of its images indicate his overall appreciation for the visual arts. Naturally woodcuts produced in Cranach's workshop benefited Luther's movement in that they helped propagate evangelical faith. But additionally, Luther's commitment to a "gospel beauty" as described earlier translates into an approval of visual arts in worship.

His perspective, which singles out imaging as inescapable for all human understanding, along with his conviction that God's revelation comes only

2. "Preface to the Wittenberg Hymnal" (1524), in LW 53:316 (WA 35:475.4–5).
3. Carl Christensen, "Luther's Theology and the Use of Religious Art," *LQ* 22 (1970): 147.
4. See Steven Ozment, *The Serpent and the Lamb: Cranach, Luther, and the Making of the Reformation* (New Haven: Yale University Press, 2011). Ozment highlights how Cranach was a mentor for Luther, helping Luther navigate the complex politics of sixteenth-century Europe in a savvy way. Likewise, Cranach's workshop assisted the Reformation by helping to "market" Luther. See also Christoph Weimer, "Luther and Cranach on Justification in Word and Image," *LQ* 18 (2004): 387–405.

as mediated through physical things, reinforces a theological backdrop that nurtures rather than inhibits the visual arts and finds a place for them in public worship and private devotion. Hence, the September Testament (1522), Luther's translation of the New Testament as a fruit of his sojourn in the Wartburg for his own protection, and his translation of the entire Bible (1534), were illustrated with woodcuts in full color and were crafted in Cranach's workshop.[5] Likewise, the Small Catechism was also often illustrated, along with hymnody, as Robin Leaver has indicated,[6] and Luther preached on St. Christopher, using images, and took his staff to be the Word of which we learn.[7] While both the Anabaptists and Reformed accorded no place for the visual arts in worship, Luther insisted on their propriety once they have been set free of any aura of works-righteousness or of having divine magical powers. Hence, it is an overstatement to assert that Luther "never went beyond the Gregorian notion of art as educative, which ultimately leaves art with an auxiliary rather than a central role."[8] For Luther, God is always "covered" and the word is always embodied.[9] Thus physical things, including human artistic creations, are fit vehicles for God's address to sinners. While God may work upon humans through human artistry, God chooses only ever to work upon humans through physical means, whether in nature, historical events, sacramental means, or human artifacts.

Luther developed his theology of imaging in debate with two opponents: (1) iconophiles who treasured relics, images, and icons as essential features in normative spirituality and that had had a long precedent in the church,[10] and

5. For a complete full-color facsimile edition of the 1534 Luther Bible, see *Biblia, das ist die ganze heilige Schrifft Deudsch*, trans. Martin Luther (Wittenberg, 1534; repr., Cologne: Taschen, 2002).

6. See Robin Leaver, "Luther's Catechism Hymns," *LQ* 11 (1997): 397–410; 12 (1998): 78–99, 161–80, 303–23.

7. See Johann Anselm Steiger, "Luther on the Legend of St. Christopher," *LQ* 25 (2011): 125–44.

8. Tonkin, "Word and Image," 48.

9. See Oswald Bayer, *Theology the Lutheran Way*, trans. Jeffrey Silcock and Mark Mattes (Grand Rapids: Eerdmans, 2007), 101, 139.

10. Most recently, Caroline Walker Bynum in *Christian Materiality: An Essay on Religion in Late Medieval Europe* (New York: Zone Books, 2011) has highlighted the power that icon veneration held for late medieval Europeans—icons were virtually alive for many of the devout. In a wider scope, Bynum claims that such icon veneration was a way that European Christians affirmed the significance and value of matter. She writes, "When [icons] insistently display—and even comment on—their own materiality, they show that they are matter. In other words, they show that they are not God. But matter is God's creation—that through and in which he acts. Matter is powerful. In their insistent materiality, images thus do more than comment on, refer to, provide signs of, or gesture toward the divine. They lift matter toward God and reveal God through matter" (ibid., 35).

(2) aniconocists, including iconoclasts, whether humanists, such as Erasmus, or other Reformers, such as Andreas Bodenstein von Karlstadt or Ulrich Zwingli, who saw such practices as idolatrous and superstitious. With respect to the first, Luther claimed that such practices led to a false trust in works, since, in this view, believers received merit in exchange for their veneration of the saint or holy one represented by the icon. The second group, those opposed to icons, assumed that they were in league with Luther's own agenda of reform, which appealed to the word alone and simplified the Mass. In contrast to Luther, however, aniconocists saw icons or relics as violating the biblical prohibition against graven images because they saw them as inseparable from their traditional, superstitious use. Ultimately this led to a different numbering of the Ten Commandments among the Reformed, who itemized the prohibition against graven images as the second commandment while Luther, following Augustine, enfolded it within the first commandment.[11] Hence, the iconoclasts, both those who literally went to the streets to break the images and others who only opposed their use, desired spirituality to be purified of any physical aids offered by icons or even stained glass. For the iconoclasts, God is Spirit and relates to human spirituality only apart from any reference to the body. At a deeper level, iconoclasts denied the ability of finite things to convey infinite truth (*finitum non capax infiniti*), and this eventually became expressed pointedly in the debate with Luther over the real presence of Christ in the Lord's Supper.[12]

Countering icon veneration, Luther's stance was not that of Erasmus, who saw the veneration of images as outright superstition. Instead, Luther's objection centered on misplaced trust in an icon instead of in Christ alone.[13]

11. Question 98 of the Heidelberg Catechism asks, "But may not images be permitted in churches in place of books for the unlearned?," and answers, "No, we should not try to be wiser than God. God wants the Christian community instructed by the living preaching of his Word—not by idols that cannot even talk" (http://www.crcna.org/welcome/beliefs/confessions /heidelberg-catechism).

12. While wholly rejecting any veneration of icons as if they could supplement the efficacy of Christ, Luther's and the Lutheran tradition's affirmation of the *finitum capax infiniti* echoes the late medieval iconic tradition that material things can disclose "the sacred through material substance" (Bynum, *Christian Materiality*, 41). Indeed, Bynum notes,

> from the perspective of the absolute disproportionality between God and man, the Lutheran tradition has also fiercely defended the incapacity of the finite regarding the infinite. Following Luther in his view that the lost human nature completely *non est capax divinitatis*, the later Lutheran tradition could simply state: *finitum non est capax infiniti*. Lutherans, however, also agree with Luther in assuming that nature is full of God's presence. All things can serve as a mask behind which God is hiding himself. From this perspective, then, the *finitum capax infiniti* is valid as well. (415–16)

13. "Superstition meant for Erasmus a misplaced faith in the external forms of religion. He was especially upset by practices in which the sacred was treated as magical, as if divine

But with respect to iconoclasts, Luther believed that evangelical liberty was at stake. When images lose saving import, they can be permitted, even welcomed, in worship and spirituality, since they teach, illustrate, and adorn the word. After all, when the word portrays Christ, it imparts Christ to believers through images, thereby regenerating believers and leading them to do the good works appropriate to their vocations. In the tradition following Luther, that such imaging can take a specific and tangible form that enhances worship can be seen in numerous artifacts, one example being Lucas Cranach's 1547 altarpiece in the city church in Wittenberg, which teaches and proclaims the gospel in its four panels.[14] The tangibility of grace is a requisite feature of Luther's sacramental theology: "But the highest form of worship He [God] requires is your conviction that He is truthful. . . . Nor does He confirm this with spiritual proofs; He confirms it with tangible proofs. For I see the water, I see the bread and the wine, and I see the minister. All this is physical [*corporalia*], and in these material forms [*figures carnalibus*] He reveals Himself."[15]

Hence, Luther's debate with the iconoclasts raises a deeper issue about the nature of the gospel. For the Reformer, there is no imageless word: the word actually portrays, pictures, or images Christ as the only way in which it can give Christ. The Reformer acknowledged no distinction set in stone between the word as imaging and artistic creations as imaging. But that raises a much wider question about how God relates to humanity and is part of the larger understanding of the concreteness, and boundedness to time and to stuff, that forms Luther's definition of being human. For Luther, God relates to humans only and always through physical means. As he noted in his *Lectures on Genesis*, "In the same way it was necessary that man, as a physical being, also have a physical or external form of worship by means of which he might be trained according to his body in obedience to God."[16]

The view that God as Spirit relates to humans only through spirit (like knows like), unencumbered by matter, is as problematic for the Reformer as the self-righteousness that he saw advocated in the school of Gabriel Biel. Such "enthusiasm" can offer no assurance of salvation, since for it the word is tethered neither to the oral word of absolution nor to the physical signs of water in baptism or bread and wine in the Lord's Supper, where God specifically

---

favors could be obtained by following prescribed formulae" (Carlos M. N. Eire, *War against the Idols: The Reformation of Worship from Erasmus to Calvin* [Cambridge: Cambridge University Press, 1986], 37).

14. Tonkin, "Word and Image," 51.

15. *Lectures on Genesis*, in LW 5:49 (WA 43:462.15–21).

16. *Lectures on Genesis*, in LW 1:94 (WA 42:72.10–12).

has promised to give grace. Thus the imaginations of anxious consciences are set adrift to seek consolation within their own spiritual ecstasies or practices bereft of God's tangible promise. Not only can that lead to further despair, but it can also feed further self-righteousness.

As Luther developed his own theology, he became more and more convinced that God comes to humans only as "covered" through physical means because (1) humans are sinful and have no direct access to the holy God, (2) they are intrinsically physical creatures and not "ghosts in machines," as Gilbert Ryle put it in his description of Descartes's theory of the relation between mind and body,[17] and (3) they have runaway imaginations and thus need their consciences to be tethered to grace, which, as promised, comes to us in a graspable, tangible way. Counter to the "Enthusiasts," he opposed a vision of spirituality that excludes the material because God's favor as *pro nobis* (for us) is always accompanied by physical signs. There is a gnosticism embedded in the aniconism or iconoclasm of Erasmus, Karlstadt, and Gabriel Zwilling (1487–1558), along with their idealistic, even utopian, programs of social and moral reform, which Luther found dangerous to the conscience.[18] As self-giving, God attaches himself to earthly things—particularly the sacraments. But, as we shall see, when Luther saw God as "covered," God is covered not only in all created things but also in human artifacts of craftsmanship and beauty.

The Role of Images in the Early Church

The Jewish faith from which Christianity came was aniconic in the sense that it tolerated no representation of God. This stance is a consequence not only of the biblical prohibition against images (Exod. 20:3–5) but also of the prophetic opposition to idolatry, in tandem with an acknowledgment of divine apophaticism in which God transcends any human characterization.[19] Even

17. Ryle, *The Concept of Mind*, new ed. (Chicago: University of Chicago Press, 2002), 22–32.

18. Of Erasmus, Richard Klann notes, "Part of the cultural program of Erasmus was the humanizing of religion—that is, fitting the Christian faith into a general program for the improvement of mankind—not essentially different from the aims of some eighteenth century leaders of the Enlightenment. The chosen means were a process of moral training and the assimilation of the literary and philosophical treasures bequeathed by antiquity" ("Human Claims to Freedom and God's Judgment," *CTQ* 54 [1990]: 247). And this modern philosophical gnosticism is carried on in the philosophy of Kant. See Mark Mattes and Roy A. Harrisville, "Translators' Epilogue," in *A Contemporary in Dissent: Johann Georg Hamann as a Radical Enlightener*, by Oswald Bayer, trans. Roy A. Harrisville and Mark Mattes (Grand Rapids: Eerdmans, 2012), 209–23. See also chaps. 7 and 9 of Bayer, *Contemporary in Dissent*.

19. There is no question that Luther was influenced by apophatic theology. Even so, the preacher in him acknowledged that it was necessary to anthropomorphize when speaking of

so, the fact that ancient Israel had an artistically adorned temple and priests clothed in attractively designed vestments bore witness to a God who ever desires to make his covenant promise concrete and embedded tangibly and pleasingly in worship. In Christian perspective, such worship is a type of the promise made incarnate in Jesus Christ. In antiquity, both Jews and Christians adorned their places of worship with themes drawn from the Bible. But because early Christians were a persecuted minority in the Roman Empire, the visual arts did not flourish among them. Since early Christians were subject to discrimination, their art was crafted and exhibited out of the limelight. "It was only in the fifth century that Christian art emerged from the shadowy world of ciphers and cemeteries to become established as a regular part of Christian life."[20]

Christian defenders of the visual arts noted that the Scriptures themselves gave examples of artistic representations appropriate for worship. Hence, Moses's bronze serpent (Num. 21:9), the cherubim over the ark of the covenant (Exod. 25:18–20), and the various decorative furnishings in Solomon's Temple (1 Kings 6–7) were used to justify Christian iconography. In his dispute with iconoclasts, Luther too would use this line of reasoning.[21] In antiquity, Christian visual arts included images of saints, statues or bas-reliefs of Christ as the Good Shepherd, decorated sarcophagi (with palms, peacocks, vines, or the chi-rho monogram), and statues of leaders such as Hippolytus of Rome or the apostle Peter.[22] But early Christians, such as

---

God. Of anthropomorphism he wrote in the *Lectures on Genesis*: "Indeed, how could men speak otherwise of God among men? If it is heresy to think of God in this manner, then a verdict has been rendered concerning the salvation of all children, who think and speak of God in this childlike fashion" (LW 1:14; WA 42:12.10–12).

20. John A. McGuckin, "Art," in *The SCM Press A–Z of Patristic Theology* (London: SCM, 2005), 32–33.

21. See "Eight Sermons at Wittenberg" (1522), in LW 51:82 (WA 10/3:27.30–28.6):

But let us go further. They say: Did not Noah, Abraham, Jacob build altars? [Gen. 8:20; 12:7; 13:4, 18; 33:20]. And who will deny that? We must admit it. Again, did not Moses erect a bronze serpent, as we read in his fourth book (Num. 22 [21:9])? How then can you say that Moses forbade the making of images when he himself made one? It seems to me that such a serpent is an image, too. How shall we answer that? Again, do we not read also that two birds were erected on the mercy seat [Exod. 37:7–9], the very place where God willed that he should be worshipped? Here we must admit that we may have images and make images, but we must not worship them, and if they are worshipped, they should be put away and destroyed, just as King Hezekiah broke in pieces the bronze serpent erected by Moses [2 Kings 18:4].

22. "The first Christians were accustomed to see statues of emperors, of pagan gods and heroes, as well as pagan wall-paintings. So they made paintings of their religion, and, as soon as they could afford them, statues of their Lord and of their heroes, without the remotest fear or suspicion of idolatry" (Adrian Fortescue, "Veneration of Images," in *The Catholic Encyclopedia* [New York: Appleton, 1910], http://www.newadvent.org/cathen/07664a.htm).

Clement of Alexandria, wanted to make sure that Christian contributions to art would seek a higher ethical standard than that of their pagan neighbors: art should not be pornographic.[23] Some variance among Christians must be noted: while icons developed in both East and West, the use of statues developed in the Latin-speaking West but was never accepted in the Greek-speaking East, and this continues to be a characteristic differentiating Roman Catholicism and Eastern Orthodoxy.

A standard justification for images that came to prevail among Christians, and which Luther approved, is that of images as offering a "Bible for the laity," the illiterate and poor (*biblia pauperum*), which would help them strengthen their memories and stimulate their devotion. Gregory the Great expressed it thusly to Serenus of Marseilles, an iconoclast bishop:

> Not without reason has antiquity allowed the stories of saints to be painted in holy places. And we indeed entirely praise thee for not allowing them to be adored, but we blame thee for breaking them. For it is one thing to adore an image, it is quite another thing to learn from the appearance of a picture what we must adore. What books are to those who can read, that is a picture to the ignorant who look at it; in a picture even the unlearned may see what example they should follow; in a picture they who know no letters may yet read. Hence, for barbarians especially a picture takes the place of a book.[24]

From the tradition of remembering saints and martyrs the practice of venerating images gradually developed. Icons were seen not merely as representations of a saint or Christ but as access to that saint or holy one. In this view, the icon so participates in the reality it represents that it is a window through which the sacred reaches out to the believer. In both East and West, icons were deemed to be "mediating signs by which we reach out to worship

---

23. Clement of Alexandria attacked the licentiousness in Roman art:
> And of what kind . . . are your other images? Diminutive Pans, and naked girls, and drunken Satyrs, and phallic tokens, painted naked in pictures disgraceful for filthiness. And more than this: you are not ashamed in the eyes of all to look at representations of all forms of licentiousness which are portrayed in public places, but set them up and guard them with scrupulous care. (*Exhortation to the Heathen* 4 [ANF 2:189])

Even so, that did not rule out any sense of the possibility of decoration or illustration for Clement:
> And let our seals be either a dove, or a fish, or a ship scudding before the wind, or a musical lyre, which Polycrates used, or a ship's anchor, which Seleucus got engraved as a device; and if there be one fishing, he will remember the apostle, and the children drawn out of the water. For we are not to delineate the faces of idols, we who are prohibited to cleave to them; nor a sword, nor a bow, following as we do, peace; nor drinking cups, being temperate. (*The Instructor* 3.11 [ANF 2:285–86])

24. Epistle 9.105 (PL 77:1027); quoted in Fortescue, "Veneration of Images."

God and venerate his saints."[25] Specifically, icons "are channels of prayer and adoration; they mediate between the earth-bound worshiper and the transcendent realities of heaven which 'stand behind' the icon. When the believer looks at an icon, it is, as it were, a look through a window into the world of the mysteries of salvation."[26] For Luther, such associations with icons would lead us to something other than Christ as saving and so is to be rejected. But where Luther remains on a similar page with this iconophilism is his conviction that all reality, including humanly crafted artworks, masks and conveys God's address to sinners, in spite of the fact that icons do not mediate grace or provide a pathway to manipulate the holy.

With its rise in the seventh century, Islam took a stricter aniconic stance than what had developed among either Eastern or Western Christians. Responding to the Islamic critique of icons, a number of Eastern Christian leaders agreed with Muslims that icons violate the biblical prohibition against making graven images. But more was at stake than the mere biblical prohibition. Iconoclasts often assumed that "matter, found in a fallen state and alienated from God, cannot possibly become a means expressive of truth, and especially of saving and divine truth."[27] That is a sentiment wholly foreign not only to the iconophiles but also to Luther. The defenders of icons noted that Christ himself is the "exact icon" of God (Col. 1:15). In their mind, God permits icon making in spite of the prohibition against graven images because icons extend Christ's incarnation. Since God became human with a physical body in Jesus's earthly ministry, which, in principle, could have been visually portrayed at the time, then the practice of making icons is justified. That veneration of icons follows suit is guaranteed by the fact that Jesus's own resurrected body was adored. For the better part of a century, vigorous debate ensued among Eastern Christians, ultimately resulting in the triumph of the pro-icon party at the Seventh Ecumenical Council, Nicaea II (787). The council followed the thinking of theologians such as John of Damascus (ca. 676–749), who defended icon veneration by making a distinction between veneration and worship.[28] Hence, John McGuckin notes, "worship was due to God alone, but veneration could be made through the medium of holy icons."[29]

25. Lawrence S. Cunningham, *The Catholic Heritage* (New York: Crossroad, 1983), 132.
26. Ibid., 133.
27. Ambrosios Giakalis, *Images of the Divine: The Theology of Icons at the Seventh Ecumenical Council* (Leiden: Brill, 2005), 65.
28. See John of Damascus, *Apologia against Those Who Decry Holy Images*, in *St. John Damascene: On Holy Images*, trans. Mary H. Allies (London: Thomas Baker, 1898), http://legacy.fordham.edu/Halsall/basis/johndamascus-images.asp.
29. McGuckin, "Art," 33.

Critique of Medieval Veneration of Icons

Contemporary Protestants can hardly imagine the hold that veneration of statues and icons had over late medieval Christians, and the opposition that such practices invoked in humanists and various Protestants. Carlos M. N. Eire notes:

> The image and the prototype often became indistinguishable in the mind of the supplicant. Ulrich Zwingli later listed the acts commonly performed before images: People would kneel and bow, remove their hats, burn incense and candles, kiss them, decorate them with gold and jewels, call them merciful and gracious, touch them as if they could really heal or forgive sins. Erasmus complained of people who "bowed the head before them, fell on the ground, crawled on their knees, kissed and fondled the carvings."[30]

For Erasmus, such practices were simply superstition through and through. "Superstition meant for Erasmus a misplaced faith in the external forms of religion. He was especially upset by practices in which the sacred was treated as magical, as if divine favors could be obtained by following prescribed formulae."[31]

The early Luther found the veneration of images and relics to be unsettling to his conscience, and this became a factor in his challenging these practices. But for the Reformer, the core issue was not primarily the existence of images per se, but the question of idolatry, the attribution of divine power to something, which raises the question: Upon what does the heart ultimately repose?[32] The Reformer's charge against such veneration is less a matter of superstition like Erasmus and more an internal matter about what the heart relies on: Christ alone or something else? More specifically, that something else would be the merit accrued for achieving the good work of veneration. But we are not to trust in good works—specifically veneration of an image. Speaking against contemporary iconoclasts, he highlights this point:

> For whoever places an image in a church imagines he has performed a service to God and done a good work, which is downright idolatry. But this, the greatest, foremost, and highest reason for abolishing images, you have passed by, and fastened on the least important reason of all. For I suppose there is nobody, or certainly very few, who do not understand that yonder crucifix is not my

---

30. Eire, *War against the Idols*, 21.
31. Ibid., 37.
32. For the early Luther's concern about idolatry, see his *Lectures on Romans* (1515–16), in LW 25:158–59, 164 (WA 56:178–79, 183).

God, for my God is in heaven, but that this is simply a sign. But the world is full of that other abuse; for who would place a silver or wooden image in a church unless he thought that by so doing he was rendering God a service? Do you think that Duke Frederick, the bishop of Halle, and the others would have dragged so many silver images into the churches, if they thought it counted for nothing before God? No, they would not bother to do it. But this is not sufficient reason to abolish, destroy, and burn all images. Why? Because we must admit that there are still some people who hold no such wrong opinion of them, but to whom they may well be useful, although they are few. Nevertheless, we cannot and ought not to condemn a thing which may be in any way useful to a person.[33]

For Luther, Christ was not only necessary but also sufficient in all spiritual matters. The veneration of images, along with the veneration of the saints, takes believers away from Christ, makes them believe they could achieve merit, and so thus undermines God's goodness and grace. But, as Luther argued, nothing in the image as such necessitates idolatry, and images may be useful for some Christians. The standard for the appropriateness of images in worship is whether they honor Christ. As Gene Veith notes, "Luther rejected only the art that interfered with the message of Christ. Images of Mary and the legendary saints were removed, with all of the attendant devotions and 'works' associated with them. Crucifixes, depicting the all-sufficient atonement for sin, and other Biblical paintings and church decorations were retained."[34]

Critique of Iconoclasm

While Luther was sequestered in the Wartburg for his own protection following his inquisition at the Diet of Worms (1521), his erstwhile friend and colleague Karlstadt and others such as Gabriel Zwilling sought to implement their versions of reform in Wittenberg. Among other things, that involved destroying images in the churches and breaking stained glass windows. This iconoclasm disturbed Luther both pastorally and politically. Pastorally Luther saw this move as insensitive to illiterate believers who could not follow the theological debates over the merit or demerit of icons, and as holding the possibility of undermining their faith. Politically he saw it as disturbing the peace, leading to rebellion and social upheaval. He left the security of the Wartburg and returned to Wittenberg to stop this approach to reformation. As Carlos Eire

---

33. "Eight Sermons at Wittenberg," in LW 51:84 (WA 10/3:31.3–32.7).
34. Veith, *State of the Arts: From Bezalel to Mapplethorpe* (Wheaton: Crossway, 1991), 62.

puts it, while Luther's presumed coworkers sought to cast out Roman idols, Luther himself moved to cast the iconoclasts out of Wittenberg.[35] Better said, Luther tried to dissuade the iconoclasts and restore evangelical unity. Zwilling eventually became a loyal Lutheran pastor in Altenburg. At stake for Luther was the question of evangelical liberty. Since images have no intrinsic power to save or damn the human soul, they should be permitted—provided they are not worshiped. Luther's approach was very different from that of Karlstadt or the Swiss Reformers a little later. They "forbad anything not authorised in Scripture, while Luther authorised everything not forbidden in Scripture. There was a world of difference between these two perspectives. The one leads towards Puritanism, the other towards a reformed Catholicism."[36] Hence, in light of Romans 14:23, Luther permitted everything that did not stem from unfaith.

Theologians cut their teeth on those positions with which they profoundly disagree. In Luther's case, his opponents forced him to specify his view of *matter*—the physical stuff out of which visual arts are made. Deeply Platonic, Karlstadt's position sought a pure spirituality devoid of material associations; hence, images were idols pure and simple. He believed that the very presence of images guaranteed that worship would be impure. His appeal to the Spirit as the locus and guide in worship, apart from the trappings of images or any traditional features of the Mass, reminds us of the stance that George Fox (1624–91), the founder of Quakerism, would later take. It finds an echo in René Descartes (1596–1650), whose approach to reason likewise is divested of materiality and history.[37] Unlike this modern gnosticism, Luther could conceive of no spirituality apart from material associations. Human beings are not designed to be pure spirits. As noted above, if God is to relate to humanity at all, it will be through physical means.

For Luther, the whole matter raises an important principle about how God works with sinners:

35. Eire, *War against the Idols*, 2.
36. Tonkin, "Word and Image," 47.
37. Hence, Descartes in his "Third Meditation" in *Meditations on First Philosophy* wrote, I will now shut my eyes, stop my ears, and withdraw all my senses. I will eliminate from my thoughts all images of bodily things, or rather, since this is hardly possible, I will regard all such images as vacuous, false and worthless. I will converse with myself and scrutinize myself more deeply; and in this way I will attempt to achieve, little by little, a more intimate knowledge of myself. I am a thing that thinks: that is, a thing that doubts, affirms, denies, understands a few things, is ignorant of many things, is willing, is unwilling, and also which imagines and has sensory perceptions. (*Classics of Philosophy*, vol. 2, *Modern and Contemporary*, ed. Louis P. Pojman [New York: Oxford University Press, 1998], 471)

Now when God sends forth his holy gospel he deals with us in a twofold manner, first outwardly, then inwardly. Outwardly he deals with us through the oral word of the gospel and through material signs, that is, baptism and the sacrament of the altar. Inwardly he deals with us through the Holy Spirit, faith, and other gifts. But whatever their measure or order the outward factors should and must precede. The inward experience follows and is effected by the outward. God has determined to give the inward to no one except through the outward. For he wants to give no one the Spirit or faith outside of the outward word and sign instituted by him, as he says in Luke 16[:29], "Let them hear Moses and the Prophets."[38]

Obviously, this stance, which places the external prior to the internal, has broad implications for worship and spiritual life. In a word, it is decidedly anti-gnostic and pro-matter. God's revelation comes ever covered and God's grace comes ever mediated—through physical means. For Luther, Karlstadt reversed or inverted the whole order of how God deals with sinners:

With all his mouthing of the words, "Spirit, Spirit, Spirit," he tears down the bridge, the path, the way, the ladder, and all the means by which the Spirit might come to you. Instead of the outward order of God in the material sign of baptism and the oral proclamation of the Word of God he wants to teach you, not how the Spirit comes to you but how you come to the Spirit. They would have you learn how to journey on the clouds and ride on the wind. They do not tell you how or when, whither or what, but you are to experience what they do.[39]

At stake for Luther is the question of where God has promised to be—most specifically in the worship service.[40] God tethers himself to tangible things. Otherwise, the human imagination runs wild and can have no certainty in its relation to God. The results can be disastrous for consciences. Implicit in Luther's reasoning here is that material, finite things can be fit vessels for God's mercy. Likewise implicit here is an affirmation of matter—so crucial for a robust theology of the visual arts.

Luther's response to Karlstadt's antimatter spirituality bears upon his debate with Zwingli, who shared Karlstadt's iconoclasm, over Christ's bodily presence in the Lord's Supper. The debate is well known and requires no extensive elaboration. But it is important to recognize that Karlstadt's rejection

38. *Against the Heavenly Prophets* (1524–25), in LW 40:146 (WA 18:136.9–19).
39. *Against the Heavenly Prophets*, in LW 40:147 (WA 18:137.12–19).
40. Bayer writes, "Divine service (*Gottesdienst*) is first and last God's service to us, the sacrifice he made for us in Christ, which he distributes to us in the particular divine service: 'Take and eat! I am here for you!' (compare 1 Cor. 11:24 with Gen. 2:16)" (*Theology the Lutheran Way*, 90).

of images as physical things as deleterious to genuine spirituality parallels Zwingli's rejection of the real presence of Christ's glorified body in the Supper. Both perspectives seek a spirituality liberated from physicality. In Zwingli's perspective, "body and spirit are such essentially different things that whichever one you take it cannot be the other."[41] In this dichotomization, spirit is to be preferred to body. That view devalues the need for a physical sign to accompany the spiritual reality in the sacrament. To summarize, for Zwingli, Christ cannot be bodily present in the Lord's Supper because the dichotomy that exists between the flesh and the spirit as radically different entities entails that Christ's bodily presence in the Supper is neither necessary nor beneficial. What counts is a spiritual communion with Christ, so the Lord's Supper is primarily a memorial.

In response to the Reformed, Luther used the same reasoning as he did with Karlstadt: "The Holy Spirit cannot be present with believers . . . except in material and physical things such as the Word, water, and Christ's body and in his saints on earth."[42] This is because God promises to be in the earthly elements. Indeed, human salvation is completely and absolutely dependent on matter—as the flesh of Christ:

> If the flesh of Christ is not spirit, and therefore is of no avail since only the Spirit is profitable, how can it be profitable when it was given for us? How can it be useful if it is in heaven and we believe in it? If the reasoning is correct and adequate, that because Christ's flesh is not spirit it must be of no avail, then it can be of no avail on the cross or in heaven either! For it is quite as far from being spirit on the cross and in heaven as in the Supper. But since no spirit was crucified for us, therefore Christ's flesh was crucified for us to no avail. And since no spirit, but Christ's flesh ascended into heaven, we believe in an unprofitable flesh in heaven. For wherever Christ's flesh may be, it is no spirit. If it is no spirit, it is of no avail and does not give life, as Zwingli here concludes.[43]

The point to be taken here is that Luther's contention that God's word is embodied is central to his entire approach to the gospel and not merely a subsidiary claim focused on images.[44] For the Reformer, humans are physical

---

41. Ulrich Zwingli, *Commentary on True and False Religion*, ed. Samuel Macauley Jackson and Clarence Nevin Helle (Durham, NC: Labyrinth, 1981), 214.

42. *That These Words of Christ, "This Is My Body," etc., Still Stand Firm against the Fanatics*, in LW 37:95 (WA 23:194).

43. *Confession concerning Christ's Supper* (1528), in LW 37:246–47 (WA 26:369.26–370.5).

44. For a helpful discussion of Luther's view of the sacrament that bears upon the role of images in Lutheranism, see Kurt K. Hendel, "*Finitum capax infiniti*: Luther's Radical Incarnational Perspective," *CurTM* 35 (2008): 420–33. Hermann Sasse writes:

creatures who require a tangible sign of God's grace, such as we receive with the bread and the wine accompanying Christ's body and blood, if the word is to be secured as the haven in which anxious consciences can rest.

Now, it is important to note that, in spite of the fact that the Reformed were iconoclasts like Karlstadt, such iconoclasm in worship did not translate into a rejection of art in everyday life. Veith notes:

> The Reformed churches of Calvin and Zwingli objected to the religious use of art, but not to art as such. "I am not gripped by the superstition of thinking absolutely no images permissible," writes Calvin, "but because sculpture and paintings are gifts of God, I seek a pure and legitimate use of each." Zwingli, an extreme iconoclast, even permitted paintings of Christ as long as they were not in churches or offered reverence. According to Zwingli, "Where anyone has a portrait of His humanity, that is just as fitting to have as to have other portraits."[45]

For Luther, iconoclasts seek a spirituality out of step with human nature as God has made it. Humans are inescapably and substantively physical beings. God does not ask humans to step outside their skin and to become something other than what they are if they are to fellowship with him. Instead, God comes deeply and wholly within human flesh just so that he might redeem this good creation from the deleterious effects of sin and renew the creation. In light of God's becoming flesh, as well as creation's status as good, matter can be a fit medium for divine self-disclosure. Such a perspective can make no distinction between visual art outside of church or inside. Provided that Christ is honored in it, the visual arts are welcome in public worship and private devotion.

Word as Portrayal

Luther's case for retaining images, provided they are neither worshiped nor yoked to a system of merit, is strongest when he makes his point that the word itself is conveyed through images. That is, the word portrays its truth through

---

If the old question is asked how the finite human nature can comprise the infinite divine nature, the answer can only be that, according to John 1:14, the Word became flesh, which cannot mean that part of the Word did not become flesh. The use of the terms "finite" and "infinite" shows that the Incarnation is being understood in terms of quantity. This must not be done; the miracle of the Incarnation is beyond all mathematics and beyond all philosophy. (*This Is My Body: Luther's Contention for the Real Presence in the Sacrament of the Altar*, rev. Australian ed. [Adelaide: Lutheran Publishing House, 1977], 120)

45. Veith, *State of the Arts*, 59.

pictures. Luther thereby undermines a strict dichotomy between word and image. Instead, he sees a continuum between the two. If the word is saturated with linguistically formed images, even as images can be understood and described only through words, then the visual arts that represent such images cannot and indeed should not be ruled out. Indeed, for Luther, even reason can only do its work of thinking in and through images. Likewise, there can be no genuine spirituality that is image-free. Of course, Luther does not see icons as offering humans an entrance or gaze into a higher world beyond this one. Instead, the true gaze is nothing other than that of God as he interprets humans through the word, whose images both present Christ and disclose humans' own true identities.

> Now there are a great many pictures in those books, both of God, the angels, men and animals, especially in the revelation of John and in Moses and Joshua. So now we would kindly beg them to permit us to do what they themselves do. Pictures contained in these books we would paint on walls for the sake of remembrance and better understanding, since they do no more harm on walls than in books. It is to be sure better to paint pictures on walls of how God created the world, how Noah built the ark, and whatever other good stories there may be, than to paint shameless worldly things. Yes, would to God that I could persuade the rich and the mighty that they would permit the whole Bible to be painted on houses, on the inside and outside, so that all can see it. That would be a Christian work.[46]

For Luther, imaging is an intrinsic way that the mind works:

> But it is impossible for me to hear and bear it in mind without forming mental images of it in my heart. For whether I will or not, when I hear of Christ, an image of a man hanging on a cross takes form in my heart, just as the reflection of my face naturally appears in the water when I look into it. If it is not a sin but good to have the image of Christ in my heart, why should it be a sin to have it in my eyes? This is especially true since the heart is more important than the eyes, and should be less stained by sin because it is the true abode and dwelling place of God.[47]

Luther's sketches of biblical events in his narratives present pictures in motion.[48] For Luther, a pure spirituality or imageless faith is an illusion.

46. *Against the Heavenly Prophets*, in LW 40:99 (WA 18:82.23–83.5).
47. *Against the Heavenly Prophets*, in LW 40:99–100 (WA 18:83.7–15).
48. See Robert Kolb, *Luther and the Stories of God: Biblical Narratives as a Foundation for Christian Living* (Grand Rapids: Baker Academic, 2012).

But that is no liability. Instead, the fact that the Scriptures establish mental images in the heart provides the very basis for new life. Such images govern the mind and the will and so establish a new person in Christ. "Therefore we should know that God neither disapproves of nor abolishes the natural affections which he imparted to nature in creation, but that He arouses and fosters them."[49]

Looking at a wider context, this gives us some insight into how for Luther the senses, specifically those of hearing and sight, the ear and the eye, are involved in human salvation. Again, Luther wanted to highlight the tangibility of God's grace and its ability to saturate "ears, eyes, and heart." As he put it in the *Lectures on Genesis*:

> You have no reason to complain that you have been visited less than Abraham or Isaac. You, too, have appearances, and in a way they are stronger, clearer, and more numerous than those they had, provided that you open your eyes and heart and take hold of them. You have Baptism. You have the Sacrament of the Eucharist, where bread and wine are the species, figures, and forms in which and under which God in person speaks and works into your ears, eyes, and heart. Besides, you have the ministry of the Word and teachers through whom God speaks with you. You have the ministry of the Keys, through which He absolves and comforts you.[50]

As is well known, hearing (the ear) was the primary sense for Luther since it has the capacity to hear God's word and it is through such hearing that faith is born. In his *Lectures on Hebrews* (1517), the early Luther claimed that "the ears alone are the organs of a Christian man, for he is justified and declared to be a Christian, not because of the works of any member but because of faith."[51]

Against the grain of Scholastic theology, he ruled out the centrality of sight in theology and often used the metaphor of "darkness," appropriated from his early studies in mysticism, in order to situate the ear and not the eye as the organ that receives the gospel. For instance, as we saw in chapter 5, he did this in the *Commentary on the Magnificat* (1521) by appealing to a tripartite anthropology in which the human is composed of spirit, soul, and body. He contrasted the spirit—"the highest, deepest, and noblest part of man" by which "he [humanity] is enabled to lay hold on things incomprehensible, invisible, and eternal . . . in brief, the dwelling place of faith and the Word of God"—with the soul, whose "nature [is] to comprehend not incomprehensible

---

49. *Lectures on Genesis*, in LW 8:20 (WA 44:594.4–9).
50. *Lectures on Genesis*, in LW 5:21 (WA 43:443.15).
51. LW 29:224 (WA 57:222.7–9).

things but such things as the reason can know and understand."[52] He noted that "his Spirit is the holy of holies, where God dwells in the darkness of faith, where no light is; for he believes that which he neither sees nor feels nor comprehends. His soul is the holy place with its seven lamps, that is, all manner of reason, discrimination, knowledge, and understanding of visible and bodily things."[53] That is, in ultimate matters such as human justification *coram deo*, human sight falters; that God loves unlovable sinners who are most unlike him in thought, word, and deed, is unfathomable to human reason. But Spirit-wrought faith does receive this gospel, which means that, with respect to salvation, faith is not only necessary but is also sufficient.

But as he elaborated much later in the *Lectures on Galatians* (1535) and the *Lectures on Genesis*, believers in the face of the accusing law need to grasp, apprehend, or take hold of—metaphors associated with *sight*—Christ. But Christ can be apprehended—seen or known—only because he is portrayed or imaged in the gospel. Outside the gospel, God is wholly hidden, but within the gospel, the eyes of faith are opened: "So it seems that God is completely forsaking us and casting us away, because He is hidden to us and we are hidden along with Him. But in faith, in the word, and in the sacraments He is revealed and seen [*conspicitur*]."[54] The gospel is received by hearing, but it grants sight—indeed, knowledge. "Thus faith is a sort of knowledge or darkness that nothing can see. Yet the Christ of whom faith takes hold is sitting in this darkness as God sat in the midst of darkness on Sinai and in the temple."[55] The gospel word portraying Christ grants right knowledge of God by joining believers with Christ.

In the context of the *Lectures on Galatians*, this is because the believer shares in the form of Christ, and in medieval thought, following Aristotle, the form is what is shared between the knower and the known. Baldly put, Luther even said that faith is knowledge, and so he constantly admonished believers to "grasp," "take hold of," or "apprehend" Christ, who is the heart and content of faith. The portrait of Christ is received through the ear and thereby is implanted in the heart. That oral portrait of Christ is made available for faith, which then grasps Christ and clings to him and thus sees or

52. *Commentary on the Magnificat*, in LW 21:303 (WA 7:538.28–30).
53. *Commentary on the Magnificat*, in LW 21:304 (WA 7:539.19–24).
54. *Lectures on Genesis*, in LW 6:148 (WA 44:110.32–33). Luther expands this: "Reason, wisdom, righteousness of the flesh, and this light of the sun God regards as dark and misty, but here the Word comes forward like a little flame shining in the midst of darkness and scattering its rays through its doctrine and the sacraments; these rays God orders to be apprehended. If we embrace them, God is no longer hidden to us in the spirit but only in the flesh" (LW 6:148; WA 44:110.34–38).
55. *Lectures on Galatians*, in LW 26:129–30 (WA 40/1:229.1–2).

knows Christ. Such a view of faith and knowledge differs from not only the premodern Augustinian heritage that valued *intellectum* over *fides* but also the modern heritage stemming from Immanuel Kant (1724–1804). Kant sought to establish the limits of knowledge just so he could "make room for faith,"[56] but in so doing he cut theology off from any claim to knowledge or reality itself for that matter. But this is exactly the opposite of Luther's view, for which faith is in fact knowledge.

A Covered God

It is well known that Luther saw that outside the gospel God is always hidden (*deus absconditus*), often appearing as wrathful or even indifferent to human plight. But a category wider than that of God's hiddenness that also bears upon the topic of imaging is that of God as "covered," never nakedly manifest to humans. As the Reformer put it, God is present at all times and places and in all things. Whether or not they are aware of it, humans ever deal with God in all their affairs and transactions. For Luther, unlike for modern people, there truly is no secular space (other than one we fancy): God is masked in all things. So, in a sense, all creation images God, but not in any way that gives clarity apart from the gospel. God communicates himself to people throughout creation, in events, and surprisingly in specific artifacts and human creations. Hence, Luther wrote:

> Perhaps God appeared to Adam without a covering, but after the fall into sin He appeared in a gentle breeze as though enveloped in a covering. Similarly he was enveloped later on in the tabernacle by the mercy seat and in the desert by a cloud and fire. Moses, therefore, also calls these objects "faces of God," through which God manifested Himself. Cain, too, calls the place at which he had previously sacrificed "the face of God" (Gen. 4:14). This nature of ours has become so misshapen through sin, so depraved and utterly corrupted, that it cannot recognize God or comprehend His nature without a covering. It is for this reason that those coverings are necessary.[57]

Thereby God communicates to people—not always clearly but always certainly—and not merely in the creation but also in human artifacts, such as the mercy seat in the tabernacle. Sometimes God's message is threat: human impotence in the face of matters over which we have no control. Sometimes

---

56. Kant, *Critique of Pure Reason*, trans. Norman Kemp Smith (New York: St. Martin's Press, 1929), B xxx, p. 29.
57. *Lectures on Genesis*, in LW 1:11 (WA 42:9.34–10.2).

it is accusation: human guilt exposed through the rustling of a leaf.[58] Some-times it is protection: the rainbow as a specific promise of God's commit-ment not to destroy the earth through a flood.[59] In that way, all people know something about God, but apart from Christ people have no certainty about whether God loves them. Clarity about that matter is given only in the gospel: a gift-word of promise that in Jesus Christ, God is for us. Here God reveals his goodness, will, and purpose for humanity, which otherwise is masked in creation or human events, roles, or artifacts. But that God must come to us as wrapped is intrinsic and not accidental to his relation to humans.[60] This is for two reasons. First, sinful humans cannot have a direct rapport with God. Second, God gives himself in tangible ways to humans since they are physical and require physical tokens.

It is not quite appropriate to speak of God's presence in creation and human events and artifacts as "sacramental" since God's speaking under such masks is not always gracious, but often threatening, disorienting, or seemingly indifferent. But, as mentioned, Luther's cosmos is no secular place. It is "enchanted"[61] even if it violates a Neoplatonic view that advocates an analogy of being in which all things conform to or participate in some way in God as the highest being. Luther undermines this ladder or stairway from the lowest to the highest in creation because it lends itself to a self-righteousness in which nature can be perfected by grace when we mimetically participate to greater degrees in divine glory.

Luther provides us with a model of God's relation to the world other than that advocated by his Neoplatonic forebears or the more secular, Epicurean approach (which reduces matter to inert, spiritless, atomic machines) that some later Europeans and Americans would advocate.[62] As in Neoplatonism, God is present in all things, and all things express God's purposes. But, un-like it, we have no criterion outside of Christ by which to determine how any given thing participates in God more or less than other things. Thus we have

58. *Lectures on Genesis*, in LW 3:8 (WA 42:127.26).

59. *Lectures on Genesis*, in LW 2:148 (WA 42:365.33).

60. "When God reveals Himself to us, it is necessary for Him to do so through some such veil or wrapper and to say: Look! Under this wrapper you will be sure to take hold of me. When we embrace this wrapper, adoring, praying, and sacrificing to God there, we are said to be praying to God and sacrificing to Him properly" (*Lectures on Genesis*, in LW 1:15 [WA 42:12.21–25]).

61. On "disenchantment," see Max Weber, *Essays in Sociology*, trans. and ed. H. H. Gerth (London: Routledge, 2009), 139. For a response, see Charles Taylor, *A Secular Age* (Cambridge, MA: Belknap Press of Harvard University Press, 2007), 25–27, 29–43, and other places. Of course, Taylor's point is that Luther was an inadvertent contributor to disenchantment. As will be shown in the next chapter, this conclusion does not hold.

62. See Matthew Stewart, *Nature's God: The Heretical Origins of the American Republic* (New York: Norton, 2014).

no basis for grading where one's status would be on some heavenly ladder. Thwarting all such self-righteousness is the fact that believers justified by faith alone are *simul iustus et peccator*. But unlike the secular perspective, nothing we encounter in the world is devoid of God because everything in the world speaks of God in one way or another. Everything speaks of God and communicates God, not because some analogy is in place that would secure the status of humanity's mimetic participation in the divine, but because God wants to address his creatures, humanity, ultimately to resituate them to be creatures defined by and grounded in faith.[63] The creation indeed bears witness to its Creator. All things participate in God, not through an analogy that grades them on a stairway to the eternal, but instead as masks of God—and by God sending messages that threaten unrepentant sinners or secure the penitent in his mercy. All we ever deal with in creation is, at its deepest level, God. Creation, then, is no stairway to the eternal but instead is an address of God to his people.[64]

Conclusion

While Luther's perspective fails to offer specific criteria for beauty in the visual arts, other than that they must witness to Christ, it offers an environment conducive to the making of such artifacts when they are divested of any salvific status. Counter to Augustinian *proportio*, Dionysian light and color, and Thomistic integrity or perfection, the gospel grants a beauty similar to the delight that a parent sees in a child even if errant and wayward. The impact of the Reformation on the visual arts was to acknowledge that we are not to be led beyond this world in some Neoplatonic scheme; instead, we are to see God's work in the ordinary, everyday stuff of life. Properly understood, the Reformation does not secularize art so much as sacralize the ordinary and raise its status as the locus where God works. The secular/sacral distinction is an attempt to abstract what must be seen concretely in the relationship of the person of the Creator to both personal and nonpersonal creatures.

In opposition to the imageless spirituality advocated by the "heavenly prophets," the gospel images. Hearing the gospel as it is given externally to

63. In contrast to Hans Boersma, *Heavenly Participation: The Weaving of a Sacramental Tapestry* (Grand Rapids: Eerdmans, 2011).

64. Here John Milbank's conviction in *Theology and Social Theory: Beyond Secular Reason* (Oxford: Blackwell, 1990)—i.e., "Between nihilistic univocity and Catholic analogy (which includes the 'convertibility' of truth, beauty and goodness) there is no longer any third liberal path" (318)—needs to be challenged. It may be that there is no third liberal path, but there is a theological path, and that is Luther's.

the ear in preaching suggests images of the saving Christ, which hold the imagination in their grasp. An incurvated imagination guarantees the spiritual perversity of "human reason" and "free will even though it may be of the highest quality."[65] It is what leads philosophers and theologians to become lost in the "mazes of the Divine Being" instead of being tethered to the "manger of Christ the Man."[66] Luther constantly admonishes believers to "take hold" of this imaged Christ as they apprehend, gaze upon, and indeed know him. In this way, Christ's favor is exchanged for our sinful liabilities, and the believer is united with Christ. Hence, such imaging is not merely didactic but also regenerative, even transformative. The preached or scriptural word holds forth images of Christ and God's action for redemption not just for human imitation but primarily for the believer's assurance and even identity as a new person in Christ.

65. *Lectures on Genesis*, in LW 2:41 (WA 42:291.26).
66. *Lectures on Genesis*, in LW 2:45 (WA 42:293.30–31).

≫8≪

Luther and *Nouvelle Théologie*

The last half century has seen a renewal of the topic of beauty in theology, led by those following the work of Hans Urs von Balthasar (1905–88) and David Bentley Hart,[1] and whose work is dependent on the *nouvelle théologie* of Henri de Lubac and others. These theologians have sought to recover beauty in response to modern and postmodern thinking that focuses not primarily on aesthetics but on epistemology, on whether the conditions for knowing anything can be met. For Kant, whose philosophy has dominated modern thinking, humans can know how they experience the world (the phenomenal), but they have no access to reality as such (the noumenal). In this view, beauty belongs not properly to reality but instead is a feature that the human mind brings to experience.[2] In contrast, for von Balthasar and Hart, modern

---

1. See Hans Urs von Balthasar, *The Glory of the Lord: A Theological Aesthetics*, 7 vols. (Edinburgh: T&T Clark, 1982–91); and David Bentley Hart, *The Beauty of the Infinite: The Aesthetics of Christian Truth* (Grand Rapids: Eerdmans, 2003). For other studies, see Frank Burch Brown, *Good Taste, Bad Taste, and Christian Taste: Aesthetics in Religious Life* (Oxford: Oxford University Press, 2000); Anthony J. Ciorra, *Beauty: A Path to God* (New York: Paulist Press, 2013); Thomas Dubay, *The Evidential Power of Beauty* (San Francisco: Ignatius, 1999); Robert MacSwain and Taylor Worley, eds., *Theology, Aesthetics, and Culture: Responses to the Work of David Brown* (Oxford: Oxford University Press, 2012); Richard Viladesau, *The Beauty of the Cross: The Passion of Christ in Theology and the Arts, from the Catacombs to the Eve of the Renaissance* (Oxford: Oxford University Press, 2008); Viladesau, *Theological Aesthetics: God in Imagination, Beauty, and Art* (Oxford: Oxford University Press, 1999); and, for a Reformed perspective, Belden C. Lane, *Ravished by Beauty: The Surprising Legacy of Reformed Spirituality* (Oxford: Oxford University Press, 2011).

2. See Immanuel Kant, *Critique of Judgment*, trans. J. H. Bernard (New York: Hafner, 1951), 37–81. For Kant, beauty is defined by four aspects. First, it is disinterested: we take pleasure in

and postmodern skepticism about knowing is unwarranted and unproductive: skepticism presumes at least some knowledge as a basis from which to determine the knowable from the unknowable. Indeed, mathematics and the hard sciences, those disciplines less vulnerable to skepticism, imply the need for some kind of ontology, drawing inferences about underlying structures of reality as such, regardless of how it should be articulated. For these thinkers, like many ancient Greek fathers (and presumably Augustine and Aquinas at their best), all beautiful things point to the transcendental reality of Beauty itself. The Christian faith witnesses to this beauty: the gospel is inherently attractive. God is the ultimate end or purpose for which humanity can find the fulfillment of its deepest hunger and desire. Grace helps creatures reach their perfection. Appreciating beautiful things directs us "upward" to seek God as the source and goal of beauty. In order to restore beauty as a proper theological topic, von Balthasar and Hart oppose Thomistic Scholasticism, which, beginning in the sixteenth century, separated the "natural" from the "supernatural" and so offered a trajectory of thought that, along with trends in modern philosophy, unintentionally bifurcated public and private spheres. In such bifurcation, the public realm is secular, independent of God as its final end, and religious experience is private, affecting people's inner lives without bearing on public life.

Influenced by the Roman Catholic *nouvelle théologie* of Henri de Lubac and others, these theologians interpret beauty through the lens of the analogy of being (*analogia entis*), which as formulated by the Fourth Lateran Council (1215) reads: "One cannot note any similarity between Creator and creature, however great, without being compelled to note an even greater dissimilarity between them."[3] The analogy of being, as developed for instance in the work of Erich Przywara (1889–1972),[4] acknowledges an approach to God in which ontologically realistic propositions can be made about God while simultaneously honoring God's apophatic mysteriousness. Attempts to reclaim beauty

---

it because we judge it to be beautiful; we do not judge it beautiful because we find it pleasurable. Second and third, it is universal and necessary. However, these features are not objective properties of beautiful things but instead are how the mind perceives things. Finally, beauty appears to be purposive but without purpose. Beautiful things affect us as if they had a purpose, but the purpose cannot be found or established. For more, see Douglas Burnham, "Immanuel Kant: Aesthetics," *Internet Encyclopedia of Philosophy*, ed. James Fieser and Bradley Dowden, http://www.iep.utm.edu/kantaest/. Luther would surely take issue with the second, third, and fourth of these propositions.

3. See Stephen H. Webb, "The End of the Analogy of Being: Przywara's Proportionality Problem," *First Things*, January 27, 2015, http://www.firstthings.com/web-exclusives/2015/01/the-end-of-the-analogy-of-being.

4. See Przywara, *Analogia Entis: Metaphysics; Original Structure and Universal Rhythm*, trans. John R. Betz and David Bentley Hart (Grand Rapids: Eerdmans, 2014).

in contemporary theology have sought in various ways to appropriate the Neoplatonic heritage latent in patristic theology. Through this Christianized Neoplatonism, beauty is retrieved as a way to reclaim mystery for the world, a "sacramental ontology," in the face of the modern tendency to disenchant the cosmos by mapping or carving up all reality through quantification, and in the process nihilistically flatlining it, rendering it a cadaver for dissection. The appropriation of a Christianized Neoplatonism is said to provide depth and meaning in contrast to nihilism, since God is the mystery present in all reality. All particular things are in some way or another icons of God, directing us above to find our ultimate happiness in God. Hence, these theologians claim beauty as a transcendental, descriptive of and instantiated in all finite things, in opposition to modern tendencies that make beauty a private, subjective matter, latent not in reality as such but only in how the mind works. So David Bentley Hart employs the analogy of being in order to show metaphysically that beauty is definitive of infinity, the basis from which to quell postmodern descriptions of competitive violence allegedly lying at the core of all relationships.[5] All this raises questions for a contemporary appropriation of Luther: If Luther is not on the same page with these scholars on the analogy of being, then does he lead us to a disenchanted view of the cosmos? Is he a contributor to secularism? Apart from the analogy of being, is Luther able to offer a satisfying account of beauty in which beauty accords with reality and is not a mere accidental epiphenomenon of human mental processes? The purpose of this chapter is to critique contemporary theologies of beauty in light of Luther's approach. Contrasting Luther's view with current thinking will bring out aspects of his theology that have been ignored by existentialist interpretations of Luther and will help position the Reformer as offering a path more faithful to the gospel than recent theologians of beauty. In contrast to contemporary theologies that tend to default either to a Platonism, such as

5. Hart writes,
  A God whose very being is love, delight in the glorious radiance of his infinite Image, seen in the boundlessly lovely light of his Spirit, and whose works are then unnecessary but perfectly expressive signs of this delight, fashioned for his pleasure and for the gracious sharing of his joy with creatures for whom he had no need (yet loved even when they were not), is a God of beauty in the fullest imaginable sense. In such a God beauty and the infinite entirely coincide, for the very life of God is one of—to phrase it strangely— infinite form; and when such a God creates, the difference between created beauty and the divine beauty it reflects subsists not in the amphiboly of multiplicity and singularity, shape and simplicity, finitude and indeterminacy, but in the analogy between the determinate particularities of the world and that always greater, supereminent determinacy in whose splendor they participate. (*Beauty of the Infinite*, 131)
Again, for Luther it is problematic that the unity of infinity and beauty can be determined unambiguously on metaphysical grounds.

the *nouvelle théologie*, or to a Kantianism, such as mainline Protestantism, Luther offers a third path.

The Ambiguity of the Infinite

The analogy of being has a long history in theology, including Lutheran Orthodoxy.[6] But an important strand of Luther's thinking could identify the analogy of being as a form of the "theology of glory," how sinners seek to accrue merit before God through offering something of their own to God, something analogous to God, a theology that should be contrasted with the "theology of the cross," God's work to humble sinners and bring them to mercy. Would not the analogy of being be one culprit that the early Luther attacked in his *Heidelberg Disputation* (1518)? Specifically, theses 19 and 20 read: "That person does not deserve to be called a theologian who looks upon the invisible things of God as though they were clearly perceptible in those things which have actually happened. He deserves to be called a theologian, however, who comprehends the visible and manifest things of God seen through suffering and the cross."[7] So, for Luther, in contrast to David Bentley Hart's metaphysical approach to infinity, it is clear that outside of or apart from Christ, infinity is ambiguous; it is not clear that it is good or beautiful. It may well be tantamount to Hegel's "bad infinite": one damn thing unendingly following another.[8] That Luther, similar to his nominalist teachers, is skeptical of the ability of metaphysics to solve the problems it generates does not make him to be "postmetaphysical." His world and Kant's are light years apart. For Luther, in contrast to Kant, we have access to

6. See Johannes Andreas Quenstedt's discussion defending analogical speech as opposed to univocal or equivocal speech in Heinrich Schmid, *The Doctrinal Theology of the Evangelical Lutheran Church*, trans. Charles Hay and Henry Jacobs (Minneapolis: Augsburg, 1961), 115–16. Johann Gerhard alludes to the analogy of being when he writes, "Whatever has being [*est*] of and through itself is the cause of those things that have being [*sunt*] by participation. God, then, is called 'Jehovah' . . . not only because He is but also because he is the cause for being of all things that are. He is the limitless and vast sea of being" (*On the Nature of God and on the Trinity*, trans. Richard J. Dinda [St. Louis: Concordia, 2007], 8).

7. *Heidelberg Disputation* (1518), theses 19 and 20, in LW 31:40 (WA 1:354.17–20).

8. See Hegel, *The Science of Logic*, trans. A. V. Miller (London: Allen & Unwin, 1969), 137:
   The infinite, however, is held to be absolute without qualification for it is determined expressly as negation of the finite, and reference is thus expressly made to limitedness in the infinite. . . . But even so, the infinite is not yet really free from limitation and finitude; the main point is to distinguish the genuine Notion of infinity from spurious infinity, the infinite of reason from the infinite of the understanding; yet the latter is the finitized infinite and it will be found that in every act of keeping the infinite pure and aloof from the finite, the infinite is only made finite.

God. But outside of the promise, God is hidden. Even in Christ's cross, God remains hidden "under the sign of the opposite" (*sub contrario*), particularly in Christ's crucifixion.[9] It is our ability to know God with certainty outside of the promise that is open to challenge. This is due not just to the limits of human knowledge in divine matters but also to God actively hiding himself, thwarting people who want a different rapport with God other than grace. But for Kant, there is no access to God at all. Instead, God is a regulative idea,[10] or a "postulate of pure practical reason."[11] Hence, when Kant speaks of "making room for faith,"[12] he has an entirely different enterprise in mind than Luther. Faith for Luther is trust in a word of promise grounded in and handed on from apostolic testimony, while for Kant it is an exercise of the imagination.

With David Bentley Hart we certainly can surmise that the infinite is beauty and that it makes a space for all finite things so that they need not jostle, hurt, or violate one another. But can we be sure of it? Philosophers are prone to highly inventive strategies devised to solve metaphysical problems. But for Luther such paths give no assurance. If we want security with respect to the eternal status of beauty, we must look to Jesus Christ. The "office of Jesus Christ is to make us certain of God."[13] Luther put it this way in *De servo arbitrio* (1525) with his famous description of the "three lights":

> By the light of nature it is an insoluble problem how it can be just that a good man should suffer and a bad man prosper; but this problem is solved by the light of grace. By the light of grace it is an insoluble problem how God can damn one who is unable by any power of his own to do anything but sin and

9. Brian A. Gerrish, "To the Unknown God: Luther and Calvin on the Hiddenness of God," in *The Old Protestantism and the New: Essays on the Reformation Heritage* (Edinburgh: T&T Clark, 1982), 131–49, distinguishes in Luther a Hiddenness I, where God's love is hidden *sub contrario* or paradoxically as wisdom in folly or life in the death of Christ, from Hiddenness II, where God is hidden even behind Jesus's manger or cross in God's inscrutable will, in which God's goodness is not always apparent. For a recent study of God as hidden, see Joshua C. Miller, *Hanging by a Promise: The Hidden God in the Theology of Oswald Bayer* (Eugene, OR: Pickwick, 2015).

10. Kant writes: "This unconditioned is not, indeed, given as being in itself real, nor as having a reality that follows from its mere concept; it is, however, what alone can complete the series of conditions when we proceed to trace these conditions to their grounds. This is the course, which our human reason, by its very nature, leads all of us" (*Critique of Pure Reason*, trans. Norman Kemp Smith [New York: St. Martin's Press, 1929], A584/B612; cf. A584/B612n).

11. Kant, *Critique of Practical Reason*, trans. Lewis White Beck (Indianapolis: Bobbs-Merrill, 1957), 137–39.

12. Kant, *Critique of Pure Reason*, B xxx, p. 29.

13. Oswald Bayer, *Theology the Lutheran Way*, trans. Jeffrey G. Silcock and Mark C. Mattes (Grand Rapids: Eerdmans, 2007), 75.

be guilty. Here both the light of nature and the light of grace tell us that it is
not the fault of the unhappy man, but of an unjust God; for they cannot judge
otherwise of a God who crowns one ungodly man freely and apart from merits,
yet damns another who may well be less, or at least not more, ungodly. But
the light of glory tells us differently, and it will show us hereafter that the God
whose judgment here is one of incomprehensible righteousness is a God of most
perfect and manifest righteousness. In the meantime, we can only believe this,
being admonished and confirmed by the example of the light of grace, which
performs a similar miracle in relation to the light of nature.[14]

Now, a "God of most perfect and manifest righteousness," a God who gives
the gospel, a righteousness grounded in his own fidelity in Christ to his own,
is a God of beauty, gospel beauty. But such beauty, like God's righteousness,
will for us finite, sinful creatures be manifest, or made indisputably clear,
eschatologically, in glory and not through metaphysics. Until then, we walk
by faith and not sight (2 Cor. 5:7).

With respect to beauty, then, Stephen John Wright (interpreting Robert
Jenson's aesthetics) offers an insight we can appropriate: "Beauty is not alien
to the object in which it is perceived—such as in a naïve idealism—but is
proper to each creature as that creature has its being in the life of Christ.
Creaturely beauty is not participation in a transcendent and eternal form
or divine idea but in the life, death, and resurrection of Jesus."[15] Or we can
say that Jesus defines the category of "form" and not "form" the identity of
Jesus. Jesus Christ is the lens through which to enjoy beauty and discern the
status of beauty in creation or human creativity, "cooperation with God,"[16]
and which will be confirmed eschatologically.

An Enchanted World

For Luther, the world is not a disenchanted place, because all creaturely activity *masks* God: God works through specific creatures as his channels or
instruments upon other creatures.[17] Thus God is accessible in creation as one
who addresses sinners in all things. So, for Luther, we do not properly understand the world if we see it as devoid of wonder and mystery. The natural and

14. *The Bondage of the Will* (1525), in LW 33:292 (WA 18:785.28–38).
15. Wright, *Dogmatic Aesthetics: A Theology of Beauty in Dialogue with Robert W. Jenson*
(Minneapolis: Fortress, 2014), 26.
16. *The Bondage of the Will*, in LW 33:242 (WA 18:753.33).
17. For a similar position, see Ronald F. Thiemann, "Sacramental Realism: Martin Luther
at the Dawn of Modernity," in *Lutherrenaissance Past and Present*, ed. Christine Helmer and
Bo Kristian Holm (Göttingen: Vandenhoeck & Ruprecht, 2015), 156–73.

the supernatural are not separated for Luther as they are for neo-Thomistic Scholastics. But this is not due to the fact that *sinners* are properly "ordered" to God and so are perfectible through mimicking truth, beauty, and goodness. Humanity as such, prior to the fall, was indeed designed to enjoy union with God. But sinners unfortunately seek to pay with something of their own for what God gives freely and is enjoyed by grace alone. As Luther put it in *De servo arbitrio*, "Before man is created and is a man, he neither does nor attempts to do anything toward becoming a creature, and after he is created he neither does nor attempts to do anything toward remaining a creature, but both of these things are done by the sole will of the omnipotent power and goodness of God, who creates and preserves us without our help."[18] The divine depth present in all creation does not ride on the creature's quest to perfect itself *coram deo*, but instead is established in that God works in and through some creatures to provide for other creatures and accomplish his will in and for them. So, for Luther, unlike Karl Barth, an "analogy of faith" is not to be played off the "analogy of being."[19] It is not as if there is no truth to natural theology. Through analogies, creation indeed witnesses to its Creator (Rom. 1:19–23), not so as to inspire human self-righteousness before the divine but instead to accuse sinners of their idolatry and injustice. So it is not certain or unambiguous from natural theology that God is gracious. As we shall see, Luther finds certainty and clarity for analogical reasoning in theology and preaching on the basis of the gospel as an ex post facto encounter with God's mercy. Unlike the law, the gospel opens horizons of experience through which people can unambiguously discern analogies of God's love and beauty: singing birds are gospel preachers for true Christians,[20] and good trees bear good fruit.[21] So we should agree with those theologians who deplore modern disenchantment. After all, "The heavens declare the glory of God, / and the sky above proclaims his handiwork. / Day to day pours out speech, and night to night reveals knowledge" (Ps. 19:1–2). Even more to the point, the Holy

18. *The Bondage of the Will*, in LW 33:242–43 (WA 18:754.1–5).

19. This debate is recorded in numerous places, most recently in D. Stephen Long, *Saving Karl Barth: Hans Urs von Balthasar's Preoccupation* (Minneapolis: Fortress, 2014).

20. See *The Sermon on the Mount* (LW 21:197–98; WA 32:462.26–35):
Whenever you listen to a nightingale, therefore, you are listening to an excellent preacher. He exhorts you with this Gospel, not with mere simple words but with a living deed and an example. He sings all night and practically screams his lungs out. He is happier in the woods than cooped up in a cage, where he has to be taken care of constantly and where he rarely gets along very well or even stays alive. It is as if he were saying: "I prefer to be in the Lord's kitchen. He has made heaven and earth," and He Himself is the cook and the host. Every day He feeds and nourishes innumerable little birds out of His hand. For He does not have merely a bag full of grain, but heaven and earth.

21. *The Freedom of a Christian*, in LW 31:361 (WA 7:61.30–31).

Spirit works through the beauty of the gospel (*"enlightens* me with his gifts")[22] to bring sinners to faith and grant them new life. This new life is not in name only. Instead, the word re-creates reality anew. It opens people of faith to beauty in the world, allows them to treasure and enjoy it, and moves them to give gratitude to God and engage in service on behalf of God (as synergy with God) to those in need.

That said, we should challenge the misperceptions about the nature of beauty that have arisen in modern and postmodern perspectives. Contemporary views of beauty such as von Balthasar's and Hart's are indebted to the *nouvelle théologie* or *ressourcement* movement, whose publications would easily fill a small library. Nevertheless, we can find an accurate overview of the *nouvelle théologie* in the work of the contemporary evangelical scholar Hans Boersma, who retrieves de Lubac's work in order to establish a "sacramental ontology"[23] for Protestant theology. For the sake of convenience, we will rely here on Boersma's work in our attempt to situate *ressourcement* thinking with respect to Luther's. In a word, to critique contemporary views of beauty arising from the analogy of being, it is necessary to critique the *nouvelle théologie*. As mentioned, a Lutheran critique of this approach is apt to see it as offering a "theology of glory" instead of a "theology of the cross." That said, in contrast to the New Testament scholar Rudolf Bultmann (1884–1976),[24] a theology of the cross properly understood releases a genuine appreciation for the world as creation (God's address to creatures through creatures, as Johann Georg Hamann [1730–88] put it),[25] an openness to beauty intertwined with sense experience, which reframes desire so that we desire what God desires and treasure what God treasures in contrast to self-gratifying

22. The Small Catechism, in BC 355:6 (BSELK 872:15).

23. See Boersma, Nouvelle Théologie *and Sacramental Ontology: A Return to Mystery* (Oxford: Oxford University Press, 2009); and Boersma, *Heavenly Participation: The Weaving of a Sacramental Tapestry* (Grand Rapids: Eerdmans, 2011). The first volume is meant to be a more scholarly approach and the second volume a more popular approach. Nevertheless, both are beneficial for our purposes.

24. Note David Bentley Hart's critique of Bultmann in *Beauty of the Infinite*, 21–24.

25. In "Aesthetica in nuce," Hamann wrote, "Speak, that I may see you!—This wish was fulfilled by creation, which is a speech to creatures through creatures; for day unto day utters speech, and night unto night shows knowledge. Its watchword traverses every clime to the end of the world, and its voice can be heard in every dialect" (*Writings on Philosophy and Language*, trans. and ed. Kenneth Haynes [Cambridge: Cambridge University Press, 2007], 65). For further commentary, see Oswald Bayer, *A Contemporary in Dissent: Johann Georg Hamann as a Radical Enlightener*, trans. Roy A. Harrisville and Mark C. Mattes (Grand Rapids: Eerdmans, 2012), 74–77. See also Bayer's discussion of Luther's sermon on *ephphatha* in *Martin Luther's Theology: A Contemporary Interpretation*, trans. Thomas Trapp (Grand Rapids: Eerdmans, 2008), 108, 112–14. See also Mark Mattes and Ron Darge, "Ephphatha: Be Open," in *Imaging the Journey* (Minneapolis: Lutheran University Press, 2006), 50.

desire.[26] Liberated from the compulsion to earn condign merit, believers can enjoy an aesthetic of freedom, loving God for his own sake, others for their own sakes, and appreciating creation as gift.

The Strange Beauty of the Cross

Not asked in the *nouvelle théologie*'s analysis of aesthetic experience is whether infinity is encountered as grace or law, mercy or expectation. This theory conflates the two. But should it? For this theory, beauty evokes desire, and desire is at the core of all human endeavor: the quest to fulfill desire and do those things that would satiate desire, especially our desire for union with the divine. In this view, whether or not humans are aware of it, ultimately their desire is to find fulfillment in God, and so perfect themselves. But this perspective on beauty would seem to be far more indebted to Plato than to Paul. It operates from a stance of contemplation of and not conflict with God.[27] If it were to acknowledge that sinners are in conflict with God, it would have to change its view of beauty. The scriptural witness throughout is that sinners are in conflict with God because they wish, in Luther's description, to establish their own divinity (*ambitio divinitatis*) over against God.[28] For this reason, God's accusing law crushes sinners so that they are bereft of their self-reliance and thus can be opened to faith in God. As Paul writes,

> Has not God made foolish the wisdom of the world? For since, in the wisdom of God, the world did not know God through wisdom, God decided, through the foolishness of our proclamation, to save those who believe. For Jews demand signs and Greeks desire wisdom, but we proclaim Christ crucified, a stumbling block to Jews and foolishness to Gentiles, but to those who are the called, both Jews and Greeks, Christ the power of God and the wisdom of God. For God's foolishness is wiser than human wisdom, and God's weakness is stronger than human strength. (1 Cor. 1:20b–25 NRSV)

26. *Lectures on Genesis*, in LW 1:337 (WA 42:248.12–13). In *De servo arbitrio*, Luther notes how the Holy Spirit in the gospel works to resituate the human will: "When God works in us, the will is changed under the sweet influence of the Spirit of God. Once more it desires and acts, not of compulsion, but of its own desire and spontaneous inclination. Its bent still cannot be altered by any opposition; it cannot be mastered or prevailed upon even by the gates of hell; but it goes on willing, desiring and loving good, just as once it willed, desired and loved evil" (*The Bondage of the Will*, trans. J. I. Packer and O. R. Johnston [New York: Revell, 1957], 103 [WA 18:634.37–635.2]).

27. Bayer, *Theology the Lutheran Way*, 59–65.

28. For *ambitio divinitatis*, see the reference above in *De servo arbitrio*. See also LW 49:337 (WA BR 5:415.41–46); LW 31:10 (WA 1:225); and LW 26:257–58 (WA 40/1:404–5).

Insofar as wisdom or strength can be associated with beauty, and foolishness or weakness with ugliness, we can paraphrase Paul: "For God's ugliness is more beautiful than human beauty." But clearly, such a beauty—that of the cross, which, as we saw, lacks the standard medieval criteria of beauty (proportion, clarity, and integrity) because it marked Christ by deformity, darkness, and death—is strange indeed. It is the beauty of grace, the same beauty that the waiting father gave his prodigal son (Luke 15:11–32) or that Christ gave the woman caught in adultery (John 8:2–11), a beauty based on God claiming sinners as his own, enduring the penalty of death in order to grant sinners new, eternal life, a beauty grounded not in what is lovely or desirable but in the forgiving and rescuing generosity of the one who loves. The outcome of both the prodigal's and the adulteress's desire led to their being crushed. But these sinners are granted pardon and a relationship with their Lord, which reawakens a new hunger, a resituated desire: to hear again and again that they are forgiven and that a new path in life is opened to them ("Go and sin no more"). It is a beauty that confirms their place and status in this world, in spite of the pharisaical quest for purity, or the condemnation of the adversary. It is a beauty that secures the gift of being at home in this world.[29]

In the cross, then, is granted a strange beauty, where *kenōsis* (emptying) is expressed not as a humility that sinners could establish for themselves but as Christ becoming sin for sinners, dying for them, precisely so that sinners may have forgiveness and eternal life. God hidden under the "sign of the opposite" is a strange and oddly beautiful matter because it is a generosity that absorbs the worst that sinners can bring so that sin can be buried in a tomb where no one—especially God—can ever find it. God's beauty precisely is his fidelity and commitment to those enslaved by sin and harassed by law. In the *nouvelle théologie* and its spin-offs, such as Radical Orthodoxy, Plato is everywhere implicit.[30] Plato is de facto canonized and receives his place among the saints and martyrs. Indeed, in this perspective, what "secularism" primarily means is the dismantling of Plato's influence on Western thought. But Plato could not conceive of a kingdom, or a Lord, without the law, and that law must of course itself be infinite, the order or pattern of beauty. In this way, the mystery and wonder of the world are defined in hierarchical terms as a grand scale

29. With reservations about both the Platonism and Kantianism in Roger Scruton's work, I find his metaphor of "at home" a useful way to describe the benefit that beauty gives us. See Scruton, *Beauty* (Oxford: Oxford University Press, 2009), 174–75.

30. See, for example, Catherine Pickstock, *After Writing: On the Liturgical Consummation of Philosophy* (Oxford: Blackwell, 1998), esp. 3–46. No doubt Plato is to be preferred to the French postmodernist philosopher Jacques Derrida (1930–2004), but the effort represented in this chapter is to offer a better alternative to both—one that affirms grace in opposition to the synergism *coram deo* latent in Neoplatonic Christianity and in opposition to postmodern nihilism.

of being stretching from the lowest bit of insignificant, trivial matter to the heavenly, eternal heights.

With Luther, we can and should affirm a depth to material reality. His is no protosecular perspective. Indeed, God as masked is ever working through creatures to provide for creaturely needs or to impose consequences upon creatures who overstep their bounds. But law alone is not definitive of reality. Reality is defined by the gospel as well. The gospel undermines the hierarchical scheme as a scale that alone traverses reality, particularly when it is interpreted as a ladder by which sinners can climb to God. From the perspective of the gospel, if the cosmic ladder should abide as a helpful heuristic tool to interpret reality, then it can only be a one-way ladder from God to sinners. Indeed, law as accusatory comes to an end in Christ (Rom. 10:4). Beauty, then, is not a self-perfecting of nature by means of supernatural aid; instead, it is calling forth a new creation into being through grace (2 Cor. 5:17). Grace alone brings creatures to their ultimate fulfillment in the future life, finishes them as new creations. God's action establishes freedom because God is doing what sinners could not do. It extinguishes the human disposition to disdain one's own creatureliness expressed in the defensive attempt to achieve a perfection based on one's own standards and accomplished through one's own merit.[31] Paradoxically, the more one desires such security for oneself, the more one cannot enjoy the world, filled as it is with all its contingencies, unforeseen and uncontrollable factors. God's beauty is given to sinners in that it reassures them that Christ is sufficient. In this way, it is the beauty of freedom, not perfection, at least as a human achievement. Christ frees humans not only from bad desires of the old creature but also from even the good ones whereby sinners attempt self-justification. As a result, all of life is situated in God's good hands. Humans can then be at home in the world. God has truly made creation good, a place where Sabbath rest, unguarded enjoyment of God's good gifts, and innocent delights make sense.

The beauty of freedom looks and feels different from the beauty of perfection: it comes as a gift, not an achievement. This beauty starts as hearing. It is awakened by the gospel promise before it can be perceived with any other sense. It opens love for God from the heart—a heart given over to God in faith—and resituates us to desire what God desires.[32] But this alters the opposition between *eros* and *agapē* as presented by Anders Nygren. Wilfried Härle notes,

31. "The remedy for curing desire does not lie in satisfying it, but in extinguishing it" (*Heidelberg Disputation*, in LW 31:54 [WA 1:363.9–14]).
32. *Lectures on Genesis*, in LW 1:337 (WA 42:248.12–13).

It is an indispensable element of *agapē* that it comes "from the heart," indeed that it—as divine love—burns with passion (Hos. 11:8–9; Luke 15:20). Thus, there is an erotic element implanted in *agapē* itself. Biblical *agapē* is devotion to another person, devotion that for the other person's sake comes from the heart. Where the happiness of the other person is experienced as one's own happiness, there *agapē* and *eros* arrive at unity. There heaven and earth touch each other.[33]

As free from the attempt to secure its own destiny, *eros* expresses joy and creativity, receiving joy in others' joy. Contrary to Plato, it has no ability to lead humans beyond this world. But, no doubt, for the redeemed, the "future life"[34] situates *eros*, providing it meaning and direction. The "future life" leads *eros* away from self-centered security and achievement and allows it to be a part of God's ongoing creation as it honors the good of others. *Agapē*, then, not only gets rid of the bad part but also, through God's alien work over time, eliminates the entire diseased body, a surgery that no doctor can perform, since it eventuates in the resurrection from the dead, with joy and love for God attendant on that renewal.[35] New beings are restored to creation such that they can see anew the wonder and beauty, given through proportion, light, and integrity, in creation.

The Goals of the *Nouvelle Théologie*

As Boersma explains it, the *nouvelle théologie* is an attempt to overcome a rupture between theology and life by achieving three goals: (1) to treat God as God, not as an object, but as the Subject par excellence; (2) to return to the church fathers, particularly the Greeks such as Irenaeus, Origen, Gregory of Nyssa, and Latin fathers prior to Augustine (who was deemed too individualistic), all of whose work was largely commentary on Scripture; and (3) to reintroduce earlier patterns of liturgical celebration that honored spiritual realities hidden behind sacramental signs.[36] The movement was a reaction against Thomistic Scholasticism, which separated nature from grace, or the supernatural, seen for example in the separation of the *praeambula fidei* (such as the "proofs" for God's existence, based on Aristotle) from the supernatural

---

33. Wilfried Härle, *Outline of Christian Doctrine: An Evangelical Dogmatics*, trans. Ruth Yule and Nicolas Sagovsky (Grand Rapids: Eerdmans, 2015), 201–2.

34. *Lectures on Genesis*, in LW 1:131 (WA 42:98.22–24).

35. The discussion here about the relation between *eros* and *agapē* is based on a discussion with Steve Paulson, email correspondence, July 16, 2015.

36. Boersma, Nouvelle Théologie *and Sacramental Ontology*, 2. Oswald Bayer notes that Luther weaves together monastic spirituality with Scholastic erudition and thus keeps the life of the mind in tandem with the life of the heart (*Theology the Lutheran Way*, 83).

truth of the gospel. In de Lubac's perspective, neo-Thomistic Scholasticism's separation of nature and grace unintentionally contributed to secularism because it legitimated the view that nature could be interpreted as autonomous or independent of God. In this perspective, creatures are internally related to God in that their ultimate purpose is achieved when they advance their supernatural ends in God.[37] In other words, secularity is tied to the rejection of "final causality" in the modern world. This rejection permits modern people to be *autopoietic*, self-defining. In contrast, for Luther, human good is to be found in receiving God's gifts. For humans, "final causality" is nothing other than God's judgment rendered in the present in the words of absolution and that has efficacy to carry creatures through to their completion in eternal life.

By upholding a belief in "pure nature" (*natura pura*), which defines creatures not with respect to God but with respect to their achieving their earthly ends or purposes, Thomistic Scholasticism helped create secularity as a space independent of God. But by the same token, when such a secular space is created—*as if* humans in their fullness could in fact be rightly understood apart from God by academic disciplines such as sociology, psychology, anthropology, political science, or biology—then faith becomes a private matter disconnected from life. "In other words, according to [Jean] Daniélou and the other *nouvelle* theologians, neo-Thomism ended up endorsing modernity's acceptance of the autonomy of nature as well as the Enlightenment belief in human progress in this independent (or immanent) realm of nature."[38] Another way of putting it is that neo-Thomism contributed to a disenchanted world, in which nature is subject to human mapping—whether a cartography of the earth or space, the human genome, the periodic table of elements, and the like—and is divested of any sense of wonder or mystery within it.[39] The rationale behind the neo-Thomists was that it was "impossible for human beings to have the innate desire for the supernatural beatific vision without also having the connatural means to attain it."[40] Building on what in Lutheran terms would be a reasoning from the law and not the gospel, the neo-Thomists concluded that "there was no *desiderium naturale* [natural

37. For a concise summation of de Lubac's thinking, in his own words, see de Lubac, *A Brief Catechesis on Nature and Grace*, trans. Richard Arnandez (San Francisco: Ignatius, 1980).
38. Boersma, Nouvelle Théologie *and Sacramental Ontology*, 5.
39. The late Klaus Schwarzwäller noted that wonder and mystery are most definitively expressed in Jesus's cross: "Unless we are internally defined by the cross and resurrection and externally keyed to it, our general perception will never suspect that the cross and resurrection of Jesus Christ do in fact bear the wonder and mystery of *God's own self*" (*Cross and Resurrection: God's Wonder and Mystery*, trans. Ken Jones and Mark Mattes [Minneapolis: Fortress, 2012], 95; italics original).
40. Boersma, Nouvelle Théologie *and Sacramental Ontology*, 92.

desire] for a supernatural end."[41] This was their way of protecting the gratuity of grace.

Because, according to the *ressourcement* view, human nature can only be understood in terms of its supernatural final end, its ultimate union with God in the beatific vision, nature has something to contribute to grace. Building on von Balthasar, Boersma notes that "revelation was primary, was supernatural in character, and did come from above. At the same time, the gift of supernatural revelation through Christ made it legitimate to turn the hourglass upside down, so that nature, too, made its genuine contribution, in and through Christ."[42] Erich Przywara would characterize Luther's way of thinking as "theo-pan-ism" since the denial of free will *coram deo* rejects the human capacity to contribute toward reaching the humans' own supernatural end.[43] De Lubac and Henri Bouillard (1908–81)

> both emphasized the "upward" direction of the natural world as it pointed towards the supernatural. . . . De Lubac's insistence on a natural desire for the vision of God, as well as his opposition to the notion of "pure nature," served to overcome neo-Thomism's dualism between nature and the supernatural. In this way, he wanted to recover a sense of the mystery that constituted the core of each human being.[44]

As we saw in our discussion about goodness, Luther was insistent that it is not God who needs our good works but the neighbor. Hence, the visions of God among the *ressourcement* theologians and that of Luther are significantly different. For Luther, God is not one before whom we could offer merit; instead, all matters of salvation center on Christ. Both *ressourcement* theologians and Luther agree that salvation hinges on Christ, but they differ over whether nature can offer merit on its own behalf to God. For *ressourcement* theologians, Christ is necessary, but he is not sufficient; nature too must make its contribution to human perfectibility. For Luther, Christ is not only necessary for salvation but also sufficient, our wisdom and righteousness and sanctification and redemption (1 Cor. 1:30). Redeemed nature offers nothing meritorious upward for God, but instead offers good deeds outward for those in need. Christians advance in their life of faith not through performing deeds approximating perfection (as if that were any longer their concern), but by trusting in Christ's sufficiency to sustain them from day to day. Likewise,

41. Ibid.
42. Ibid., 5.
43. Przywara, *Analogia Entis*, 165, 218–19.
44. Boersma, Nouvelle Théologie *and Sacramental Ontology*, 32.

Luther has his own way of expressing mystery and wonder within nature through the metaphor of "masking," but without any sense that we contribute to grace. Free will does not make one free; after all, it only expresses the desires of the self. It is self-will. Instead, only Christ makes one free. Insisting on maintaining free will is not freeing; instead, to be given trust that sees one's life as unfolding entirely within God's gracious care is freedom indeed.

Human nature needs liberation, not self-perfection—precisely if it is to come to its fulfillment.[45] Human teleology or fulfillment is outside humanity's hands, but is in the best of hands, God's, nail scarred though they be. Our fulfillment, living with God eternally, can be claimed "in ever so weak a manner; but in the future life we shall attain it fully."[46] How could it not be if we are indeed God's "workmanship" (Eph. 2:10)? Such fulfillment will not be accomplished through achieving condign merit either in this life or the next. Truly we are freed from a perfection established through works; we await a fulfillment solely in faith, one where through daily dying and rising we will be conformed to the image of the crucified. Of course, such liberation does not to lead to sloth. For the sake of the neighbor we daily struggle against sin, striving to love not only our friends but also our enemies.[47] Through God's promise, human life will be congruent with this image when the old Adam or Eve is completely dead; the new person in Christ will be completely unfettered to the old, and so in human life God will be all in all (1 Cor. 15:28).

The Question of Participation

The key concept from *nouvelle théologie* that Boersma sees as requisite for contemporary theology is "participation."[48] Indeed, secularity is a result of

45. Luther sees human perfection as occurring in the afterlife. See *The Freedom of a Christian*, in LW 31:358 (WA 7:59.31).

46. *Lectures on Genesis*, in LW 1:131 (WA 42:98.22–24).

47. See *The Sermon on the Mount*, in LW 21:129 (WA 32:406.31–39):

So I am called a truly perfect man, one who has and holds the doctrine in its entirety. Now, if my life does not measure up to this in every detail—as indeed it cannot, since flesh and blood incessantly hold it back—that does not detract from the perfection. Only we must keep striving for it, and moving and progressing toward it every day. This happens when the spirit is master over the flesh, holding it in check, subduing and restraining it, in order not to give it room to act contrary to this teaching. It happens when I let love move along on the true middle course, treating everyone alike and excluding no one. Then I have true Christian perfection.

48. There are many references to this concept in Boersma, *Heavenly Participation*, but one that ties participation to Paul is the following:

The heavenly identity of believers is, according to Paul, already a present reality. The rather realized eschatology of the letters to the Ephesians and the Colossians is emphatic about

our inability to affirm the participation of all created realities in God—giving these realities an independence or autonomy that in fact is not in accord with their very being. For Boersma, when Protestants interpret justification in forensic terms as an external divine judgment of forgiveness administered to sinners rather than an infusion of superadded spiritual gifts into the human heart, they undermine such participation.[49] Boersma is keen to find references to human participation in God through Christ in Scripture. Presumably, we participate first in various "forms" and beyond those in the transcendentals in which the forms participate, and through the transcendentals we participate in Christ. But Boersma's focus on participation is strongest when he agrees with Paul that it is through the word (Rom. 10:14–15) that we specifically and directly participate in Christ's own death and resurrection (Rom. 6:5–11), and not by means of the forms or universals as such. For Paul, Christ defines sinners, claims them as his own, and, when Christ is "put on" (Gal. 3:27), works through them for service in the world. In spite of these inconsistencies, Boersma has a point when he argues that "participation in heaven changes life on earth: paradoxically, only otherworldliness guarantees proper engagement in this world."[50] The cosmos finds its meaning only in reference to its Creator who has granted it space and time.

For Boersma, following de Lubac, the philosophy most congenial to maintaining the conviction that the earthly participates in the heavenly is Neoplatonism. For instance, the Neoplatonist view of an *exitus-reditus* schema, in which the cosmos "goes out" from God and "returns" to him, is seen as "broadly compatible" with Pauline Christianity.[51] If Christian faith is to have a more robust countervailing rejoinder to secularism, it must retrieve this Neoplatonic approach. It is Neoplatonism that acknowledges a depth and meaning behind the visible world, which modern approaches to knowledge tend to flatline through quantification and analysis, presumably for the sake of a greater harnessing of resources for human flourishing. In the Neoplatonic scheme, all material things participate in a deeper, truer heavenly reality that gives meaning to material things. The material thing "sacramentally" points

---

this present reality. For Paul, it is not as though believers here on earth somehow identify with a faraway place called "heaven." Rather, they have a real or participatory connection with heaven. The central paschal event—Christ's death, resurrection, and ascension—is something Christians participate in: God "made us alive with Christ," Paul insists. (4)

49. Boersma notes, "We do not want merely a nominal relationship; we desire a participatory relationship. In fact, a sacramental ontology maintains that the former is possible only because of the latter: a genuinely covenantal bond is possible only because the covenanting partners are not separate or fragmented individuals" (*Heavenly Participation*, 25).

50. Ibid., 5.

51. Ibid.

beyond itself to a transcendent reality. It is this metaphysic of hidden depth, where all created things are iconic of a deeper spiritual reality, that makes Neoplatonism valuable for a theory of beauty. As icons, all created realities are pointed *upward* by means of developing their full potential at their own level to conform to beauty, truth, and goodness as they are able. Boersma is eager to claim that Christian Neoplatonism brings a much higher regard for matter than non-Christian versions.[52] But even at its best, there seems to be a subtle undermining of the value of created matter. Hence, as Boersma notes about Augustine's view of beauty, "physical beauty . . . is a good created by God, but it is a temporal, carnal good, very low in the scale of goods."[53] Its center of gravity shifts entirely away from the physical to the intellectual and ultimately to the eternal. The question of whether the cosmos could be conceived as participating in God but shorn of eudaimonism—that is, the attempt to prioritize and achieve *self*-fulfillment through exercising one's potential toward perfection, and its attendant hierarchy—needs to be raised. Participating in God non-eudaimonistically is the direction to which Luther leads.

Boersma is convinced that this retrieval of the Platonic roots of patristic theology, which interprets creation as primarily "a sacramental sharing or participating in the life of God,"[54] is the best way to countervail the secular supposition that "the created order carries its own truth, its own goodness, and its own beauty"[55] and modernity's having made the created order into an idol. Here there are strong parallels with the critique of Hamann, who noted that modernity tends paradoxically to make the creation both a "sacrifice" and an "idol."[56] For Hamann, nature is made into a "sacrifice" in that we reduce it to a Cartesian "extended thing" (*res extensa*) for the purpose of mapping, quantifying, and controlling it. Conversely, appalled at our own reduction of nature to a corpse, we then romantically valorize it as a partner with whom we can imaginatively engage, converse—even adore and worship.[57] But, as

52. Boersma itemizes the following as Christian alterations of Platonism. First, "God did not *have* to create but was *free* to create." Second, "Christians had a much higher regard for matter than did the Platonists" ("matter was . . . located at the very bottom of the hierarchy of being"). Finally, "Neo-Platonism functioned on the basis of a principle of absolute oneness." Christians "agreed that Scripture reflects the principle of hierarchy; thus were they ready to ally themselves with Neo-Platonism on that point. But they did not accept that the one implied perfection while the many implied imperfection. The doctrine of the Trinity provided a strong counterbalance to an unhealthy form of divine monarchy. . . . The one and the many both went back to the heart of who God is" (*Heavenly Participation*, 33–35).
53. Ibid., 7.
54. Ibid., 31.
55. Ibid.
56. Hamann, "Aesthetica in nuce," in *Writings on Philosophy and Language*, 78.
57. Bayer, *Contemporary in Dissent*, 82–84.

much as the Platonism that *nouvelle théologie* wants to appropriate seems like the answer to secularism, is it not problematic as a tool for conveying the gospel? Platonism has a built-in hierarchicalism that favors the intellect over the body, form over matter, eternity over time, and the transcendent over the immanent. For Luther, all such polarities should instead be interpreted through the lens of God's alien work and God's proper work.

From the perspective of the gospel, God became human not only so that humans might become divine but also that they might become more human, "perfectly free lords subject to none, and dutiful servants subject to all." It is not that we participate in truth, beauty, and goodness, but that we die and rise with Christ. Only then can we have a clue to the nature of truth, beauty, or goodness. Humans are related to one another not primarily because they share the same Platonic form or universal, but because, as con*form*ed to the crucified, they are to serve one another. It is not clear that Plato can accommodate the death of the old Adam or Eve attendant upon such faith; that would be to acknowledge the law not as something doable but instead as accusatory and killing.

The Question of Hierarchy

We can be grateful for the attempt of de Lubac and his followers to reaffirm wonder and mystery at the heart of all created things. But when entering mystery's hidden depths, we need to ask: Do we enter a securing presence providing tranquility or a threatening abyss in which all is lost? Can we truly know (outside of Christ) whether this mystery is good or beautiful? If nature is sacramental, do we eat and drink it to our damnation or salvation when we enter into it (1 Cor. 11:29–32)?[58] Likewise, must the affirmation of mystery come with a hierarchy, a series of intermediaries between humans and the divine, inviting human ascent to God even though the divine is unattainably beyond humanity? Even if there is some hierarchy, how can we be assured that we could ever climb it? If we made progress, would we have a basis for looking down on others, all the while being looked down on, given that others have made better progress? No doubt God is not only within all things but also above all. In light of the gospel, though, the humanity of Jesus Christ is not merely or only an icon of God (Col. 1:15) but is the embodiment of God (John 1:14). If there is a ladder between God and the cosmos, it is a "down staircase" in which God descends to sinners instead of sinners presuming that

58. See, for instance, the *Catechism of the Catholic Church*, 2nd ed. (Rome: Liberia Editrice Vaticana, 2000), 350 (no. 1457).

they can raise themselves to God.[59] Hence, an approach to hierarchy that feeds self-righteousness is undermined in Christ's incarnation and ministry. The key is to find a way to affirm the mystery at the heart of all things without baptizing a hierarchical approach that implicitly undermines the integrity of the physical, the material, the immanent, the contingent, and the particular.

For the Reformer, the challenge of the hierarchy and the implicit self-righteousness that the old Adam or Eve brings to the table with it go much further than the ancients. Strikingly, Luther undermined hierarchy as a path by which we can reach perfection. He noted that "unless God is in the balance and throws his weight as a counterbalance, we shall sink to the bottom of the scale. . . . If it is not true that God dies for us, but only a man died, we are lost. But if God's death and God dead lie in the opposite scale, then his side goes down and we go upward like a light or empty scale."[60] Luther maintained that the apophatic, transcendent dimension of God thwarts the desire to control by peering into God and to know his workings from the inside out for the purpose of bargaining or negotiating with God. Yet, at the same time, for the Reformer, the man Jesus Christ is the presence of God and no mere pointer to or reflection of God. Christ's humanity is no mere analogue of the divine but an incarnation of the Second Person of the Trinity.

While Boersma's interpretation of the *nouvelle théologie* does not primarily focus on beauty, the concept inescapably surfaces. For instance, he quotes C. S. Lewis: "We want . . . to be united with the beauty we see, to pass into it, to receive it into ourselves, to bathe in it, to become part of it."[61] Although played out in a different way, a study of Luther's view of beauty can affirm with Boersma that "the truth, goodness, and beauty of all created things is grounded in Christ, the eternal Logos of God. In other words, because creation is a sharing in the being of God, our connection with God is a participatory, or real connection—not just an external, or nominal, connection."[62] With Luther we deal with a *verbum reale*, a word that does

59. Gerhard O. Forde, *Where God Meets Man: Luther's Down-to-Earth Approach to the Gospel* (Minneapolis: Augsburg, 1972), 7–31.

60. *On the Councils and the Church* (1539), in LW 41:103 (WA 50:590.11–16).

61. Boersma, *Heavenly Participation*, 25.

62. Ibid., 24. However, referring to Peter Leithart's critique of the *ressourcement* movement, Kevin Vanhoozer counters the charge that grace is "external" to nature:

> [According to Leithart,] the problem is that both neoscholastics and their *nouvelle* detractors appear to chalk up humanity's distance from God to their createdness, not fallenness. On the contrary: the problem is not that God (or the supernatural) is "external" to creation but rather that the whole realm of creation has become alienated from God through sin. Stated differently: the gospel is the good news that men and women can be adopted as children of God, not because human nature has by grace been "elevated," but because human sinners (persons) have by grace been forgiven. (*Biblical Authority*

what it says and says what it does[63] and that places sinners firmly and securely in Christ, since through it we participate in Christ's death and resurrection in the sacrament of baptism. Luther's doctrine of justification is not only forensic but also effective.[64]

But the word is effective, precisely because it is "external" with respect to sinners. That the word comes externally (*verbum externum*) is due to the fact that sinners have nothing of their own to bring to God, certainly not their awareness of truth, goodness, and beauty, which simply condemns them (because they use such matters to bargain with God—with whom no bargaining can suffice). But the major difference between Luther and Neo-platonism is not over participation. Instead, it is over the conviction that we genuinely have something that we can sacrificially offer God. If that were true, then we would have a basis for climbing a ladder to heaven. For the Reformer, the view of God latent in this supposition is wrong, but not because God is sheer, arbitrary will as nominalists maintained.[65] After all, there is nothing arbitrary about God's proper work; it is to seek and save the lost. Instead, that view of God is wrong because when God re-creates, he does so from nothing (*ex nihilo*), just like the way he creates. Hence, all creatures participate directly in God because their existence is moment by moment completely dependent upon God's continuously creative word: "God's nature is to create everything out of nothing. And his most proper nature is to call into being that which is not."[66] The fact that "the creature comes into being from nothing" reinforces the truth that "all things of which the creature is capable are nothing."[67] In this sense, creation is patterned after justification: "God rejoices in making light out of darkness, out of nothing. . . . So

---

after Babel: Retrieving the Solas *in the Spirit of Mere Protestant Christianity* [Grand Rapids: Brazos, 2016], 49)

63. "In the case of God to speak is to do and the word is the deed" (LW 12:33; WA 40/2:231.28).

64. See Mark Mattes, "Luther on Justification as Forensic and Effective," in *The Oxford Handbook to Martin Luther's Theology*, ed. Robert Kolb, Irene Dingel, and L'ubomir Batka (Oxford: Oxford University Press, 2014), 264–73.

65. Of course we must acknowledge that there is an element of "voluntarism" in Luther's approach to the divine will. Hence, in his *Antinomian Disputations* (1537), Luther said, "All men are under the law. The Lord of the law can grant dispense for whom and however he wishes; his will is law. When they, therefore, married several women with the approval of the Holy Spirit, they did not sin, but the law ceased. That sentence did not sound forth from God. Wishing to do so, if he commanded to commit adultery, then it would be law" (Holger Sonntag, ed. and trans., *Solus Decalogus est Aeternus: Martin Luther's Complete Antinomian Theses and Disputations* [Minneapolis: Lutheran Press, 2008], 389).

66. "On Psalm 125:1" (1540) (WA 40/3:154.11; translation from Hans Schwarz, "Creation," in *Dictionary of Luther and the Lutheran Traditions*, ed. Timothy Wengert et al. [Grand Rapids: Baker Academic, 2017], 176).

67. *Lectures on Genesis*, in LW 4:61 (WA 43:178.42–179.1).

he helps the forgotten, justifies the sinners, brings the dead to life, saves the condemned."[68]

No doubt for Luther, as for *analogia entis* theology, there is an apophatic character to God in which God is always greater. But for Luther that indicates that there is no merit that we could offer God—even with the help of Christ. If we could offer something, then Christ would no longer be necessary. God's incomprehensibility thwarts the human presumption to give God anything. God's goodness is such that God is sufficient. Likewise, Neoplatonist Christianity is unable to see how sinners, through God's word of forgiveness, could be totally sinful *coram mundo* and totally just *coram deo* at the same time. Instead, for Neoplatonism, we ever are invited to climb a hierarchical itinerary to grow ever more godlike. It posits an eternal law, but has no place for an eternal gospel.[69] For Luther, the growth in the hierarchy is sidelined by a God who embraces sinners and clothes them with the righteousness of Christ. Having nothing to give God, we are free to give what we have to our neighbors—those in need.

As an apologetic, no doubt the Neoplatonist vision is on to something. It seeks to reclaim wonder and mystery as at the core of all reality, including created reality. Mystery refers to "realities behind the appearances that one could observe by means of the senses. That is to say, though our hands, eyes, ears, nose, and tongue are able to access reality, they cannot fully grasp this reality. They cannot comprehend it."[70] The upshot of this perspective is that "the created world cannot be reduced to measureable, manageable dimensions."[71] Now, the Reformer agrees with the medieval assumption that everything perceived is a manifestation of the divine, but he models a different, non-Platonic approach. Indeed, he counters Neoplatonism, with its tendency to see matter as something to be superseded by intellect or spirit, at work in Karlstadt, Zwingli, and the *Schwärmerei*. Luther has no disenchanted worldview. But his enchanted world is free of the attempt to self-justify through merit by climbing the itinerary of the spiritual ladder. As we saw in the chapter on images, for Luther, in contrast to the Platonism operative in the antimatter stances of either the "fanatics" or the "prophets," the Spirit "cannot be with us except in material and physical things."[72] Hence, "all that our body does outwardly and

68. "On Psalm 125:1" (WA 40/3:154.15; trans. Schwarz, "Creation").
69. The law does have its limits—at least for believers. "Paul speaks about the damning law. When we arrive in heaven, then we will no longer preach the law" (Sonntag, *Solus Decalogus est Aeternus*, 214).
70. Boersma, *Heavenly Participation*, 21.
71. Ibid.
72. *That These Words of Christ, "This Is My Body," etc., Still Stand Firm against the Fanatics* (1527), in LW 37:95 (WA 23:193.31–33). See also Richard Strier, "Martin Luther and the Real Presence in Nature," *JMEMS* 37 (2007): 271–303.

physically, if God's Word is added to it and it is done in faith, is in reality and in name done spiritually. Nothing can be so material, fleshly, or outward that it does not become spiritual when done in the Word and in faith."[73] For Luther, the physical "kernel" is not to be separated from the material "shell."[74] "God is present in all creatures, and I might find Him in stone, in fire, in water, or even in a rope, for He is certainly there, yet He does not wish that I seek Him there, apart from the Word, and cast myself into the water or fire. . . . He is present everywhere, but He does not wish that you grope for Him everywhere. Grope rather where the Word is. There you will lay hold of Him right."[75]

Luther paradoxically describes God's presence everywhere and in every particular thing as God's hiddenness. Sometimes this hiddenness is threatening, but often it is seen as providential. That God works through all earthly things affirms the enchanted outlook that Luther had on the world. "Our parents and all authorities—as well as everyone who is a neighbor—have received the command to do us all kinds of good. So we receive our blessings not from them, but from God through them. Creatures are only the hands, channels, and means through which God bestows all blessings. For example, he gives to the mother breasts and milk for her infant or gives grain and all sorts of fruits from the earth for sustenance—things that no creature could produce by itself."[76] Hence, "all creatures are God's masks and costumes which God wants to work with him to help create all manner of things, yet he can and does also work without them."[77] Likewise, from the perspective of the gospel, nature is not devoid of analogies for God. Luther goes so far as to claim that even the fields and the trees can be sermons better than most preached in churches. In commenting on this, Vítor Westhelle cautions: "But this knowledge is only of an exemplary character. It is only right and proper for us to follow this path once we have been led in the right direction; once we have already been turned around."[78]

Through the gospel, humans are granted new birth; this opens them to receive creation as a gift, and not merely as something to conquer or worship.

73. *That These Words of Christ, "This Is My Body," etc., Still Stand Firm against the Fanatics*, in LW 37:92 (WA 23:188.8–11).
74. *Confession concerning Christ's Supper* (1528), in LW 37:219 (WA 26:333.17).
75. "The Sacrament of the Body and Blood of Christ—Against the Fanatics" (1526), in LW 36:342 (WA 19:492.19–24).
76. The Large Catechism, in BC 389:26–27 (BSELK 938:20–25).
77. "Sermon on Matthew 4:1–11," in *Fastenpostille* (1525) (WA 17/2:192.28–30; translation from Hans Schwarz, *True Faith in the True God: An Introduction to Luther's Life and Thought*, rev. and exp. ed. [Minneapolis: Fortress, 2015], 101).
78. Westhelle, *The Scandalous God: The Use and Abuse of the Cross* (Minneapolis: Fortress, 2006), 52. Luther's claim in the previous sentence is found in WA 42:156.24–26.

Opened to creation, humans can treasure and thank God for it and through it serve their neighbors. As gift, creation is not a stepping-stone to a more godlike experience. Our experience as sinners is mixed: we experience God's hiddenness, in which it is not always clear that the universe is governed by a teleology or is a reflection of beauty. Such divine hiddenness is a challenge to the pancalism (everything is beautiful) embraced by Neoplatonic aesthetics. In contrast, it is only through the gospel that we can unconditionally affirm that the cosmos is beautiful and good. Pancalism cannot be affirmed outside of Christ or outside the lens of the promise. As an aspect of God's gifting, we receive enjoyment and pleasure in this world, all the while without having to secure enjoyment and pleasure. It is not as if God wants to withhold anything good from us. The security with respect to eternal life permits us to affirm the best in what this life has to offer. As new creatures, human desire is resituated: desiring what God desires and not what kind of reward one receives from God. Thus God is loved for his own sake, and likewise our neighbors can be loved for their own sakes instead of being used to secure rewards. Enjoyment is granted in the gospel as concurrent with gratitude; it accords with nature; *using others to gain merit with God fails to accord with nature*. Even so, the question is still raised: Does God desire that we desire him? And yet that question is far too weak; after all, we are commanded to love God! But as is proven over and over such commands cannot deliver, cannot transform those who in their sinful human nature hate God, hold bitterness toward him. Such renewal of the heart happens only through the word that grants and reassures sinners that for Christ's sake they are loved. Only then will love and desire for God arise spontaneously in the heart.

The Question of Pure Nature

The *nouvelle théologie* deplores how well-intentioned sixteenth-century Thomists contributed to the rise of secularism by extricating or isolating the natural from the supernatural. Seeking to affirm the gratuity of grace, scholars such as Juan Francisco Suárez (1548–1617) and Robert Bellarmine (1542–1621) postulated that humans prior to the fall existed in a state of "pure nature" (*natura pura*). Such a state acknowledges that the desire to obtain the beatific vision leading to ultimate human fulfillment is not integral to human nature but instead must be added by grace. In this view, humans are capable of reaching a this-worldly happiness, but only grace can elevate humans to attain eternal happiness. There is nothing that humans can do that can merit this grace. The *nouvelle théologie* claims that the unintended consequence of the theory of pure nature was to secularize nature—to permit it to be understood on its own terms independently of God—because it accorded the natural realm an autonomy or independence from God as nature's final good. For the *nouvelle théologie*, desire for the beatific vision understood as built into human nature is the necessary link that maintains an "enchanted" nature.

Luther's approach is entirely different from these Thomists. For Luther, in the *Lectures on Genesis*, the prelapsarian Adam is *saturated* with and content with God's love. That is, in Eden, grace already and thoroughly permeated nature, righteousness was truly a part of human nature, and there was sheer joy in God's presence.[79] There is nothing autonomous about nature, either before or after the fall, because it is understood not on its own terms independently of God but as the venue for God's enlivening and joy-awakening presence. Adam's final end, indicated by his mathematical abilities (see chap. 5),[80] is not the only or necessary bond between nature and God, since prelapsarian nature is animated by God's presence. Even though the theology of "pure nature" intends a non-Pelagian view of grace, it continues to adhere to a view of human pilgrimage (*viatores*) as defined by a ladder on which humans climb ever closer to God, in contrast to a journey outward through freely serving neighbors based on the truth that one's position with God is already secure through grace.

Likewise, as is well known, Luther made a distinction between "two kingdoms" or spheres, the earthly and the heavenly. While such a distinction designates the earthly as penultimate and the heavenly as ultimate, it is not defined by means of a separation of nature from grace or rendering nature autonomous in any way. As mentioned earlier, God is "masked" or hidden in the earthly sphere, hidden not only in the ominous, threatening sense of an "absconded" God but also in the sense of providentially providing order through governing authorities and generously offering sustenance for all creatures so that their lives can flourish whether or not they are aware of such care. Hence, under the surface in all dealings, one ever deals with God. No doubt, the earthly realm has an integrity as the means by which God works through creatures to tend to the needs and desires of other creatures, but it is the heavenly realm that secures sinners' status before God through the gospel and so provides them deep joy. So these two spheres should not be understood as running parallel, with the earthly sphere granted a measure of autonomy.

79. "Let us rather maintain that righteousness was not a gift which came from without, separate from man's nature, but that it was truly part of his nature, so that it was Adam's nature to love God, to believe God, to know God, etc. These things were just as natural for Adam as it is natural for the eyes to receive light" (LW 1:165; WA 42:124.4–7).

80. *Lectures on Genesis*, in LW 1:46 (WA 42:35–36); 1:126 (WA 42:94.33–37).

Instead, the earthly exists for and is, in a way, subordinate to the heavenly: God created humans precisely in order to redeem them.[81] God graciously provides for and sustains creatures in the earthly realm as a context in which they might hear the gospel, believe it, and so receive God's favor.

Even so, the alleged desire for the supernatural latent or embedded in the natural, advocated by the *nouvelle théologie*, runs roughshod over the fact that sinners' primary mode of dealing with God is conflictive and not contemplative. With Luther's discussion of Adam in the *Lectures on Genesis*, we can affirm that at their origin humans were indeed "ordered" to something greater, eternal life with God, as indicated by humans' mathematical abilities. The problem of course is that this side of the fall, apart from participating in Christ's death and resurrection, one will not receive God as the fullness of joy. That said, earthly goals have a penultimate significance; hopefully they reflect service to our neighbor, whether done from a heart of gratitude or done by coercion of the law.

For Luther, the dissimilarity between the Creator and the creature, between "being" and "beings," outweighs any similarity between the two, apart from Christ, in whom Creator and creature, infinite and finite, are one. With respect to divine ontology, Luther's critics are apt, wrongly, to identify him with the nominalist school, which, following John Duns Scotus, affirmed the "univocity of being." For the univocity theory, being is an objective, neutral category encompassing both God's being and created being and making them identical in kind, although on the scale of being, God is incontestably and supremely greater or more powerful than finite realities. Boersma claims that the doctrine of the "univocity of being" served as one of the blades of modernity's scissors that cut the real, sacramental presence of God in the natural world.[82] This doctrine posited that being is the overarching category that both God and creatures share. Consequently, earthly objects autonomously possess their own being. For Boersma and the *nouvelle théologie*, the loss of analogy is equivalent to the loss of sacramentality in nature.

Defenders of Scotus's theory of univocity have responded with important critiques of the *nouvelle théologie*'s construal of univocity as a perceived neutral third by which to understand God and creatures, the infinite and the finite.[83] But if this theory of univocity is taken seriously, it would seem that

81. The Large Catechism, in BC 439:64 (BSELK 1068:5).
82. Boersma, *Heavenly Participation*, 74.
83. Most recently, Daniel Horan has written that Scotus does not reject analogy as such, but instead convincingly argues from the vantage point of a logician that a univocal concept of some sort is axiomatically necessary to maintain any analogical discourse. "Analogy, Scotus asserts, is simply equivocation without an a priori univocally predicable concept" (*Postmodernity and*

such univocity actually gets rid of God and gives language over to humans plain and simple, or that it produces dialectical theologies that separate nature and revelation. In response, for *nouvelle théologie*, "participation" is supposed to be that middle that allows both nature and supernature to be connected, as the imperfect is to the perfect. But this is quite literally beauty as glory, an aesthetics of perfectibility and not receptivity, attempting an ascent into God. Luther should be interpreted through neither the lens of univocity nor that of analogy. Instead, God sets the conditions for everything that exists, including being. Only through Christ do we have access to God as merciful and loving. Nor can Luther be accused of contributing to a "nominalist fragmentation of created order,"[84] which regards sensible objects as separate from and in competition with one another and separate from their transcendent origin. For Luther, creatures are properly related to God through faith, which permits God to be God for them, and they are properly related to each other *when they serve* (thus, when they are not in constant antagonism with each other), such as the mother feeding her baby, as we noted.

Is it true, as the *nouvelle théologie* contends, that secularization is a result of the loss of final causality? As mentioned above, for Luther, mathematics indicates that humans are designed for ultimate fulfillment in God. Likewise, the cosmos is enchanted, but it is not clear that the mystery behind all created things outside of Christ is transparently benevolent. Only through Christ is that made certain. Even so, we should not assume that Plato's teleology is the key to a nonsecular world. How else would we conceive of Platonism prior to the rise of the Christian faith, if not as "secular," independent of the biblical God, or at least pagan, an unbaptized approach to eternity?

No doubt, Platonic perspectives helped many early Christians sort through many aspects of the doctrines of Christ and the Trinity. But Christians should not take their stand on the value of Plato's philosophy. The current North American religious milieu has been described as "gnostic," more than anything honoring a "sacred self" or core within each individual.[85] Truth be told, many contemporary gnostics are fairly Platonic-like, valuing the nebulous, intangible, and everlasting "self" in place of the ancient category of "soul," but obviously are not Christian. It would seem that the heart of the question of secularity is the fact that Platonism can be packaged in nonbiblical formats. So secularity is best understood not as the dismantling of the Platonic

---

Univocity: A Critical Account of Radical Orthodoxy and John Duns Scotus [Minneapolis: Fortress, 2014], 185).

84. Boersma, Nouvelle Théologie *and Sacramental Ontology*, 16.

85. Harold Bloom, *The American Religion: The Emergence of the Post-Christian Nation* (New York: Touchstone, 1992).

infrastructure of Western thought (since, as Alfred North Whitehead put it, it is a series of footnotes on Plato), but as the dismantling of a biblical worldview. Modern philosophers and literati have offered unrelenting critiques of a biblical worldview so that the "self" may be unencumbered by "tradition," "authority," and ultimately God. Such matters should not intervene in its quest for greater self-discovery and self-awareness however it achieves those ends, provided no harm is done to others.

Surely all secular views hold little or no regard for worldviews shaped by the Bible. Even more than foreclosing on Plato, undermining or eliminating a biblical worldview—as happened in the thinking of Thomas Hobbes (1588–1679) and Baruch Spinoza (1632–77)—guarantees a secular outlook. Hence, not primarily Plato (even though his work has significantly influenced Christian theology), but the Bible, with the various ways of experiencing the world that it discloses, is the alternative to secularism. Christianity is not, as Friedrich Nietzsche (1844–1900) put it, Platonism for the people,[86] but, if properly understood, Christ for the masses. Thus the Scriptures are not a heteronomous or oppressive external authority; within its pages, written over several thousand years, human experience is given voice through lament and wisdom, threat and promise, poetry and prose testifying to humanity's relation to God.

Conclusion

Luther's view of beauty is tied to freedom because it is tied to the gospel. The gospel sets the conscience free; but in so doing it opens humans to receiving nature as creation, as gift, and as this gift is given through the senses. The ladder between humanity and God is not one that beauty tempts us to raise toward perfection. Instead, it is a downward staircase in which God overthrows the self-righteousness, ingratitude, and insensitivity by which sinners close themselves off from the wealth of good things God crafts into the creation. The creation is composed of creatures who are channels through which God cares for other creatures abundantly and graciously, indeed beautifully. Hence—in spite of the fact that creation is marred by sin—proportion, clarity, and integrity still apply as criteria by which to discern beauty in creation, although they do not apply to the strange beauty of Christ or the beauty of the new creation that clothes believers in the righteousness of faith. Analogy often says too little to describe God's works; that creatures are channels of

86. Nietzsche, *Basic Writings*, trans. Walter Kaufmann (New York: Modern Library, 2000), 193.

his providential care is no mere analogical relation but a means of God's love. Through beauty—given most clearly in Jesus's death and resurrection, which confirms encounters with beauty in creation and human creativity—God assures his creatures that they are at home in this world. All things mask God, but not all things are beautiful. Through Jesus Christ believers can have confidence that ultimately we will see that reality is truth, goodness, and beauty in its fullness, and that we will be brought to our fulfillment; but presently that is a conviction of faith, which eschatologically will be given over to sight.

» 9 «

Luther for a Contemporary Theology of Beauty

It is a commonplace to assert that Protestant theology offers little for a theory of beauty or theological aesthetics because it gives prominence to the word and not the image. Likewise, Luther's retrieval of the Pauline understanding of baptismal participation in Christ as dying and rising with Christ—discontinuity and not continuity with respect to human life—violates or undermines desire as the agent that moves the beholder on a journey toward union with Beauty as such. Unfortunately, there are indeed some Protestant perspectives that feed this misperception of Protestant thinking as a wasteland when it comes to the question of beauty.

That sentiment, for instance, is echoed with a vengeance in the theology of Rudolf Bultmann:

> The idea of the beautiful is of no significance in forming the life of Christian faith, which sees in the beautiful the temptation of a false transfiguration of the world which distracts the gaze from "beyond." . . . If the beautiful is an image in which, in a certain sense, the puzzling, confused motion of life is brought to a halt and is made surveyable for the eye set at a distance from it, thus disclosing the deeper meaning for him (i.e., for man), then it is true for the Christian faith that it is not art that discloses the depths of reality, and that this is not grasped in a distanced act of seeing, but rather that this is grasped in *suffering*. The reply to the question posed in the human lot can never be objectified in a work of art but is always to be found in the enduring of suffering itself.

> The beautiful . . . is therefore, as far as the Christian faith is concerned, always
> something that lies beyond this life.[1]

Bultmann misreads beauty as a means by which sinners seek to circumvent the cross, to avoid the suffering that leads to their own demise, and so they adorn the cross with roses. Obviously, any theologian influenced by Luther will recognize that God's alien work of crushing self-satisfied and self-securing sinners is inexorable and unavoidable. No doubt Bultmann has a sense for the truth that sinners united with Christ through baptism die with Christ. Some sinners may wish to forestall such death, defend themselves from death, by clinging to beauty—whether in nature, art, or a beloved. True, it can be a sinner's avoidance tactic used to maintain self-continuity. But the problem lies in the sinner, not in beauty. Beauty is of God's making. It is nothing to be trivialized or sneered at. Bultmann should be asked: What of human rising with Christ, the flip side of dying with Christ? How might those, shorn of their defenses built up to shield them from death, experience the world anew after having undergone dying with Christ? Would they experience the world differently? It is not uncommon for those who have experienced encounters with death to find themselves renewed in their appreciation of life, daily, unguardedly, savoring life's experiences as they would a rich dessert. How much greater appreciation could be expected from those who have plunged into death itself in the waters of baptism (Rom. 6)? Not having to (mis)use things in the world to secure their identity in the face of death, might they see those very same things in a new and different light: perhaps as gifts or matters inviting stewardship or innocent delight in beauty? In fact, might they experience such beauty as sheer gift and give glory to God for it?

Given what Bultmann wrote, it makes sense to ask whether the beauty one encounters both in the arts and in nature is nothing other than deceit or illusion. For surely people, whether of faith or not, value beauty. No doubt such beauty finally condemns those who fail to give God glory for it. But where Bultmann is wrong, more than anywhere, is in his failure to acknowledge that the gospel is beautiful. "How beautiful upon the mountains / are the feet of him who brings good news, / who publishes peace, who brings good news of happiness" (Isa. 52:7). Evangelists' feet are beautiful precisely because they bring gospel beauty. Of what does that beauty consist? Simply the good news of freedom. It is God's embrace of sinners: the God who "exalted them of low degree" (Luke 1:52 KJV). As Miikka Anttila puts it,

---

1. Bultmann, *Glauben und Verstehen: Gesammelte Aufsätze* (Tübingen: J. C. B. Mohr, 1975), 2:137, cited in David Bentley Hart, *The Beauty of the Infinite* (Grand Rapids: Eerdmans, 2003), 23.

In the cross of Christ there is supreme beauty concealed beneath the most abominable ugliness. Yet there is no ugliness in God. The ugliness of the cross belongs to us, whereas the beauty is God's. God is most beautiful not only when compared to us. He proves to be most beautiful when he makes us beautiful, that is, gives his beauty to us. This is an aesthetic variation on the doctrine of justification.[2]

Crushed by the law, sinners cannot get enough of this good news! It allures and comforts those to whom it ministers. If the gospel is indeed the "power of God for salvation" (Rom. 1:16), does not that power (*dynamis*) include an element of beauty? Do we not see it operative in Jesus's granting mercy and liberating those in need? Anttila is far truer to Luther than Bultmann is: "The greatest gifts of God are so obvious that we often forget to give thanks for them. What would happen if the light of the sun would fail us for a moment? Faith opens the human mind to see and appreciate the goodness of God in everything. Thus, faith is a *deeply aesthetic* way to look at the world."[3]

Bultmann is right to note that receiving the gospel is not without pain, a dying to self and a rising with Christ. But that is just the point: there is resurrection life. The flip side of the theology of the cross is a theology of resurrection.[4] But if so, what might the contours of resurrection life be like? No doubt many Christians who find their lives sung, if you will, *in a minor key*, beset with sin or hurt or pain, will resonate with Luther's theology of the cross and find it descriptive of their own life experiences. But talk of "contours" might trigger a reaction in some who are attuned to the proper distinction between law and gospel: Is the question about the contours of the new life in Christ simply a retreat to order, more law? Is it not incompatible with freedom, tantamount to some kind of standard to which we must live up? But these questions fail to take into account that God is making a

2. Anttila, "Music," in *Engaging Luther: A (New) Theological Assessment*, ed. Olli-Pekka Vainio (Eugene, OR: Cascade, 2010), 218.

3. Ibid., 219 (italics added).

4. As James Nestingen once put it in a seminar lecture on the theology of the cross (Luther Seminary, spring 1984). But we should be cautious of Karl Barth, who claimed, "There is no preaching of the cross or faith in the cross *in abstracto*. For that reason there are serious objections to all representations of the crucified Christ as such. There is no going back behind Easter morning. To the extent that they may contain or express such a going back, all theologies or pieties or exercises or aesthetics which center on the cross—however grimly in earnest they may be—must be repudiated at once" (*Church Dogmatics* 4/1, trans. Geoffrey Bromiley [Edinburgh: T&T Clark, 1956], 344). It is not as if the Resurrected One does not carry his wounds. In baptism, which conveys an ongoing daily dying and rising, sinners are conformed more and more to Christ's death and resurrection. Barth's fundamental error is that he acknowledges but one word of God and not two, law and gospel.

new creation and that new creation does in fact have an impact on life and the world. Luther says that new life is nothing less than a "form of God."[5] Following Philippians 2, Luther spells out what this means in life: "Although the Christian is thus free from all works, he ought in this liberty to empty himself, take upon himself the form of a servant, be made in the likeness of men, be found in human form, and to serve, help, and in every way deal with his neighbor as he sees that God through Christ has dealt and still deals with him. This he should do freely, having regard for nothing but divine approval."[6] There is an analogy between the incarnational Christ and the incarnational Christian. The inner logic is that of abundance. Because God is so generous to people, Christians can afford likewise to be generous. Though sinners are unworthy, God gives them "all the riches of righteousness and salvation without any merit . . . out of pure, free mercy."[7]

Christians receive their identity from Christ, not from the world, not from the law, not from the accuser. But that identity reorients and resituates them, makes them to live like Christ. It shapes their whole disposition: "Behold, from faith thus flow forth love and joy in the Lord, and from love a joyful, willing, and free mind that serves one's neighbor willingly and takes no account of gratitude or ingratitude, of praise or blame, of gain or loss."[8] But the gospel not only makes one to be Christ to the neighbor, it also opens one to the world as gift—as creation. It entails a "conversion to the world, a turning toward the creature."[9] In Luther's words, "the more intimately one knows God, the more one understands the creatures and is attached to them."[10] The gospel opens believers with the word *Ephphatha* ("Be open"; Mark 7:34), which enlivens their senses to God's goodness within creation so that, with human defenses now dead in Christ, they need not define Christian life.[11] Unguardedly, people of faith experience the world with new eyes and open ears. We do experience its wonder and mystery even prior to the "beyond" of this life. That the senses are opened is a result of the fact that incurvation no longer defines the new being in Christ. It is not a standard of regeneration, something that we on our own could achieve, but instead is the effect on the senses of a heart finding its safety and security in God's word. Such new life does not

5. *The Freedom of a Christian* (1520), in LW 31:366 (WA 7:65.27).

6. *The Freedom of a Christian*, in LW 31:366 (WA 7:65.32–36).

7. *The Freedom of a Christian*, in LW 31:367 (WA 7:65.37–38).

8. *The Freedom of a Christian*, in LW 31:367 (WA 7:66.7–9).

9. Oswald Bayer, *Martin Luther's Theology: A Contemporary Interpretation* (Grand Rapids: Eerdmans, 2008), 107.

10. *Lectures on Genesis*, in LW 4:195 (WA 43:276.18–20).

11. Bayer, *Martin Luther's Theology*, 108. Bayer's interpretation is based on "Predigt am Sonntag nach Trinitas" (September 8, 1538), a Luther sermon found in WA 46:494.15–495.21.

supplant the fact that, for many, life is often lived in a minor key. But it does help them appreciate the beauty of that minor key since it is the Spirit, that triune person of eschatological hope and power, who helps them pray in their "weakness . . . with groanings too deep for words" (Rom. 8:26).

In our current world marred by ecological challenges and inequities between rich and poor, the powerful and the power-deprived, and skepticism about wonder and mystery, Luther's views on beauty can speak. This final chapter will draw out Luther's view of beauty in order to show its vitality for theology and ministry today. We will summarize the results of our research into Luther's theological aesthetics and show how it bears on some modern aesthetic concerns, such as the Romantic view of beauty as salvific, how beauty relates to the sublime (often seen as a threat to beauty), the recurring question of beauty as form, and the impact of beauty on preaching.

Summary of Results

It will be valuable first of all to summarize the results of our research so far. Luther's work falls short of a grand, unified theory of beauty. However, as we have seen, the topic of beauty appears at important junctures in his assessment of the impact of justification by grace alone through faith alone on doctrine and spirituality. Although beauty as such is not a primary locus of his work, it bears on his work throughout because he countered an important aspect of medieval spirituality. Medieval spirituality looked to the human disposition of desiring what is attractive as a basis for understanding human salvation. Because Luther evaluates theology through the lens of law and gospel and draws out the ramifications of that doctrine for all of his thinking, medieval views of beauty are reworked in his theology. God loves the base, ignoble, and unattractive, resituating their hearts to trust God's promise, reestablishing desire as treasuring God for God's own sake and longing for the well-being of the other. We can summarize our conclusions from the work of the previous chapters thusly:

- The theology of the cross, unlike that of glory, recognizes that God reaches out to sinners through unattractive means, such as the crucified Jesus Christ and the mortification resulting from the accusing law, which thwarts sinners' presumption that fulfilling their desires will ultimately unite them with God.
- On the basis of the theology of the cross we can distinguish a theological aesthetics of perfectibility from a theological aesthetics of freedom. The

aesthetics of perfectibility looks to fulfilling the law as a way to achieve the desire of ultimate union with God in the beatific vision, while the aesthetics of freedom receives God's favor given to sinners, which unites them with Christ as a bride is united to her groom. It appreciates this world as a locus of God's goodness and refuses to disparage it as secondary or inconsequential to the heavenly. It acknowledges that "in the future life" God will bring his creatures to their fulfillment.

- Christ as promise is inherently attractive and thus draws sinners to himself; through Christ, God is seen for the beauty that God is. "The ugliness of the cross belongs to us, whereas the beauty is God's."[12]

- God's promise opens sinners to live outside themselves and in God, others, and creation as Christs and so to treasure the beauty that is about them.

- All of life, including the crosses one bears, melodies played or sung in minor keys, is made holy or beautiful in that through such crosses God is constantly shaping believers, as a potter shapes a pot, into what God finds most pleasing: people of faith.

- Human desire—even at its most elevated—is resituated; human life is no longer primarily about self-fulfillment. But even so, the promise does in fact fulfill the human longing to be one with God. This is not a union that obliterates believers' identities, but one that assures them not only that God is for them but also that Christ is present in them. Heaven is granted to earthly creatures, and so creation as creaturely is restored.

- Finite things can convey God's infinite grace. Beauty is analogous to grace; it is profligate. One will sell all one has in order to buy the field in which the treasure is buried (Matt. 13:44).

- Indwelt by Christ, Christians share in God's beauty by grace.

- Idolatry is properly in the heart and not the eyes (or ears). While the ear is the proper organ of faith, Christians who trust in God can count on the fact that the eyes of faith will eventually behold God face-to-face in eternal life.

- In addition to gospel beauty in which sinners are clothed in Christ, there is also a creation beauty fashioned into the cosmos and characterized by proportion, clarity, and integrity. Though deformed through sin, this beauty can be seen and enjoyed by those granted new life through grace.

- The analogy of being says too little; in the Large Catechism, the mother is not merely analogous to God's parental care but instead is the very

12. Anttila, "Music," 218.

means whereby God provides milk for infants. Beauty is given, as is goodness, by means of created, finite things: "Even the grain would talk to us: 'Be joyful in God, eat, drink, use me and serve your neighbor with me.'"[13]

- Beauty does not begin in the context of a theology of glory since the glory perspective feeds an egoism that makes it impossible to appreciate beauty fully. Instead, it is opened by a theology of the cross that provides not only comfort but also fulfillment as a gift to those who die to their status as *viatores* (pilgrims). Theologians of the cross can appreciate beauty because they receive it as a gift; and this gift transforms them from the outside in, renews them, and leads them both to gratitude and service. The pilgrimage of theologians of the cross is that of service.

- Music is an innocent pleasure available for human enjoyment; Christ is the *cantus firmus* or definable, recognizable melody that identifies and empowers Christian people.

- Images are not necessary for worship but are valuable as teaching aids and tangible indicators of God's incarnate grace.

Clearly those who are seeking a well-refined theory of theological aesthetics in Luther will be disappointed. The Reformer's work in aesthetics tends to be an offshoot of his primary work in Christian doctrine. But the fact that Luther falls short of offering a comprehensive aesthetic upheld by a single principle or series of principles applicable for all times and places actually rings true with David Bentley Hart's contention that the word "beauty"

> *indicates* nothing: neither exactly a quality, nor a property, nor a function, not even really a subjective reaction to an object or occurrence, it offers no phenomenological purchase upon aesthetic experience. And yet nothing else impresses itself upon our attention with at once so wonderful a power and so evocative an immediacy. Beauty is there, abroad in the order of things, given again and again in a way that defies description and denial with equal impertinence.[14]

In spite of its lack of comprehensiveness, there are sufficient family resemblances among the threads of Luther's thought about beauty from which we can feel and see its texture.

13. Bayer, *Martin Luther's Theology*, 109. The reference is to Luther's sermon on *ephphatha* in WA 46:494.15–17.
14. Hart, *Beauty of the Infinite*, 16.

Beauty of Christ, Revisited

In our quest for a contemporary view of beauty informed by Luther, we can expand on the conclusions above by outlining how Christ is beautiful, how humans are beautiful, and how God is beautiful. First, to elaborate on the beauty of Christ, it is fascinating to realize that some medieval people believed that they had in their possession a supposed eyewitness report of Christ's physical traits, based on a "translation into Latin in the thirteenth or fourteenth century of a Greek manuscript" that contained "a description of Christ's features supposedly given in a letter by a governor of Judea before the time of Pontius Pilate."[15] It reads:

> A man of average or moderate height, and very distinguished. He has an impressive appearance, so that those who look on him love and fear him. His hair is the color of a ripe hazel-nut. It falls straight almost to the level of his ears; from there down it curls thickly and is rather more luxuriant, and this hangs down to his shoulders. In front his hair is parted into two, with the parting in the center in the Nazarene manner. His forehead is wide, smooth and serene, and his face is without wrinkles or any marks. It is graced by a slightly reddish tinge, a faint color. His nose and mouth are faultless. His beard is thick and like a young man's first beard, of the same color as his hair; it is not particularly long and is parted in the middle. His aspect is simple and mature. His eyes are brilliant, mobile, clear, splendid. He is terrible when he reprehends, quiet and kindly when he admonishes. He is quick in his movements but always keeps his dignity. No one ever saw him laugh, but he has been seen to weep. He is broad in the chest and upstanding; his hands and arms are fine. In speech he is serious, sparing and modest. He is the most beautiful among the children of men.[16]

It is not necessary to see how this description would favorably compare with the criteria of proportion, color, and integrity outlined by Aquinas. The image is crafted in the light of those criteria to reinforce a view of Jesus as someone who would draw us into his life, lead us to want to grow more like him, reinforce those habits by which we could be transformed so as to become more like him, and ultimately find that grace perfects nature as it seeks to perfect itself—the beauty of perfection that we have been critiquing.

But for Luther the piety latent in the description above (ironically not so very different from the lyrics of "praise songs" heard from contemporary

15. Richard Viladesau, *The Beauty of the Cross: The Passion of Christ in Theology and the Arts, from the Catacombs to the Eve of the Renaissance* (Oxford: Oxford University Press, 2008), 57.
16. Ibid., 57–58.

Christian rock bands or solo "artists") is exactly what Luther found problematic and led him to label it as "theology of glory." No doubt the old Adam and Eve are convinced that they would discern the beauty of Christ and be led in devotion to follow him with all their hearts. And they would likewise be desirous of the heavenly reward that should accompany such devotion. But it is not Christ's handsomeness to which Luther looks. Instead, what is unavoidable (since the Gospels tend to be "passion narratives with lengthy introductions")[17] is Jesus deformed by human rejection, beating, and scorn. God (whom through faith we acknowledge as beauty) comes in Christ, but only as "under the sign of the opposite," as one "despised and rejected by men, / a man of sorrows and acquainted with grief" (Isa. 53:3). There is nothing dainty, pretty, or petite about the beauty of Christ. This is due to the fact that love "bears all things, believes all things, hopes all things, endures all things" (1 Cor. 13:7), including human violence toward the neighbor and rebellion against the Creator. Such a beauty is resilient, enduring, and even triumphant in the face of everything that would challenge or seek to derail it.

So it is not the continuity between human desire and God that humans can claim for themselves but instead the guilt and shame of their sin that they must admit, at least before the cross. The cross indeed shatters human conceptions of beauty. It is nothing less than an "attack" on beauty, as Steven Paulson puts it.[18] But, conversely, the accusing law is also an attack on postmodern attacks on beauty since many postmodern thinkers are especially conceited in their claim to unmask beauty as an illusion and goodness as power. Postmodern theorists tend to replace "beauty" with "shock" in an attempt to dismantle ideologies that keep unjustified power in place.[19] As noble, compelling, and worthy as that goal is, postmodern art tends to be moralistic with a vengeance. In contrast, even unlettered rural villagers in the Majority World understand the importance of decorative craftsmanship, folk music, and dance since those matters can hearten, empower, enliven, and unite those in dire economic straits and whose dignity would otherwise be eclipsed. But postmodern and contemporary art should not be reduced to moralism. In its willingness to engage in fragility, absurdity, abstraction, dissonance, and impersonality, as well as in its forays not only into kitsch but also into tenderness and compassion, postmodern art can be read through a Lutheran lens as an encounter with God in hiddenness (*deus absconditus*) for both

17. Martin Kähler, *The So-Called Historical Jesus and the Historic, Biblical Christ*, trans. Carl Braaten (Philadelphia: Fortress, 1964), 80, referring particularly to the Gospel of Mark.

18. Paulson, *Lutheran Theology* (London: T&T Clark, 2011), 1.

19. Gene Edward Veith, *State of the Arts: From Bezalel to Mapplethorpe* (Wheaton: Crossway, 1991), 20–21.

artists and patrons, a meeting that destabilizes and causes them to be aware of their vulnerability, pain, and capacity either to receive or to participate in injustice. Not only does postmodern representation of human finitude and vulnerability indicate a hidden God, it also presents the fragility and sinful marring of the natural and social realms into which the Son of God became incarnate. Insofar as contemporary art displays warmth and tenderness, it can testify to God's mercy granted through physical means, whether or not the artist or the patron is aware of it.[20]

Most specifically, in Luther's context, the cross shatters the criteria of proportion, clarity, and integrity with which presumptuous sinners would wish to whitewash Jesus. But Christ Jesus is genuinely beautiful in that his work is "for us and for our salvation." He bears human sin and death, God's wrath and the devil's ridicule, and brings them to naught so that there may no longer be "condemnation for those who are in Christ Jesus" (Rom. 8:1). God is a liberating God, and such liberation is beautiful. Sinners cannot get enough of it; they revel in it and dance for joy in it. It is the beauty of the waiting father (Luke 15), of Jesus protecting the adulteress (John 8), of the dry bones coming to life (Ezek. 37), or of Miriam's victory dance after liberation from military threat (Exod. 15), which evokes not only gratitude to God but also hunger for more of the promise. Thankfully, the Reformer responds, "Daily in this Christian church the Holy Spirit abundantly forgives all sins—mine and those of all believers."[21]

Creaturely Beauty, Revisited

Creaturely beauty *coram deo* is not via participation in eternal forms but instead in the life, death, and resurrection of Jesus Christ. Here we can affirm with Jeremy Begbie that "creation's beauty is not . . . something that lives in a land beyond the sensual or behind the material particularity or beneath the surface, or wherever—to which we must travel. Creation's beauty is just that, the beauty of creation."[22] Obviously this is not written to discredit wonder and mystery at the core of all things, an enchanted cosmos. Instead, it is to iterate that God is not to be found in a realm that transcends this created

20. This discussion about the value of contemporary art has benefited from email correspondence with Daniel A. Siedell (October 1, 2016). For a Lutheran theologian who provides a theological interpretation of postmodern art, see Klaus Schwarzwäller, *Cross and Resurrection: God's Wonder and Mystery*, trans. Ken Jones and Mark Mattes (Minneapolis: Fortress, 2012).
21. The Small Catechism, in BC 356 (BSELK 872:20).
22. As quoted in William A. Dyrness, *Poetic Theology: God and the Poetics of Everyday Life* (Grand Rapids: Eerdmans, 2011), 22.

order. Indeed, God is accessible—albeit *hidden*—in this order of things. Creation as made by God is indeed beautiful. The traditional medieval criteria for beauty—integrity (perfection), proportion, and clarity or light—say too little because God's creation exceeds these standards. But the standards are given a modicum of validity because they become the very means by which we can tell that God's works exceed them. It is because created things have *form* as fashioned by God that thoughtful people can disagree about the degree or depth of their beauty or lack thereof. More importantly, we can infer that the new creation that God has begun in Jesus Christ will be even more beautiful than the original. Due to sin, the powers and virtues of creatures have diminished. Hence, when we see their grandeur even in this world, how much more was their power in the prelapsarian Eden, and how much more will it be in the new creation toward which God is working?

There is nothing beautiful about the law as accusing or God's hiddenness as terrifying. While one undergoes it, God's alien work is never beautiful. But ex post facto, believers can affirm that all those matters that have wrested power or control from their hands, have hounded or terrorized their consciences, and finally have brought them to Christ are those very instruments or tools through which God brings us to faith (Rom. 8:28). By such means, God crafts us as creatures whose hearts are centered in God, and in the long run, God opens our senses to delight in the wonder that he has built into the fabric of the cosmos. Few have described this "downward ascent" better than the late Edna Hong:

> The finger of the Holy Spirit has traced the call to be perfect, to be saints, to newness in Christ, on every page of the New Testament. It is written in blood on the cross. There is no evading that call! But thanks be to God, the communion of saints is not based on human perfectibility but assumes its imperfection and imperfectability. Our God has chosen to become involved in the divine failure—humanity. Our Savior chose to share with us the pain, punishments, and penalties of being imperfect humans. And God's Secret Agent of Reform chooses to help us imperfect creatures respond to the terrible call to be new creatures in Christ. For it *is* a terrible call, and it is a long, long painful journey. For there is so much to tear down before the Holy Spirit can build up. There are so many fake props to knock down. And the end of the painful road is not perfection, but perfect humility. Not morbidity and self-loathing, but a humble and contrite heart.[23]

But such humility and contrition in God's eyes is not only good but also beautiful; it is where humans become receptive to God's one-sided generosity

---

23. Hong, *The Downward Ascent* (Minneapolis: Augsburg, 1979), 50–51.

and mercy. It is at the core of the new creation, men and women who walk by faith, completely trusting in God's promise given in Jesus Christ, whose hearts thus accord with the creatureliness that is their nature. Such men and women discover that head and heart, intellect and affect, responsibilities and contingencies are integrated into the narrative of their earthly pilgrimage. Unlike Plato, they do not favor the "divine" aspect of humanity over the human but allow each to have its place.

Even so, believers know that their lives are "hidden with Christ in God" (Col. 3:3) and that they have no empirical criteria by which to measure their progress in grace and so have self-righteousness again reinforced. Luther was convinced that there is a kind of progress in the Christian life ("To advance is always a matter of beginning anew").[24] It is not primarily that we get more of God but, shall we say, that God gets more of us. In trusting Christ, we discover more and more on a daily basis just how much we need Christ and his forgiveness and love. Hence, whatever progress or growth in love that is accomplished in this life remains a matter of faith and not empirical observation (as if praying longer each day translated into greater holiness). Faith remains a matter of the heart. Indeed, faith is beautiful precisely because it gives all glory to God for life, health, and salvation. In such an admission, nothing is lost for the human since the truth of humanity is that it is totally dependent on God. Humans accord most with reality precisely when they acknowledge that and express gratitude to God that it is God who through his creative word in love and mercy sustains them moment to moment out of nothingness.

How this all bears out on the arts should be looked at. It is often claimed that the Reformation led to a "secularization" of art.[25] But, as noted, disenchantment with nature is not due to Luther's theology but is a result of early modernity's attempt to free itself from the shackles of a biblical worldview because it was perceived as heteronomous, a threat to human freedom as self-definition. But Luther's theology does not sustain secularism even by those standards, which favor a Platonic-like stance as a criterion for nonsecularity. For instance, Angus Menuge notes that Lucas Cranach the Elder (1472–1553), Luther's friend and mayor of Wittenberg, painted his subjects so as to "appear as emblems, illustrations, or emanations of a deeper and higher reality that transcends them all."[26] Hence, his work—following Luther's—honors worldly enchantment. But by the same token, Cranach affirms God's work

24. *Lectures on Romans*, in LW 25:478 (WA 56:486.7).
25. Veith, *State of the Arts*, 59.
26. Menuge, "The Cultural and Aesthetic Impact of Lutheranism," in *Where Christ Is Present: A Theology for All Seasons on the 500th Anniversary of the Reformation*, ed. John Warwick Montgomery and Gene Edward Veith (Corona, CA: NRP Books, 2015), 215.

in ordinary matters, "through creatures to creatures," as for example when mothers feed their infants—an affirmation of everyday life, especially familial life. Menuge further notes:

> It builds up the family as the primary building block for both church and society, ennobles the vocations of ordinary life, and supports the church by revealing our need for the Gospel. Here one finds neither the triumphalism nor the nihilism of modern art, where artists lurch between narcissistic self-preoccupation and cynical debasement and transgression of all boundaries. The idea that honest self-expression is necessarily "authentic" and valuable is rejected, because it may only reflect our sinful self-deception: the blind leading the blind. Like Blaise Pascal (1623–62), the Lutheran artist reveals man as both much more wretched and yet much greater than modern and postmodern minds can comprehend.[27]

God as Beautiful, Revisited

That God is beautiful will be disclosed in its fullness only in the eschaton. Presently humans encounter God first in his alien work of uprooting proud and self-secure sinners, so that they might then receive his proper work of comforting and consoling them, remaking them to be men and women of faith. This is the reason that sinners delight so much in God's proper work, administering the promise. In the consummation of all things, God's alien work—at least for believers—will no longer be necessary, and believers will freely enjoy and revel in God's beauty and love, no different from how prelapsarian Adam was "drunk" in God, and so lived outside of himself, in God and in his neighbor, a gardener for this beautiful garden, this good earth.

The eschatological beauty of God is fully expressed in the doctrine of the Trinity seen in Luther's hymn "Dear Christians, One and All."[28] God gives his dearest, most beautiful *treasure*, "his beloved Son," to ransom humankind through the shedding of his "precious blood," suffering for sinners' "good."

> God said to his beloved Son:
> "'Tis time to have compassion.
> Then go, bright jewel of my crown,
> And bring to all salvation;
> From sin and sorrow set them free;
> Slay bitter death for them that they
> May live with you forever."

27. Ibid., 219.
28. LBW, no. 299.

Here beauty is affirmed when the Son is described as a "bright jewel." And this redemptive work involves the whole Trinity. It is initiated by the Father, accomplished by the Son, and administered by the Spirit, who is given to believers in order to comfort and grant them wisdom:

> "Now to my Father I depart,
> From earth to heav'n sending,
> And, heavenly wisdom to impart,
> The Holy Spirit sending;
> In trouble he will comfort you
> And teach you always to be true
> And into truth shall guide you."

As beauty as such, all three persons of the Trinity work in tandem to bring God's beauty, along with his goodness, to the world.

Luther in Contrast to Modern Views of Beauty

Like new creatures, the old Adam and Eve are, surprisingly, people of faith. The difference is that they put their faith in some idol, an image of themselves, while new creatures trust instead in God. Similarly, the old Adam and Eve are people of desire, but ultimately what they desire is their own security, their own continuity, and their own perfection. Such desire, like idolatry, must be "extinguished" or put to death. Again, the new creation resituates desire in God and satiates longing in that it fills people with God's goodness through the promise. Modern perspectives on desire, no less than medieval perspectives, pressure humans toward perfection as the way that humans can achieve fulfillment. Even though the modern world brackets Luther's category of *coram deo* and seeks to situate the human in a purely secular, nonreligious space, it is a world no less grounded in law than the medieval world. For ancient and medieval people, desire sparked interest in and movement toward the eternal. Art in the modern world points to a beauty that is perceived as no less salvific for individuals. Appealing to Charles Taylor's interpretation of a secular salvation that developed in the Romantic period and maintained that individuals' true identity can be found in or expressed through their self-creativity, John Milbank notes that

> the basis of this [self-creativity as salvific] . . . lies in the affirmation of everyday life that comes from the Reformation, and that did so much to encourage the exploration of the world and, even in Romanticism, the expansion of creative

options. For various cultural and historical reasons, the religious background was no longer assumed, but a substantive ethical notion survived: the idea that something outside oneself can be found and captured in art which can bring fulfillment to persons—can move them beyond simple human flourishing. Notice the new and enlarged place this gives to art and aesthetic practices. These writers believed that "Beauty is what will save us, complete us." It is not hard to see the connection between Romanticism's exploration of personal creativity and the aesthetic turn that we have been tracing. In terms of our argument, the Romantics recognized that practices and objects could draw the human person out of themselves toward a higher and fuller life.[29]

While Milbank, following Taylor, sees this trend as an unintended consequence of the Reformation's valuation of daily and family life, it is hard to see it as faithful to the Reformation. Instead, it is a detachment from, distancing from, or even rebellion against the Reformation. The Reformation honored the secular sphere not as secular in the sense of a religiously vacant, neutral, or "naked" public realm but instead as another locus—other than the gospel—of God's providential agency. The tendencies outlined above can be unmasked as an aesthetics of perfectibility, albeit in a secular mode, where God serves no longer as the objective standard of perfection but as the individual's own inner compass indicating whether self-actualizing *auto-poiesis* has been achieved. It too, for Luther, would be an unnatural desire needing to be "extinguished," since it fails to accord with the truth that God's forgiveness and promise are sufficient to bring meaning and wholeness to life.

The Sublime

The modern world and particularly the postmodern world have pitted the sublime against the beautiful, usually at the expense of the value of the beautiful.[30] Usually the two are distinguished in this way: the beautiful is seen as small, smooth, and clear, while the sublime is seen as immeasurably vast, dark and gloomy, and rugged. Stephen John Wright presents Edmund Burke's definition of the two as follows:

29. Milbank, "Beauty and the Soul," in *Theological Perspectives on God and Beauty*, by John Milbank, Graham Ward, and Edith Wyschogrod (Harrisburg, PA: Trinity Press International, 2003), 19.

30. For the first-century thinker Longinus, from whom the concept of the sublime stems, the sublime is on a continuum with beauty, in contrast to eighteenth-century thinkers who tended to oppose beauty and the sublime. See Longinus, "On the Sublime," in *Critical Theory since Plato*, ed. Hazard Adams (San Diego: Harcourt, 1971), 76–102.

Writing prior to the emergence of Romanticism, Burke set the opposition of
beauty and the sublime for the Romantics. Before this time, sublimity largely
signified intense experiences of formed beauty. Burke argued that beauty is not
characterized by proportion and fitness but rather by smallness, smoothness,
gradual variation, and delicacy. Furthermore, he considered beauty to be primarily feminine in character, and in contrast to the soft and delicate "femininity"
of beauty, he positioned the powerful and great terror of the sublime. . . . For
Burke, beauty is identified with the arousal of pleasure—the sublime with the
experience of pain. Beauty, moreover, is marked by clarity, whereas the sublime
is overwhelming and inconceivable.[31]

No doubt some people's trivialization of beauty as an appropriate theme for
theology is due to the fact that they swallow Burke's configuration of it as
"feminine," and so surmise that it lacks any bite or threat that grips one's
attention. As seen in this study, such gender profiling with beauty is not fair.
No doubt there is a tenderness to beauty that offers solace and consolation.
But as seen in Christ's fidelity to his own, leading him to the cross, there is
indeed a tenacious, robust, and forceful power to beauty.

The notion of the sublime has powerfully influenced postmodern thinking,
and so the topic requires reflection. With respect to Luther, it is tempting to
translate the sublime into his view of God's hiddenness. But such a move should
not be made in haste. For Kant, not surprisingly, the sublime is configured
anthropologically, not theologically, as the human desire to affirm its own
resolute power and indestructible continuity in the face of insurmountable
threats: the human can stand before it, be enraptured by it, and yet not be
destroyed by it. Indeed, the "sublime" as presented by both Burke and Kant
iterates human autonomy: humans threatened and potentially overwhelmed
by uncontrollable natural forces or, in Kant's case, behavior such as war[32] are
able to detach themselves from the peril and contemplate the ungraspable
power and tantalizing energy manifest in it. But that does not translate into
Luther's *deus absconditus* (hidden God), which truly disempowers all who
attempt to defy it. The Neoplatonic way to relate beauty and the sublime is
to try to interpret the sublime as somehow compatible with beauty, as David
Bentley Hart indicates.[33] Stephen John Wright notes that, prior to Burke,
the sublime "largely signified intense experiences of formed beauty."[34] But if
the sublime is taken as what genuinely threatens humanity, as opposed to a

31. Wright, *Dogmatic Aesthetics: A Theology of Beauty in Dialogue with Robert W. Jenson*
(Minneapolis: Fortress, 2014), 32.
32. Kant, *Critique of Judgment*, trans. J. H. Bernard (New York: Hafner, 1951), 102.
33. Hart, *Beauty of the Infinite*, 47.
34. Wright, *Dogmatic Aesthetics*, 31.

grand test that humanity can ultimately withstand,[35] it could legitimately be seen as one manifestation of divine hiddenness—not God as providential, as God speaking through creatures to other creatures, but instead as a threat to human security, such as we see in a tornado, earthquake, volcanic eruption, or tsunami. And this is not because the sublime reinforces the noumenal inaccessibility of reality as such, but instead precisely because humans are not able to withstand the reality of God as God is in majesty. The only answer to the sublime (understood truly as the death of humans as opposed to the illusion that humans can withstand and contemplate it) is the *promissio*. The only answer to the *deus absconditus* is the revealed God. The only answer to God's alien work is God's proper work. Hence, the necessity for preachers. Such terrifying matters should not be sugarcoated or dignified with beauty. Beauty is indeed profligate and arouses hope among those in dire circumstances. But such beauty can just as well evoke resentment and bitterness in those realizing that their dreams and aspirations will never be fulfilled. Again, faith clings to the promise and even rubs God's nose in it, if it must.[36]

Revisiting Form

Now it is helpful once more to look at the concept of form since it has been the most important concept for theological aesthetics in the last six or seven decades, particularly as seen in Hans Urs von Balthasar's view of beauty as form:

> The beautiful is above all a *form*, and the light does not fall on this form from above and from outside, rather it breaks forth from the form's interior. . . . The content (*Gehalt*) does not lie behind the form (*Gestalt*), but within it. . . . In the luminous form of the beautiful the being of the existent becomes perceivable as nowhere else, and this is why an aesthetic element must be associated with all spiritual perception as with all spiritual striving.[37]

35. "But the sight of them [thunderstorms, volcanoes, hurricanes, waterfalls, the ocean] is the more attractive, the more fearful it is, provided only that we are in security; and we willingly call these objects sublime, because they raise the energies of the soul above their accustomed height and discover in us a faculty of resistance of a quite different kind, which gives us courage to measure ourselves against the apparent almightiness of nature" (Kant, *Critique of Judgment*, 100–101).

36. See Oswald Bayer, "Luther as an Interpreter of Holy Scripture," trans. Mark Mattes, in *The Cambridge Companion to Luther*, ed. Donald McKim (Cambridge: Cambridge University Press, 2003), 77.

37. Von Balthasar, *The Glory of the Lord: A Theological Aesthetics*, vol. 1, *Seeing the Form*, trans. Erasmo Leiva-Merikakis (Edinburgh: T&T Clark, 1982), 151, 153.

Engaging as this definition is, surely the question of whether the "luminous form" is that of a false, beguiling angel of light (2 Cor. 11:14) or that of the light enlightening everyone coming into the world (John 1:9) needs to be raised, not especially because we fear the Cartesian "evil genius," the master concocting the alleged illusion that bodies and other minds exist, but simply because we as responsible Christians are called to discern the spirits (1 John 4:1). That said, we should not take issue with the concept of form per se. It is valuable because it is an idea that helps identify things. That Christians have the "form of Christ" indicates that it is Christ who gives them their identity and not their lack of faith, their misdeeds, or even their good works.

Von Balthasar's view of form is far more complex than this initial definition would indicate. Indeed, von Balthasar comes as close to Luther as a Roman Catholic can when he restates the nature of form in a cruciform way on the basis of an *analogia Christi* (analogy of Christ) as a countermove to Karl Barth's christomonistic rejection of the *analogia entis* (analogy of being). Von Balthasar writes:

> Our task . . . consists in coming . . . to see [Christ's] "formlessness" . . . as a mode of his glory because a mode of his "love to the end," to discover in his deformity (*Ungestalt*) the mystery of transcendental form (*Übergestalt*). . . . What we have before us *is* pure glory, and even though it is really a concealment and really an entering into darkness . . . , it is always but a function of its opposite. What is more, for the believer who sees it is the appearance of the opposite. . . . If the Cross radically puts an end to all worldly aesthetics, then precisely this end marks the decisive emergence of the divine aesthetic.[38]

Compared to Aquinas's standards for beauty (clarity, integrity, and proportion)— or those of the other medieval thinkers we examined—von Balthasar's aesthetics offers a significant advance, a theory of beauty far more informed by the gospel. But his is an aesthetics that affirms a quest for glory instead of one that in the *verbum reale* of *ephphatha* opens humans to creation as sheer gift. For von Balthasar, the cross analogizes the inner-trinitarian life. John Webster describes von Balthasar's view of this inner-trinitarian movement:

> For it is precisely in the abandonment of the Son to death on the cross that God's Trinitarian nature is embodied—precisely, that is, in that event in which the unity of the divine life seems imperiled in the extreme. And it is only because Father and Son remain—even at the point of their furthest separation—bound

38. Ibid., 471.

together in the Holy Spirit that the divine life does not collapse into the void. For at the cross, God "proves to be so living, so mobile, that he can reveal his life precisely even in death, his Trinitarian communality even in abandonment."[39]

Thus the ugliness of Christ's death is an analogy for the eternal relationship among the triune persons, particularly the Father and the Son. Webster explains:

> And the divine life does not at this point [the crucifixion] break down; the distance between Father and Son at the cross is not a distance in which God is in opposition to himself. Rather, it is the manifestation of the mutuality of God's being, for here, too, there is played out "the commitment of the divine persons to each other" so that "the mystery of the cross is the highest revelation of the Trinity."[40]

As the concrete event of revelation, the darkness of the cross paradoxically has its own luminosity because, as Webster notes, "it is impermissible for the theologian to seek to 'go behind' the form in which God has revealed himself: the 'truth' which God shows about himself is essentially inseparable from the manner of its occurrence."[41] For von Balthasar, then, God's self-manifestation in the cross allows humans to ascend past the historical event of Jesus's crucifixion into the beauty of the eternal vision of God's love.

But the cross is no mere analogy for the inner-trinitarian life. Nor is it the path for human ascent. It is first and foremost the alien work (*opus alienum*) of God in which God delivers to sinners the wages of their sin. As Luther notes, because on the cross Jesus exchanges his righteousness for human sin,[42] Christ himself is the "greatest sinner."[43] We can know that the cross manifests God's love not because we see through it to what the cross analogizes but because the Word of God tells humans the counterfactual truth that this crucified, "formless" man is God and that his execution is a

---

39. Webster, "Hans Urs von Balthasar: The Paschal Mystery," *Evangel* 1/4 (October 1983): 7. Quotation is from Hans Urs von Balthasar, *Pneuma und Institution* (Einsiedeln: Johannes-Verlag, 1974), 402.

40. Webster, "Hans Urs von Balthasar," 7. Quotation is from Hans Urs von Balthasar, *Mysterium Paschale*, in *Mysterium Salutis* III/2, ed. J. Feiner and M. Lohrer (Einsiedeln: Johannes-Verlag, 1969), 142.

41. Webster, "Hans Urs von Balthasar," 7.

42. "Now let faith come between them and sins, death, and damnation will be Christ's, while grace, life, and salvation will be the soul's; for if Christ is a bridegroom, he must take upon himself the things which are his bride's and bestow upon her the things that are his. If he gives her his body and very self, how shall he not give her all that is his?" (*The Freedom of a Christian*, in LW 31:351 [WA 7:54.39–55.4]).

43. *Lectures on Galatians* (1535), in LW 26:100 (WA 40/1:182.15).

manifestation of God's love[44]—precisely as *sub contrario* (under the opposite). The cross, then, is not first and foremost a pathway into the inner life of God's triune love but instead is God's accusation of sinners who reject Christ's mercy given to the least and the lost, including themselves. In the cross is echoed Nathan's accusation of David: "You are the man!" (2 Sam. 12:7a). Only when that accusation cuts sinners to the quick and delivers its death knell can the cross also be heard as a promise of God, who hears Jesus's cry of dereliction, who never abandons his own, and who raises sinners with Christ from the dead.

Indeed, light as reflected through the gospel shines "in the darkness," though a darkness that has not "overcome it" (John 1:5). No doubt this darkness is often a perversion of or our rebellion against the light. But at times it is the darkness of God's own alien work designed to disempower smug, self-satisfied sinners. Apart from that darkness, humans presume apart from the cross to have transparent access into the life of God. But that surely is not the case. Jesus's death as the one who bears the sins of the world and the wrath of God, taking sin and wrath away, covering sinners in his righteousness and his blood—his fidelity to his own to the end—must be the lens through which light, beauty, and form are properly to be understood. Hence—to challenge von Balthasar—Christ so identifies with sinners that his cross is no mere analogy that grants humans access to divine glory but instead is the death of sinners, God's alien work, God consigning "all to disobedience, that he may have mercy on all" (Rom. 11:32). The fact that God is finally not beholden to a prearranged order—God as beyond or other than law, God, then, as sheer love and mercy, revealed in the cross—is the very basis by which grace can truly be mercy and gospel beauty can be established.

God gives law its place and time; its place and time is to lead sinners to Christ. Beauty is forensically granted to sinners for Jesus's sake. As God works in their lives, and in God's own way and time, sinners' lives are transformed into the image of the crucified because they learn more and more to trust in God's goodness and promise. Their lives are increasingly marked by beauty as given in and through the prism of the crucified. As a result, they are open to receiving and identifying beauty in the world, whether in music, images, or nature. In the case of sinners, it is not that one must first find preexistent luminosity before beauty can be discerned. Instead, God takes what is nothing in itself and shapes it into the creature he wishes it to be. Death is not beyond God's ability to work through and with it toward a resurrection life. But this is all because Christ himself bore sin in his body, tasted death, and assailed

---

44. This insight is indebted to Jack Kilcrease, email correspondence, September 25, 2016.

the evil one. Christ's victory, though hidden to the world, is wondrous and beautiful for believers.

That there is form within creation, seen in integrity, clarity, and proportion, permits rational inquiry into the nature of beauty. Form exists as part of creation, a structure of created existence. On that basis, taste is not purely subjective (beauty is not merely in the eye—or tongue—of the beholder) but belongs to God's creative generosity as God is shaping the world. Hence, reason need not be limited to collecting data or drawing up general laws.[45] That thoughtful people can discern order and proportion in the created order permits discussion about matters of taste, even given the fact that intelligent people of goodwill do not always see eye-to-eye about whether something is beautiful or the degree or depth to which something is beautiful.[46]

Beauty and Preaching

As a final note, we return to an important passage in *De servo arbitrio* (1525) since it gets to the heart of what is at stake for Luther's view of beauty:

> Now, God in His own nature and majesty is to be left alone; in this regard, we have nothing to do with Him, nor does He wish us to deal with Him. We have to do with Him as clothed and displayed in His Word, by which He presents Himself to us. That is His glory *and beauty*, in which the Psalmist proclaims Him to be clothed (cf. Ps. 21:5). I say that the righteous God does not deplore the death of His people which He Himself works in them, but He deplores the death which He finds in His people and desires to remove from them. God preached works to the end that sin and death may be taken away, and we may be saved.[47]

Luther is clear that God is not always experienced as beautiful. The attempt to ascend into God by means of desiring beauty leads not to the tranquility, security, and joy that the *viator* covets but to frustration and even danger. But that is not how God wishes to leave matters. God wishes instead to clothe sinners in his beauty, his righteousness. That is why God gives the church preachers: to offer God as God is clothed in the word, in the gospel. And God wants to share these clothes of righteousness with sinners, but this gift can only be received through proclamation. Not only is the cross of Jesus Christ

45. Montague Brown, *The Restoration of Reason: The Eclipse and Recovery of Truth, Goodness, and Beauty* (Grand Rapids: Baker Academic, 2006), 27.

46. Ibid., 43.

47. Luther, *The Bondage of the Will*, trans. J. I. Packer and O. R. Johnson (New York: Revell, 1957), 170 (italics added) (WA 18:685.14–24).

a strange beauty, but so also is the cross that God is imposing on all sinners' lives—all so as to lead sinners to the mercy found in Christ. God painfully tears down the castles sinners build so as to rebuild these sinners to be men and women of faith, people who rely on God and whose whole confidence is found in God. And that rebuilding project is one laden with beauty, the splendor of a righteousness established not through one's own efforts or on one's own terms, but instead as pure gift. God's righteousness is God's beauty, and it is the unique task of the preaching office to impart this beauty. The article of justification by grace alone through faith alone is not something other than or different from beauty, but instead articulates the core of what beauty most truly is, and even more importantly frees and so beautifies sinners and reveals this good earth as beautiful. Thus God offers a world focused not only on tasks but also on enjoyment—treasuring the gospel, but also treasuring innocent delights, such as song, opened up by the gospel and being thankful for them.

Works Cited

Primary Literature

Aquinas, Thomas. *Summa Theologica*. Translated by Fathers of the English Dominican Province. Westminster, MD: Christian Classics, 1948.

Aristotle. *Basic Works*. Edited by Richard McKeon. New York: Random House, 1941.

Augustine. *The City of God*. Translated by Gerald G. Walsh, SJ, Demetrius B. Zema, SJ, Grace Monahan, OSU, and Daniel J. Honan. Abridged by Vernon J. Bourke. New York: Doubleday, 1958.

————. *Confessions*. Translated by R. S. Pine-Coffin. Harmondsworth, UK: Penguin, 1961.

————. *Literal Commentary on Genesis*. Translated by John Hammon Taylor. ACW 41. New York: Newman, 1982.

Catechism of the Catholic Church. 2nd ed. Rome: Liberia Editrice Vaticana, 2000.

Descartes, René. *Meditations on First Philosophy*. In *Classics of Philosophy*. Vol. 2, *Modern and Contemporary*, edited by Louis P. Pojman, 465–90. New York: Oxford University Press, 1998.

Hamann, Johann Georg. *Writings on Philosophy and Language*. Translated and edited by Kenneth Haynes. Cambridge: Cambridge University Press, 2007.

Hegel, G. W. F. *The Science of Logic*. Translated by A. V. Miller. London: Allen & Unwin, 1969.

Heidelberg Catechism. Translated by a joint task force formed by the Reformed Church in America, the Christian Reformed Church in North America, and the Presbyterian Church (USA). 2011. http://www.crcna.org/welcome/beliefs/confessions/heidelberg-catechism.

John of Damascus. *Apologia against Those Who Decry Holy Images*. In *St. John Damascene: On Holy Images*. Translated by Mary H. Allies. London: Thomas Baker, 1898. http://legacy.fordham.edu/Halsall/basis/johndamascus-images.asp.

Junghans, Helmar. "Die Probationes zu den philosophischen Thesen der Heidelberger Disputation Luthers im Jahre 1518." *Lutherjahrbuch* 46 (1979): 10–59.

Kant, Immanuel. *Critique of Judgment*. Translated by J. H. Bernard. New York: Hafner, 1951.

—. *Critique of Practical Reason*. Translated by Lewis White Beck. Indianapolis: Bobbs-Merrill, 1957.

—. *Critique of Pure Reason*. Translated by Norman Kemp Smith. New York: St. Martin's Press, 1929.

Kolb, Robert, and Timothy J. Wengert, eds. *The Book of Concord: The Confessions of the Evangelical Lutheran Church*. Minneapolis: Fortress, 2000.

Longinus. "On the Sublime." In *Critical Theory since Plato*, edited by Hazard Adams, 76–102. San Diego: Harcourt, 1971.

Luther, Martin, trans. *Biblia, das ist die ganze heilige Schrifft Deudsch*. Wittenberg, 1534. Reprint, Cologne: Taschen, 2002.

—. *The Bondage of the Will*. Translated by J. I. Packer and O. R. Johnston. New York: Revell, 1957.

—. "Disputation on the Divinity and Humanity of Christ." Translated by Christopher B. Brown. http://www.leaderu.com/philosophy/luther-humanitychrist.html.

—. *D. Martin Luthers Werke: Kritische Gesamtausgabe; Schriften*. 73 vols. Weimar: H. Böhlau, 1883–2009.

—. *The Theologia Germanica of Martin Luther*. Translated by Bengt R. Hofman. New York: Paulist Press, 1980.

Nietzsche, Friedrich. *Basic Writings*. Translated by Walter Kaufmann. New York: Modern Library, 2000.

Pelikan, Jaroslav, and Helmut T. Lehmann, eds. *Luther's Works* (American ed.). 55 vols. Philadelphia: Fortress; St. Louis: Concordia, 1955–86.

Plato. *The Collected Dialogues*. Edited by Edith Hamilton and Huntington Cairns. Princeton: Princeton University Press, 1961.

—. *Plato: Lysis, Symposium, Gorgias*. Translated by W. R. M. Lamb. LCL. Cambridge, MA: Harvard University Press, 1933.

Pseudo-Dionysius. *Pseudo-Dionysius: The Complete Works*. Translated by Colm Luibhéid. New York: Paulist Press, 1987.

Sonntag, Holger, ed. and trans. *Solus Decalogus est Aeternus: Martin Luther's Complete Antinomian Theses and Disputations*. Minneapolis: Lutheran Press, 2008.

Tappert, Theodore, ed. *Luther: Letters of Spiritual Counsel*. Philadelphia: Westminster, 1955.

Zwingli, Ulrich. *Commentary on True and False Religion*. Edited by Samuel Macauley Jackson and Clarence Nevin Helle. Durham, NC: Labyrinth, 1981.

Secondary Literature

Aertsen, Jan. *Medieval Philosophy as Transcendental Thought: From Philip the Chancellor (ca. 1225) to Francisco Suárez.* Leiden: Brill, 2012.

Alfsvåg, Knut. "Luther as a Reader of Dionysius the Areopagite." *ST* 65 (2011): 101–14.

———. *What No Mind Has Conceived: On the Significance of Christological Apophaticism.* Leuven: Peeters, 2010.

Althaus, Paul. *The Theology of Martin Luther.* Translated by Robert C. Schultz. Philadelphia: Fortress, 1966.

Anttila, Miikka E. "Die Ästhetik Luthers." *KD* 58 (2012): 244–55.

———. *Luther's Theology of Music: Spiritual Beauty and Pleasure.* Berlin: de Gruyter, 2013.

———. "Music." In *Engaging Luther: A (New) Theological Assessment*, edited by Olli-Pekka Vainio, 210–22. Eugene, OR: Cascade, 2010.

Arand, Charles. "God's World of Daily Wonders." In *Dona Gratis Donata: Essays in Honor of Norman Nagel on the Occasion of His Ninetieth Birthday*, edited by Jon Vieker, Bart Day, and Albert Collver III, 197–215. Manchester, MO: The Nagel Festschrift Committee, 2015.

Balthasar, Hans Urs von. *The Glory of the Lord: A Theological Aesthetics.* 7 vols. Edinburgh: T&T Clark, 1982–91.

Barker, H. Gaylon. *The Cross of Reality: Luther's* Theologia Crucis *and Bonhoeffer's Christology.* Minneapolis: Fortress, 2015.

Barth, Karl. *Church Dogmatics.* Vol. 4/1. Translated by Geoffrey Bromiley. Edinburgh: T&T Clark, 1956.

Baur, Jörg. "Luther und die Philosophie." *NZSTh* 26 (1984): 13–28.

Bayer, Oswald. *A Contemporary in Dissent: Johann Georg Hamann as a Radical Enlightener.* Translated by Roy A. Harrisville and Mark Mattes. Grand Rapids: Eerdmans, 2012.

———. "Luther as an Interpreter of Holy Scripture." Translated by Mark Mattes. In *The Cambridge Companion to Luther*, edited by Donald McKim, 73–85. Cambridge: Cambridge University Press, 2003.

———. *Martin Luther's Theology: A Contemporary Interpretation.* Translated by Thomas Trapp. Grand Rapids: Eerdmans, 2008.

———. *Theology the Lutheran Way.* Translated by Jeffrey Silcock and Mark Mattes. Grand Rapids: Eerdmans, 2007.

Beardsley, Monroe C. *Aesthetics from Classical Greece to the Present: A Short History.* New York: Macmillan, 1966.

Becker, Siegbert. *The Foolishness of God: The Place of Reason in the Theology of Martin Luther.* Milwaukee: Northwestern, 2009.

Begbie, Jeremy. "Theology and Music." In *The Modern Theologians*, edited by David Ford, 719–35. Oxford: Blackwell, 2005.

Bielfeldt, Dennis. "Clarity with Respect to Realism." *Disputationes* (blog). January 10, 2009. http://disputationes.blogspot.com/2009/01/clarity-with-respect-to-realism .html.

———. "Luther's Late Trinitarian Disputations." In *The Substance of Faith: Luther's Doctrinal Theology for Today*, by Dennis Bielfeldt, Mickey Mattox, and Paul Hinlicky, 59–130. Minneapolis: Fortress, 2008.

Bloom, Harold. *The American Religion: The Emergence of the Post-Christian Nation*. New York: Touchstone, 1992.

Boersma, Hans. *Heavenly Participation: The Weaving of a Sacramental Tapestry*. Grand Rapids: Eerdmans, 2011.

———. Nouvelle Théologie *and Sacramental Ontology: A Return to Mystery*. Oxford: Oxford University Press, 2009.

Bradbury, Rosalene. *Cross Theology: The Classical* Theologia Crucis *and Karl Barth's Modern Theology of the Cross*. Eugene, OR: Pickwick, 2010.

Brecht, Martin. *Martin Luther: His Road to Reformation, 1483–1521*. Translated by James Schaaf. Minneapolis: Fortress, 1993.

Brown, Christopher Boyd. *Singing the Gospel: Lutheran Hymns and the Success of the Reformation*. Cambridge, MA: Harvard University Press, 2005.

Brown, Frank Burch. *Good Taste, Bad Taste, and Christian Taste: Aesthetics in Religious Life*. Oxford: Oxford University Press, 2000.

Brown, Howard Mayer, and Louise K. Stein. *Music in the Renaissance*. Upper Saddle River, NJ: Prentice Hall, 1999.

Brown, Montague. *The Restoration of Reason: The Eclipse and Recovery of Truth, Goodness and Beauty*. Grand Rapids: Baker Academic, 2006.

Burnham, Douglas. "Immanuel Kant: Aesthetics." *Internet Encyclopedia of Philosophy*. Edited by James Fieser and Bradley Dowden. http://www.iep.utm.edu/kantaest/.

Buszin, Walter. "Luther on Music." *MQ* 32 (1947): 80–97.

Bynum, Caroline Walker. *Christian Materiality: An Essay on Religion in Late Medieval Europe*. New York: Zone Books, 2011.

Caldwell, John. *Medieval Music*. Bloomington: Indiana University Press, 1978.

Christensen, Carl. "Luther's Theology and the Use of Religious Art." *LQ* 22 (1970): 147–65.

Ciorra, Anthony J. *Beauty: A Path to God*. New York: Paulist Press, 2013.

Clark, R. Scott. "*Iustitia Imputata Christi*: Alien or Proper to Luther's Doctrine of Justification." *CTQ* 70 (2006): 269–310.

Congdon, David W. "*Nova Lingua Dei*: The Problem of Chalcedonian Metaphysics and the Promise of the *Genus Tapeinoticon* in Luther's Later Theology." Unpublished student paper, Princeton Theological Seminary, 2011.

Crouse, Robert. "*Paucis mutatis verbis*: St. Augustine's Platonism." In *Augustine and His Critics*, edited by Robert Dodaro and George Lawless, 37–50. London: Routledge, 2000.

Cunningham, Lawrence S. *The Catholic Heritage*. New York: Crossroad, 1983.

Dalferth, Ingolf. *Theology and Philosophy*. Oxford: Oxford University Press, 1988.

Dieter, Theodor. *Der junge Luther und Aristoteles: Eine historisch-systematische Untersuchung zum Verhältnis von Theologie und Philosophie*. Berlin: de Gruyter, 2001.

———. "Why Does Luther's Doctrine of Justification Matter Today?" In *The Global Luther: A Theologian for Modern Times*, edited by Christine Helmer, 189–209. Minneapolis: Fortress, 2009.

Dubay, Thomas. *The Evidential Power of Beauty*. San Francisco: Ignatius, 1999.

Dyrness, William A. *Poetic Theology: God and the Poetics of Everyday Life*. Grand Rapids: Eerdmans, 2011.

Eco, Umberto. *The Aesthetics of Thomas Aquinas*. Translated by Hugh Bredin. Cambridge, MA: Harvard University Press, 1988.

———. *Art and Beauty in the Middle Ages*. Translated by Hugh Bredin. New Haven: Yale University Press, 1986.

Eggert, Kurt J. "Martin Luther, God's Music Man." Wisconsin Evangelical Lutheran Seminary Essay Files. Accessed July 1, 2015. http://www.wlsessays.net/bitstream/handle/123456789/1274/EggertLuther.pdf.

Eire, Carlos M. N. *War against the Idols: The Reformation of Worship from Erasmus to Calvin*. Cambridge: Cambridge University Press, 1986.

Elert, Werner. *The Christian Faith: An Outline of Lutheran Dogmatics*. Translated by Martin H. Bertram and Walter Bouman. Columbus, OH: Lutheran Theological Seminary, 1974.

Forde, Gerhard. *A More Radical Gospel: Essays on Eschatology, Authority, Atonement, and Ecumenism*. Edited by Mark C. Mattes and Steven D. Paulson. Grand Rapids: Eerdmans, 2004.

———. *On Being a Theologian of the Cross: Reflections on Luther's Heidelberg Disputation, 1518*. Grand Rapids: Eerdmans, 1997.

———. *Where God Meets Man: Luther's Down-to-Earth Approach to the Gospel*. Minneapolis: Augsburg, 1972.

Fortescue, Adrian. "Veneration of Images." In *The Catholic Encyclopedia*. New York: Appleton, 1910. http://www.newadvent.org/cathen/07664a.htm.

Freddoso, Alfred J. "Ockham on Faith and Reason." In *The Cambridge Companion to Ockham*, edited by Paul Vincent Spade, 326–49. Cambridge: Cambridge University Press, 1999.

Geertz, Clifford. *The Interpretation of Cultures*. New York: Basic Books, 1973.

Gerhard, Johann. *On the Nature of God and on the Trinity*. Translated by Richard Dinda. St. Louis: Concordia, 2007.

Gerrish, Brian. *The Old Protestantism and the New: Essays on the Reformation Heritage*. Edinburgh: T&T Clark, 1982.

Giakalis, Ambrosios. *Images of the Divine: The Theology of Icons at the Seventh Ecumenical Council*. Leiden: Brill, 2005.

Gillespie, Michael Allen. *The Theological Origins of Modernity*. Chicago: University of Chicago Press, 2008.

Grosshans, Hans-Peter. "Luther on Faith and Reason: The Light of Reason at the Twilight of the World." In *The Global Luther: A Theologian for Modern Times*, edited by Christine Helmer, 173–85. Minneapolis: Fortress, 2009.

Hägglund, Bengt. "Was Luther a Nominalist?" *Theology* 59 (1956): 226–37.

Hamm, Berndt. *The Early Luther: Stages in a Reformation Reorientation*. Translated by Martin J. Lohrmann. Grand Rapids: Eerdmans, 2014.

———. "Martin Luther's Revolutionary Theology of Pure Gift without Reciprocation." *LQ* 29 (2015): 125–61.

Härle, Wilfried. *Outline of Christian Doctrine: An Evangelical Dogmatics*. Translated by Ruth Yule and Nicolas Sagovsky. Grand Rapids: Eerdmans, 2015.

Hart, David Bentley. *The Beauty of the Infinite: The Aesthetics of Christian Truth*. Grand Rapids: Eerdmans, 2003.

Helmer, Christine. *The Trinity and Martin Luther: A Study on the Relationship between Genre, Language and the Trinity in Luther's Works (1523–1546)*. Mainz: von Zabern, 1999.

Helmer, Paul. "The Catholic Luther and Worship Music." In *The Global Luther: A Theologian for Modern Times*, edited by Christine Helmer, 151–72. Minneapolis: Fortress, 2009.

Hendel, Kurt K. "*Finitum capax infiniti*: Luther's Radical Incarnational Perspective." *CurTM* 35 (2008): 420–33.

Hoelty-Nickel, Theodore. "Luther and Music." In *Luther and Culture*, by George Wolfgang Forell, Harold J. Grimm, and Theodore Hoelty-Nickel. Martin Luther Lectures 4. Decorah, IA: Luther College Press, 1960.

Hofmann, Werner, ed. *Luther und die Folgen für die Kunst*. Munich: Prestel, 1983.

Hong, Edna. *The Downward Ascent*. Minneapolis: Augsburg, 1979.

Horan, Daniel. *Postmodernity and Univocity: A Critical Account of Radical Orthodoxy and John Duns Scotus*. Minneapolis: Fortress, 2014.

Janz, Denis. *Luther on Thomas Aquinas: The Angelic Doctor in the Thought of the Reformer*. Stuttgart: Steiner, 1989.

Jüngel, Eberhard. *The Freedom of a Christian: Luther's Significance for Contemporary Theology*. Translated by Roy A. Harrisville. Minneapolis: Augsburg, 1988.

———. *God as the Mystery of the World: On the Foundation of the Theology of the Crucified One in the Dispute between Theism and Atheism*. Translated by Darrell L. Guder. Grand Rapids: Eerdmans, 1983.

Junghans, Helmer. "Die Probationes zu den philosophischen Thesen der Heidelberger Disputation Luthers im Jahre 1518." *Lutherjahrbuch* 46 (1979): 10–59.

Juntunen, Sammeli. "Luther and Metaphysics." In *Union with Christ: The New Finnish Interpretation of Luther*, edited by Carl Braaten and Robert Jenson, 129–60. Grand Rapids: Eerdmans, 1998.

Kähler, Martin. *The So-Called Historical Jesus and the Historic, Biblical Christ.* Translated by Carl Braaten. Philadelphia: Fortress, 1964.

Klann, Richard. "Human Claims to Freedom and God's Judgment." *CTQ* 54 (1990): 241–63.

Kolb, Robert. *Bound Choice, Election, and the Wittenberg Theological Method.* Grand Rapids: Eerdmans, 2005.

———. "God Kills to Make Alive: Romans 6 and Luther's Understanding of Justification (1535)." *LQ* 12 (1998): 33–56.

———. *Luther and the Stories of God: Biblical Narratives as a Foundation for Christian Living.* Grand Rapids: Baker Academic, 2012.

———. *Martin Luther: Confessor of the Faith.* Oxford: Oxford University Press, 2009.

Kristeller, Paul Oskar. *Renaissance Thought II: Papers on Humanism and the Arts.* New York: Harper & Row, 1965.

Lane, Belden C. *Ravished by Beauty: The Surprising Legacy of Reformed Spirituality.* Oxford: Oxford University Press, 2011.

Leaver, Robin. "Luther on Music." In *The Pastoral Luther: Essays on Martin Luther's Practical Theology*, edited by Timothy J. Wengert, 271–91. Grand Rapids: Eerdmans, 2009.

———. "Luther's Catechism Hymns." *LQ* 11 (1997): 397–410; 12 (1998): 78–99, 161–80, 303–23.

———. *Luther's Liturgical Music: Principles and Implications.* Grand Rapids: Eerdmans, 2007.

Lienhard, Marc. *Luther: Witness to Jesus Christ; Stages and Themes of the Reformer's Christology.* Translated by Edwin H. Robertson. Minneapolis: Augsburg, 1982.

Lindberg, Carter. *Beyond Charity: Reformation Initiatives for the Poor.* Minneapolis: Fortress, 1993.

Loewe, J. Andreas. "Why Do Lutherans Sing? Lutherans, Music, and the Gospel in the First Century of the Reformation." *CH* 82 (2013): 69–89.

Long, C. Stephen. *Saving Karl Barth: Hans Urs von Balthasar's Preoccupation.* Minneapolis: Fortress, 2014.

Lubac, Henri de. *A Brief Catechesis on Nature and Grace.* Translated by Richard Arnandez. San Francisco: Ignatius, 1980.

Macey, Patrick, and Jeremy Noble. "Josquin des Prez." In *New Grove Dictionary of Music and Musicians*, edited by Stanley Sadie and John Tyrrell, 13:220–66. 2nd ed. Oxford: Oxford University Press, 2001.

MacSwain, Robert, and Taylor Worley, eds. *Theology, Aesthetics, and Culture: Responses to the Work of David Brown*. Oxford: Oxford University Press, 2012.

Małysz, Piotr. "Luther and Dionysius: Beyond Mere Negations." In *Re-thinking Dionysius the Areopagite*, edited by Sarah Coakley and Charles M. Stang, 149–62. Oxford: Wiley-Blackwell, 2009.

Mannermaa, Tuomo. *Christ Present in Faith: Luther's View of Justification*. Translated by Kirsi Stjerna. Minneapolis: Fortress, 2005.

Marshall, Bruce. "Faith and Reason Reconsidered: Aquinas and Luther on Deciding What Is True." *The Thomist* 63 (1999): 1–48.

Mattes, Mark. "A Contemporary View of Faith and Reason in Luther." In *Propter Christum: Christ at the Center; Essays in Honor of Daniel Preus*, edited by Scott Murray et al., 145–68. St. Louis: Luther Academy, 2013.

————. "A Future for Lutheran Theology?" *LQ* 19 (2005): 439–57.

————. "Luther on Justification as Forensic and Effective." In *The Oxford Handbook to Martin Luther's Theology*, edited by Robert Kolb, Irene Dingel, and L'ubomir Batka, 264–73. Oxford: Oxford University Press, 2014.

Mattes, Mark, and Ron Darge. *Imaging the Journey*. Minneapolis: Lutheran University Press, 2006.

McGrath, Alister. *Luther's Theology of the Cross*. Oxford: Blackwell, 1985.

McGuckin, John A. "Art." In *SCM Press A–Z of Patristic Theology*, 32–34. London: SCM, 2005.

Menuge, Angus J. L. "The Cultural and Aesthetic Impact of Lutheranism." In *Where Christ Is Present: A Theology for All Seasons on the 500th Anniversary of the Reformation*, edited by John Warwick Montgomery and Gene Edward Veith, 209–31. Corona, CA: NRP Books, 2015.

Milbank, John. *Theology and Social Theory: Beyond Secular Reason*. Oxford: Blackwell, 1990.

Milbank, John, Graham Ward, and Edith Wyschogrod. *Theological Perspectives on God and Beauty*. Harrisburg, PA: Trinity Press International, 2003.

Miller, Joshua C. *Hanging by a Promise: The Hidden God in the Theology of Oswald Bayer*. Eugene, OR: Pickwick, 2015.

Negri, Enrico de. *Offenbarung und Dialektik: Luthers Realtheologie*. Darmstadt: Wissenschaftliche Buchgesellschaft, 1973.

Nettl, Paul. *Luther and Music*. Translated by Frida Best and Ralph Wood. Philadelphia: Muhlenburg, 1948.

Nygren, Anders. *Agape and Eros*. Translated by Philip S. Watson. Chicago: University of Chicago Press, 1982.

Ozment, Steven. *The Serpent and the Lamb: Cranach, Luther, and the Making of the Reformation*. New Haven: Yale University Press, 2011.

Paolucci, Henry. Introduction to *The Enchiridion on Faith, Hope and Love*, by Augustine. Chicago: Regnery, 1961.

Pasewark, Kyle. "Predestination as a Condition of Freedom." *LQ* 12 (1998): 57–78.

Paulson, Steven. *Lutheran Theology*. London: T&T Clark, 2011.

Pickstock, Catherine. *After Writing: On the Liturgical Consummation of Philosophy*. Oxford: Blackwell, 1998.

Plass, Ewald. *What Luther Says: A Practical In-Home Anthology for the Active Christian*. St. Louis: Concordia, 1959.

Przywara, Erich. *Analogia Entis: Metaphysics; Original Structure and Universal Rhythm*. Translated by John R. Betz and David Bentley Hart. Grand Rapids: Eerdmans, 2014.

Rummel, Erika. *Biblical Humanism and Scholasticism in the Age of Erasmus*. Leiden: Brill, 2008.

Ryle, Gilbert. *The Concept of Mind*. New ed. Chicago: University of Chicago Press, 2002.

Saarinen, Risto. "Finnish Luther Studies." In *Engaging Luther: A (New) Theological Assessment*, edited by Olli-Pekka Vainio, 1–26. Eugene, OR: Cascade, 2010.

———. "The Word of God in Luther's Theology." *LQ* 4 (1990): 31–44.

Sasse, Hermann. *This Is My Body: Luther's Contention for the Real Presence in the Sacrament of the Altar*. Rev. Australian ed. Adelaide: Lutheran Publishing House, 1977.

Schmid, Heinrich. *The Doctrinal Theology of the Evangelical Lutheran Church*. Translated by Charles Hay and Henry Jacobs. Minneapolis: Augsburg, 1961.

Schumacher, William. *Who Do I Say That You Are? Anthropology and the Theology of Theosis in the Finnish School of Tuomo Mannermaa*. Eugene, OR: Wipf & Stock, 2010.

Schwarz, Hans. "Creation." In *Dictionary of Luther and the Lutheran Traditions*, edited by Timothy Wengert et al., 176–79. Grand Rapids: Baker Academic, 2017.

———. *True Faith in the True God: An Introduction to Luther's Life and Thought*. Rev. and exp. ed. Minneapolis: Fortress, 2015.

Schwarzwäller, Klaus. *Cross and Resurrection: God's Wonder and Mystery*. Translated by Ken Jones and Mark Mattes. Minneapolis: Fortress, 2012.

Schwiebert, Ernest. *Luther and His Times*. St. Louis: Concordia, 1950.

Scruton, Roger. *Beauty*. Oxford: Oxford University Press, 2009.

Seay, Albert. *Music in the Medieval World*. Englewood Cliffs, NJ: Prentice-Hall, 1965.

Steiger, Johann Anselm. "Luther on the Legend of St. Christopher." *LQ* 25 (2011): 125–44.

Stevenson, Robert M. *Patterns of Protestant Church Music*. Durham, NC: Duke University Press, 1953.

Stewart, Matthew. *Nature's God: The Heretical Origins of the American Republic*. New York: Norton, 2014.

Stolt, Birgit. "Joy, Love and Trust—Basic Ingredients in Luther's Theology of the Faith of the Heart." *SRR* 4 (2002): 28–44.

———. "Luther's Translation of the Bible." *LQ* 27 (2014): 373–400.

Strier, Richard. "Martin Luther and the Real Presence in Nature." *JMEMS* 37 (2007): 271–303.

Taylor, Charles. *A Secular Age*. Cambridge, MA: Belknap Press of Harvard University Press, 2007.

Thiemann, Ronald F. "Sacramental Realism: Martin Luther at the Dawn of Modernity." In *Lutherrenaissance Past and Present*, edited by Christine Helmer and Bo Kristian Holm, 156–73. Göttingen: Vandenhoeck & Ruprecht, 2015.

Thijssen, Hans. "Condemnation of 1277." *The Stanford Encyclopedia of Philosophy*. Edited by Edward N. Zalta. https://plato.stanford.edu/entries/condemnation/.

Tonkin, John. "Word and Image: Luther and the Arts." *Colloq* 17 (1985): 45–54.

Työrinoja, Reijo. "*Nova Vocabula et Nova Lingua*: Luther's Conception of Doctrinal Formulas." In *Thesaurus Lutheri: Auf der Suche nach neuen Paradigmen der Luther-Forschung*, edited by Tuomo Mannermaa et al., 221–36. Helsinki: Luther-Agricola-Society, 1987.

Vanhoozer, Kevin J. *Biblical Authority after Babel: Retrieving the Solas in the Spirit of Mere Protestant Christianity*. Grand Rapids: Brazos, 2016.

Veith, Gene Edward. *State of the Arts: From Bezalel to Mapplethorpe*. Wheaton: Crossway, 1991.

Viladesau, Richard. *The Beauty of the Cross: The Passion of Christ in Theology and the Arts, from the Catacombs to the Eve of the Renaissance*. Oxford: Oxford University Press, 2008.

———. *Theological Aesthetics: God in Imagination, Beauty, and Art*. Oxford: Oxford University Press, 1999.

Webb, Stephen H. "The End of the Analogy of Being: Przywara's Proportionality Problem." *First Things*. January 27, 2015. http://www.firstthings.com/web-exclusives/2015/01/the-end-of-the-analogy-of-being.

Weber, Max. *Essays in Sociology*. Translated and edited by H. H. Gerth. London: Routledge, 2009.

Webster, John. "Hans Urs von Balthasar: The Paschal Mystery." *Evangel* 1/4 (October 1983): 6–8.

Weimar, Christoph. "Luther and Cranach on Justification in Word and Image." *LQ* 18 (2004): 387–405.

Westhelle, Vítor. *The Scandalous God: The Use and Abuse of the Cross*. Minneapolis: Fortress, 2006.

White, Graham. *Luther as Nominalist: A Study of the Logical Methods Used in Martin Luther's Disputations in the Light of Their Medieval Background*. Helsinki: Luther-Agricola-Society, 1994.

Wilson-Kastner, Patricia. "On Partaking of the Divine Nature: Luther's Dependence on Augustine." *AUSS* 22 (1984): 113–24.

Wright, Stephen John. *Dogmatic Aesthetics: A Theology of Beauty in Dialogue with Robert W. Jenson*. Minneapolis: Fortress, 2014.

Zahl, Paul. *Grace in Practice: A Theology of Everyday Life*. Grand Rapids: Eerdmans, 2007.

Index of Names

217

Index of Ancient Sources

Index of Subjects

aesthetics, 4–5, 70. *See also* criteria, aesthetic
affectivity. *See* heart; senses
alien, God's work as. *See* God: alien work of
analogia entis. *See* being, analogy of
apophaticism, 16n3, 138n19, 175
apprehension. *See* faith
art
    icons and, 135–37, 140–47
    music as, 125–28
    postmodern, 191–92
    visual, 133–35, 137–40, 147–51, 189, 194–95
    See also iconoclasm; icons
atonement. *See* Christ; cross, the; justification

being, analogy of
    in contemporary theology, 13, 156–58, 172–77
    creation and, 152–53, 158–60, 179–80, 188–89
    philosophy and, 24

cantus firmus, 12, 113, 127–28
causality. *See* being, analogy of; secularism
Christ
    analogy of being and, 14, 158–60, 172–77
    beauty and, 79–80, 84–85, 111–12, 185–87, 190–92
    faith and, 99–105, 150–51
    as form, 100–104, 200–203
    goodness and, 61, 63–66
    grace and, 11, 27, 168–69
    idolatry and, 142–43
    incarnation of, 141
    justification and, 3–4, 49, 87–90, 91–99
    love of, 45n9, 165–66

pancalism and, 12, 111–12
philosophy and, 17–18, 22–23, 24n33, 29–30, 34–40
    as promise, 188
    sacrament and, 61, 120–21, 145–47, 152–53
    See also cross, the
contrary, sign of. *See* God: as hidden
covered, God as. *See* creation: visual art and; God: as hidden
creation
    beauty and, 7–8, 111–12, 192–94, 196–97
    the infinite and, 158–60, 188
    justification and, 2–3, 11, 85–90
    music and, 114–15, 120–22, 125, 130–31
    mystery and, 160–63, 166–69, 172–81
    omnipotence and, 59–60
    participation in, 170–72, 174–75
    righteousness and, 105–10
    visual art and, 134–38, 141, 143–47, 151–53
criteria, aesthetic
    Christ and, 79–80, 91–92, 97, 100–102, 190–92
    creation and, 105–6, 108–9, 111–12
    Kant's, 155n2
    medieval, 4–5, 70, 91
    music and, 126–28
    word as, 134
cross, the
    beauty and, 163–66, 184–85, 189, 191–92
    form and, 200–203
    mystery and, 167n39
    theology of, 86, 93–94, 158–60, 163–66, 187–88
    See also Christ

223